Contemporary China Studies

Series Editor
Angang Hu
Institute for Contemporary China Studies
Tsinghua University Institute for Contemporary
China Studies
Beijing, China

Shaojie Zhou • Angang Hu

China: Surpassing the "Middle Income Trap"

palgrave
macmillan

Shaojie Zhou
Tsinghua University
Beijing, P. R. China

Angang Hu
Tsinghua University
Beijing, P. R. China

Contemporary China Studies
ISBN 978-981-15-6542-7 ISBN 978-981-15-6540-3 (eBook)
https://doi.org/10.1007/978-981-15-6540-3

This Palgrave Macmillan imprint is published by the registered company Springer Nature Singapore Pte Ltd.
The registered company address is: 152 Beach Road, #21-01/04 Gateway East, Singapore 189721, Singapore

This book was realized as a result of national top think tanks' research initiative and sponsored by the Institute for National Governance and Global Governance at Tsinghua University

PRAISE FOR *China: Surpassing the "Middle Income Trap"*

"This book provides an empirical summary of how China crossed the "poverty trap" and an objective analysis of how China overcomes the "middle-income trap" by drawing China's development paths. It is worth reading by those interested in China's development."

—Jinjun Xue, *Professor of Economics Research Center at Nagoya University and Co-Director of the Institute of Global Low-carbon Economy*

"There are many disputes about the concept of "middle-income trap" in the academic community, but the "middle-income trap" has become an important perspective for understanding China's development prospects. Based on this perspective, this book gives an explanation of Chinese-style development and governance."

—Shaoguang Wang, *Emeritus Professor at the Chinese University of Hong Kong and Professor at Tsinghua University*

Contents

List of Figures

List of Tables

CHAPTER 1

What Is the "Middle Income Trap"?

1.1 Proposition of the "Middle Income Trap"

In 2007, Indermit Gill and Homi Kharas (2007), two World Bank economists, published a report titled *An East Asian Renaissance: Ideas for Economic Growth*,[1] which suggested that East Asia would soon develop into a middle-income region and proposed the concept of the "middle income trap". It should be noted that the report did not provide an in-depth interpretation of the concept, nor did it offer a clear income range for the "middle income trap". In 2011, Homi Kharas and Harinder Kohli (2011) further elaborated on the concept,[2] specifying that when a country escapes the poverty trap in the low-income development stage and enters into the middle-income development phase, the country may face growth stagnation and inability to further move up the ladder into the high-income range.

Why does the "middle income trap" phenomenon exist? They emphasized the need for different growth strategies after reaching the middle-income status through comparing the long-term performance of Latin American economies and East Asian economies. In the latter case,

[1] Indermit Gill and Homi Kharas (2007). *An East Asian Renaissance: Ideas for Economic Growth*, The World Bank.

[2] Homi Kharas and Harinder Kohli (2011). What Is the Middle-Income Trap, Why do Countries Fall into It, and How Can It Be Avoided? *Global Journal of Emerging Market Economies*, 3(3) 281–289.

S. Zhou, A. Hu, *China: Surpassing the "Middle Income Trap"*,
Contemporary China Studies,
https://doi.org/10.1007/978-981-15-6540-3_1

countries successfully shifted their growth strategies after achieving the middle-income status and adopted new growth strategies to sustain economic growth. However, economies from Latin America failed to achieve the shift.

Generally, one fundamental reason for low-income economies to break away from the poverty trap lies in the ability to create jobs for the abundant and cheap labor which promotes labor transfer from the low-productivity agricultural sector to the high-productivity sector. The structural change of labor force allocation is the key factor in sufficiently mobilizing economic potentials. However, when a country enters into the middle-income status from the low-income development stage, it loses the comparative advantages of cheaper labor cost and becomes less competitive in manufacturing exports against low-income and low-wage countries due to rising labor costs. If the country does not achieve substantial progress in technological innovation, its ability to compete with developed economies in the arena of high-tech and innovation products would be hampered, resulting in the loss of export competitiveness. Thus, the country may fall into the predicament of declining economic growth or even experience economic regression, causing the country to be trapped in the middle-income status and lose the ability to stride toward the high-income status.

After its proposal, the concept of the "middle income trap" which provided a new perspective for understanding the economic growth in developing countries, received immediate media and academia attention. In the wake of the 2008 global financial crisis, the investment-driven and export-led growth model of China faces great challenges due to the domestic structural adjustments and external demand shocks. Whether the Chinese economy could maintain its high-speed growth has raised substantial concerns.

In 2010, China surpassed Japan in gross domestic product (GDP) for the first time to become the world's second largest economy. The 2012 World Development Report listed China as a middle-income country for the first time on the basis of 2010 per capita income in China. In this sense, 2010 marked an important juncture in the course of China's economic development. Subsequently, China began the implementation of its 12th Five-Year Plan. As the world was reeling from the global financial crisis, China's economic performance came into the spotlight. Being the world's second largest economy, China's economic growth undoubtedly affects global growth, especially for countries that have China as their main trade partner. In the long run, questions of whether China can maintain a relatively high growth rate and join the ranks of high-income countries call for particular attention.

The subject of the "middle income trap" has drawn consideration attention from Chinese scholars and has provided an important perspective for understanding the prospect of China's economic growth. The number of academic papers exploring the theme of the "middle income trap" in Chinese academic journals has witnessed rapid growth in recent years. However, an examination of international academic journals reveals that the majority of research on the "middle income trap" materialized in the form of working papers with only a few published in international journals. Among existing published textbooks on development economics, the "middle income trap" has yet to be clearly defined and discussed as a coherent notion. How to understand the "middle income trap" remains an important and much contemplated subject matter in academia.

1.2 Definition of the "Middle Income Trap"

1.2.1 Absolute Criteria

Since 1978, the World Bank has been publishing the World Development Report annually (biennially on a few occasions). Although the subject of the World Development Report varies from year to year, the World Bank would consistently release data reflecting the development of each country's economy, population, education and health outcomes. In particular, the World Bank classifies all countries into different income groups based on per capita income calculated with the *Atlas* method.[3] In the 1978 World Development Report, the World Bank categorized countries into low-income countries (GNP per capita equal to or lower than $250 by *Atlas* method in 1976), middle-income countries (GNP per capita higher than $250), industrialized countries, capital-surplus oil-exporting

[3] The *Atlas* method employed by the World Bank calculates the dollar value of per capita income based on the *Atlas* conversion factor. The *Atlas* conversion factor is obtained through the synthetic exchange rate method by averaging a country's exchange rates in past three years and taking into account the changes in the country's GDP deflator relative to a weighted GDP deflator of these countries with Special Drawing Right (SDR). The advantage of the method in calculating the per capita income of a country lies in its ability to cushion the effect of exchange rate fluctuations on per capita income calculation.

countries, central-planning countries and so on.[4] Since then, the World Bank's classification of income groups has been adjusted several times. For example, countries were classified into low-income, middle-income, industrialized market economies, capital-surplus oil-exporting countries and industrialized non-market economies in 1981; Then in 1989, with the disintegration of the socialist camp in Eastern Europe, countries were classified into low-income, middle-income (including lower-middle and upper-middle) and high-income countries. Thus far, the classification of countries through per capita income by the World Bank has solidified into four categories, that is, low-income, lower-middle income, upper-middle income and high-income countries.

Currently, the World Bank classifies countries by income level based on per capita national income (GNI) calculated through the *Atlas* method.[5] Since this is calculated on the basis of the current price of dollars, the criteria for income group classification vary annually. The threshold for each income group also undergoes adjustments regularly according to changes in inflation rates and exchange rates of countries with Special Drawing Right (SDR).[6]

Although the thresholds are adjusted according to the changes in exchange rates and inflation rates, the per capita GNI thresholds calculated through the *Atlas* method can be presumed to be relatively fixed or regarded as absolute income criteria, because the adjustments of nominal value take the real value of income level of countries with SDR as the

[4] In the 1978 World Development Report, China's per capita GNP was 410 US dollars. By that measure, China should have already belonged to the club of middle-income countries which would be an apparent misrepresentation. The main reason was that at the very beginning of China's "reform and opening up", it had yet to regain its membership in the World Bank. Thus, China had yet to fully cooperate on data sharing with the World Bank. When China resumed its membership in the World Bank in 1980, the 1980 World Development Report published China's per capita GNP was 230 US dollars, based on part of official information provided by Chinese authorities.

[5] Gross national income (GNI) is equal to the sum of the gross domestic product of a country and the net inflow of such income as rent, profits and remuneration earned by residents of the country abroad. The World Bank converts the GNI, as measured by national currencies, into GNI expressed in US dollars using the exchange rate average over the last three years for the sake of eliminating the effects of exchange rate fluctuations.

[6] Since 1987, the World Bank has adjusted the income thresholds annually. For instance, the threshold for high-income countries stood at 6000 US dollars in 1987, compared to 7620 US dollars in 1990 and 9265 US dollars in 2000. Since 1996, the World Bank has announced the adjusted thresholds on July 1 every year.

Table 1.1 Classification by income group in selected years (1995–2015)

Income group	*1995*	*2000*	*2005*	*2010*	*2015*
Low-income countries	<= 765	<= 755	<= 875	<= 1005	<= 1025
Lower-middle-income countries	766–3035	756–2995	876–3465	1006–3975	1026–4035
Upper-middle-income countries	3036–9385	2996–9265	3466–10,725	3976–12,275	4036–12,475
High-income countries	> 9385	> 9265	> 10,725	> 12,275	> 12,475

Source: The World Bank

benchmark. In this sense, if a country can maintain a positive rate of real economic growth and keep the exchange rates relatively stable with countries with SDR, the country will eventually reach the threshold for high-income countries. Table 1.1 shows the thresholds of income group classifications.

According to the World Bank's income group classification of countries by the 2015 criteria, countries with a per capita GNI of more than 12,746 US dollars can be considered as high-income. Notably, high-income countries might not necessarily equate to what we commonly refer to as developed or advanced economies. According to the International Monetary Fund, there are 39 countries and regions in the world classified as developed economies.[7] However, the World Bank listed as many as 79 countries in the high-income group in the report published on July 1, 2015.

In fact, according to the World Bank,[8] among 154 countries in 1987, the numbers of high-income and middle-income countries were 41 and

[7] Including the U.S., 19 eurozone countries, Japan, the U.K., Canada and 16 other countries (Australia, South Korea, Singapore, the Czech Republic, Macau, Sweden, Denmark, New Zealand, Switzerland, Hong Kong, Norway, Taiwan, Iceland, Puerto Rico, Israel, San Marino). Source: IMF Advanced Economies List. World Economic Outlook, April 2016, p. 148.

[8] World Bank GNI per Capita Operational Guidelines & Analytical Classifications. http://siteresources.worldbank.org/DATASTATISTICS/Resources/OGHIST.xls accessed August 13, 2017.

74. Among 74 middle-income countries, the numbers of lower-middle-income and higher-income economies were 46 and 28; Among 217 economies in 2015, the numbers for high-income and middle-income countries were 79 and 107 and the numbers for lower-middle-income and higher-income economics were 52 and 55, respectively. For economies in the middle-income range in 1987, 19 of them advanced to the high-income category, accounting for one-fourth of the middle-income economies in 1987. In this sense, only a minority of middle-income countries succeeded in progressing to the club of high-income countries over time.

1.2.2 Relative Criteria

In 2012, the World Bank and the Development Research Center of the State Council of China conducted a joint study and published the book: *China 2030: Building a Modern, Harmonious, and Creative High-Income Society*. Through the Maddison Project database,[9] the study classified countries into three income groups on the basis of each country's per capita GDP as a percentage of that of the United States (U.S.) (measured by purchasing power parity, PPP), that is, low-income, middle-income and high-income economies. Thereinto, the middle-income economies were defined as those with per capita GDP equivalent to 5%–40% of that of the U.S. Those that fell below this range were classified as low-income economies while those that exceeded the range were classified as high-income economies. Therefore, we can adopt this approach of classification as the relative criteria for classifying countries by income level, that is, per capita GDP (PPP method) relative to that of the U.S. On account of this criteria, the study classified countries into nine categories during the period of 1960–2008 through comparing their per capita GDP in 1960 and 2008 with those of the U.S. (see Fig. 1.1).

Some important findings can be found by looking at Fig. 1.1. First, only approximately one-third of the countries recognized as low-income economies in 1960 upgraded to the middle-income rank in 2008, and none of them developed into high-income economies. Second, among all of the 101 countries that were classified as middle-income in 1960, only 13 successfully joined the club of high-income economies during the

[9] Maddison Historical Statistics https://www.rug.nl/ggdc/historicaldevelopment/maddison/

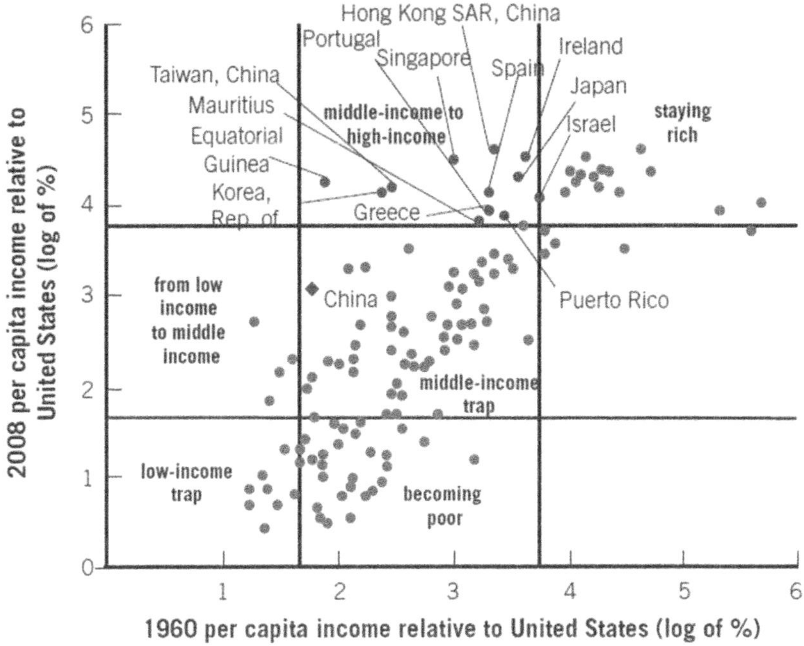

Fig. 1.1 Per capita income of countries relative to U.S. (1960–2008). (Source: World Bank 2012)

1960–2008 period.[10] In addition, a considerable number of economies classified as middle-income in 1960 downgraded to the low-income status in 2008. This fact reveals that in nearly 50 years since 1960, only a limited number of middle-income countries advanced to the high-income rank while more have fallen back into the low-income category, a phenomenon thus termed the "middle income trap". Third, most countries recognized as high-income in 1960 had remained in the category by 2008.

Further analysis on these economies that have successfully overcome the "middle income trap" reveals that many of them are small countries or economies with populations of less than 10 million. For instance, Mauritius, with a population of 1.26 million in 2016, and an urbanization

[10] Including the six Asian countries of Japan, the Four Asian Tigers (Hong Kong, Taiwan, South Korea, Singapore) and Israel, the four European countries of Spain, Portugal, Greece and Ireland, the two African countries of Equatorial Guinea and Mauritius, and Puerto Rico.

rate of only 40% in 2016, is a representative of developing economies in multiple dimensions. In fact, according to the data of 2016, Mauritius cannot be classified as high-income country based on both the absolute and relative criteria.[11]

Another case is Equatorial Guinea—with a population of only 0.82 million in 2016, the country was also excluded from high-income countries based on the two criteria.[12] In particular, although its per capita GDP is much higher than that of many developing countries, its development indicators reveal extremely unsatisfactory performance in education and health. According to the Human Development Index (HDI) rankings compiled by the United Nations Development Programme, Equatorial Guinea is still a low-HDI country ranking only 135th among the 188 countries, signaling an extremely unbalanced development of economic and human development for this country.[13]

Hong Kong and Singapore are typical small and open city economies, and their ascension to the high-income category is not representative of the broader section of middle-income countries or economies in 1960. It can be seen that with the exception of the aforementioned economies as well as China's Taiwan, the remaining countries are members of the Organisation for Economic Co-operation and Development (OECD), including Japan, South Korea, Israel, Portugal, Spain, Greece and Ireland. The vast majority of developing countries had yet to overcome the "middle income trap" in 2008 when judged based on the relative criteria. Therefore, the "middle income trap" has indeed been a common phenomenon hobbling the economic development of developing countries. The phenomenon is manifested in that the economic growth of a country is high when the country is in the low-income development stage, but the economic growth rate begins to decline, stagnate or even fall into recession once the country joins the middle-income rank, resulting in a failure to progress further into the high-income category. We can see from Fig. 1.1 that middle-income countries or economies with similar income

[11] According to the World Bank, its GNI per capita (PPP) amounted to 36 percent of that of U.S. in 2016; its GNI per capita (Atlas method) was 9770 US dollars in 2016, below the threshold of high-income group.

[12] According to the World Bank, its GNI per capita (PPP) amounted to 38 percent of that of U.S. in 2016; its GNI per capita (Atlas method) was 7180 US dollars in 2016, below the threshold of high-income group.

[13] For example, life expectancy in 2015 was only 57.9 years and the average years of education received by people aged 25 and older was only 5.5 years.

levels in 1960 exhibited a high degree of dispersion relative to the U.S. in 2008, indicating that overcoming the middle-income trap is not easy and relies on sustaining a relative high growth rate in the long run.

Employing the relevant income criteria, we reclassified 191 countries and regions with the latest World Bank data. The basic statistical results are as follows: In 2015, 53 countries' per capita GDPs (PPP, 2011 international dollars) surpassed 40% of that of the U.S. and could be regarded as high-income countries. We could also further classify these 53 countries. Among them, 33 countries and regions were OECD members and 20 were non-OECD members. These non-OECD countries and regions included (population in parentheses): Qatar (2.24 million), Macao (0.59 million), Brunei (0.42 million), Singapore (5.54 million), Kuwait (4.40 million), Bermuda (0.065 million), United Arab Emirates (9.16 million), Hong Kong (7.31 million), Saudi Arabia (31.5 million), Oman (4.49 million), Bahrain (1.38 million), Malta (0.43 million), Cyprus (1.17 million), Equatorial Guinea (0.845 million), Trinidad and Tobago (1.36 million), Puerto Rico (3.47 million), Lithuania (2.91 million), Malaysia (30.33 million), Russia (144 million) and Kazakhstan (17.5 million). Among them, the population of five countries and regions stood at less than 1 million. For those non-OECD countries and regions with a population size greater than 1 million, most of them relied on resource extraction to varying degrees for economic development, including Qatar, Kuwait, United Arab Emirates, Saudi Arabia, Oman, Bahrain, Malaysia, Russia and Kazakhstan. The four countries with a population exceeding 10 million were Saudi Arabia, Malaysia, Russia and Kazakhstan.

On the basis of 2015 per capita GDP data (PPP, 2011 international dollars), of the 191 countries with available data, 106 countries or regions belong to the category of middle-income economies (per capita GDP equivalent to 5%–40% of that of the U.S.) while the number of low-income countries stood at 32.

The above demonstrates only a classification of countries by income based on the relative criteria. Considering the disparity in population size among countries, we can narrow down the analysis of those countries with significant population scales. According to the 2015 World Bank demographic statistics, there were 59 countries with a population of more than 20 million in the world, together accounting for 90.31% of the world's population. Among them, 14 countries were classified as high-income economies, accounting for 15.42% of the world's population and 17.07% of the gross population of countries with more than 20 million people.

Among these 14 high-income countries, only Malaysia and Saudi Arabia are non-OECD members. Besides the G8 countries, the 12 OECD countries also included South Korea, Spain, Poland and Australia. It should be noted that Saudi Arabia is an oil-exporting country whose high-income hinges heavily upon the export of resources. Malaysia's per capita GDP (PPP) surpassed 40% of that of the U.S. in 2010 for the first time. However, in terms of absolute criteria, Malaysia's per capita GDP (*Atlas* method) in 2015 stood at 10,548 US dollars, which was still below the threshold for high-income countries in 2015 (12,745 US dollars).

1.3 Overcoming the "Middle Income Trap": A Comparison of East Asia and Latin America

The above analysis reveals that only a few countries or regions such as Japan and the Four Asian Tigers among East Asian economies have successfully escaped the "middle income trap" and entered into the ranks of developed countries or regions. However, the vast majority of countries in Latin America and South-East Asia are still mired in the trap. Therefore, these East Asian economies' experiences in tackling the "middle income trap" stand in sharp contrast with that of their peers in Latin America, and a comparative analysis of the two categories of countries can provide important insight into understanding the "middle income trap".

1.3.1 A Comparative Analysis of Countries and Regions in Asia in Overcoming the "Middle Income Trap"

Among the East Asian economies, Japan and South Korea both stand out as relatively populous countries. According to the 2015 World Bank statistics, their populations stood at 127 million and 50.62 million, respectively; Taiwan, Hong Kong and Singapore claimed much smaller populations and belonged to the category of small and open economies. Among them, Japan and South Korea's experiences in overcoming the "middle income trap" prove to be more instructive for China. According to the Maddison Project database, Japan's per capita GDP reached to 5668 US dollars (1990 international dollars) in 1964, equivalent to 40.1 percent of that of the U.S., and thus landing it in the category of high-income countries. In 1991, Japan's per capita GDP reached a historic high of 19,347 US dollars, equivalent to 84.7 percent of that of the

U.S. As Japan's economic bubble collapsed in the late 1990s, its per capita GDP (PPP) witnessed a significant diminution in relation to that of the U.S., to roughly 74% by the year 2000 and 10 percentage points lower than in the early 1990s. Since then, Japan's per capita GDP has remained relatively stable during the period between 2000 and 2015, fluctuating in the range of 72–74%.

South Korea's per capita GDP reached 9446 US dollars (1990 international dollars) in 1991, surpassing 40% of that of the U.S. for the first time (41.4%) and thus landing it within the category of high-income countries; it continued to gain on the U.S., reaching 71.2% of the U.S. level in 2010 and roughly matching Japan's level in 2010. Overall, Japan's per capita GDP relative to that of the U.S. rose from 20.1% in 1950 to 40.1% in 1962 within a 12-year span; South Korea's per capita GDP relative to that of the U.S. grew from 20.5% in 1976 to 41.4% in 1991 within a 15-year span.

It should be duly noted that the above data are calculated on the basis of Maddison's per capita GDP estimates (PPP, 1990 international dollars). If the World Bank's per capita GDP data (2011 PPP, international dollars) are used alternatively, discrepancies in South Korea's levels relative to that of the U.S. may surface. For instance, South Korea's per capita GDP would surpass 40% of that of the U.S. for the first time in 1995, reach 60.3% of that of the U.S. in 2010 and 64.7% in 2015, pointing to a longer time frame than if calculated with the Maddison Project database. Japan's per capita GDP relative to that of the U.S. remains fundamentally consistent across the two sources of data. In particular, we can see that after Japan and South Korea's per capita GDP exceeded 40% of that of the U.S., they then further narrowed the gap with the U.S. In a sense, only by further narrowing the gap can a country solidify its stead in the ranks of high-income countries and securely avoid the "middle income trap" (Fig. 1.2).

With reference to the relative criteria, China's per capita GDP surpassed 20% of that of the U.S. for the first time in 2008, on par with Japan's level in 1950, indicating that there still exists substantial room for catch-up in the future for China. India's per capital GDP relative to that of the U.S. was comparable to China's in the mid-1970s, but the country's economic growth lagged far behind that of China thereafter, and it failed to catch up to the U.S. with the momentum that China displayed. India's per capita GDP relative to that of the U.S. stood at only 10.5% by 2010, on par only with China's level in 1995 (Fig. 1.3).

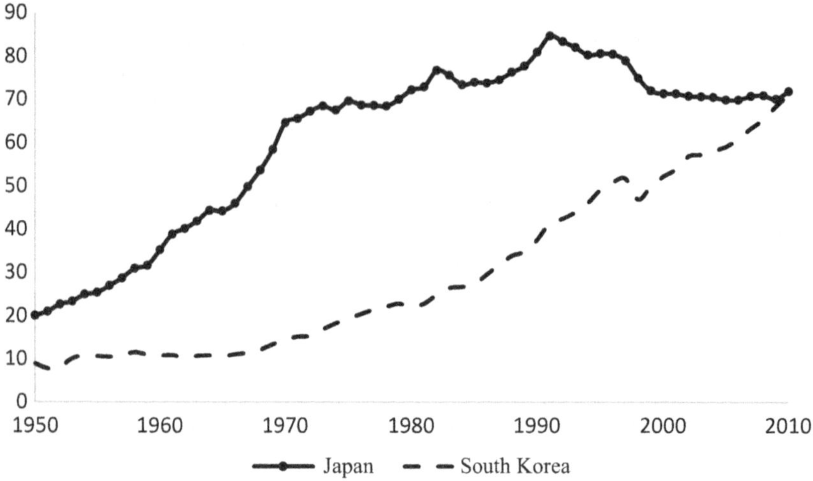

Fig. 1.2 Japan and South Korea's per capita GDP relative to the U.S. level (1950–2010). (Source: The Maddison-Project, http://www.ggdc.net/maddison/maddison-project/home.htm, 2013 version)

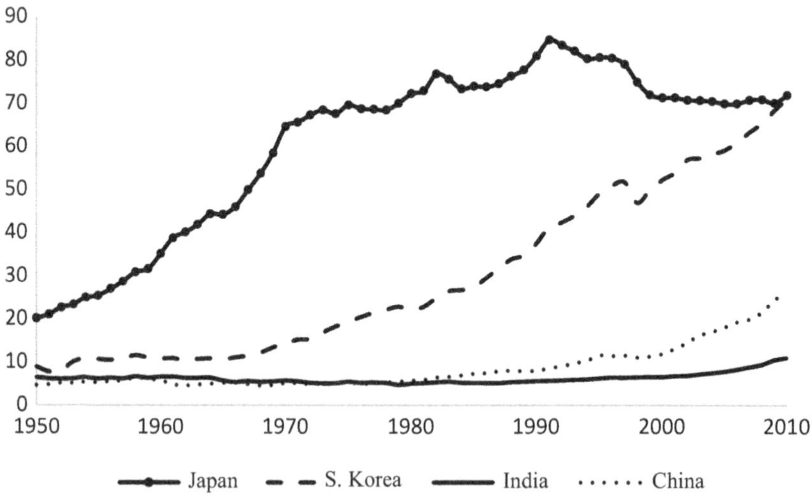

Fig. 1.3 Per capita GDP of some East Asian countries relative to the U.S. level (1950–2010). (Source: The Maddison-Project, http://www.ggdc.net/maddison/maddison-project/home.htm, 2013 version)

In addition to the East Asian countries, a number of Southeast Asian countries also performed exceptionally well in terms of economic growth, with Thailand, Malaysia, Indonesia and others being a few examples. Among them, Thailand, Malaysia and Indonesia experienced relatively rapid growth in the 20 years during 1976–1996. The average economic growth rates of the three countries during this period reached 6%, 4.6% and 5%, respectively. Although these countries experienced periods of rapid growth, their economic growth lacked sustainability and as a result failed to make the leap from middle to high-income countries.

Due to the fact that the Asian financial crisis first began in Thailand, the analysis of Thailand also provides clarity in understanding how countries hit hard by the financial crisis lost the opportunity to overcome the “middle income trap”. Before the Asian financial crisis, Thailand had maintained rapid economic growth for ten consecutive years, registering an average annual per capita GDP growth rate of around 8% during 1986–1996 and witnessing an increase in per capita GDP from 1727 US dollars to 3705 US dollars (in real 2010 dollar terms). By contrast, China claimed a per capita GDP of 1335 US dollars in 1996, only 36% of that of Thailand in the same period. However, the Asian financial crisis ended Thailand’s economic boom and ushered in a period of recession that hobbled its economy until 2002 when it returned to its pre-crisis level. In 2015, Thailand’s per capita GDP stood at 5775 US dollars (in real 2010 dollar terms), significantly lower than that of China (6497 US dollars). After reeling from the impact of the Asian financial crisis, the Thai economy has not been able to return to a high growth trajectory with its economic growth rate at a mere 3.4% during 2000–2015 if calculated on the basis of constant real dollars.

According to the relative criteria, Thailand’s per capita GDP in 1990 (PPP, 2011 international dollars) equated to 17.6% of that of the U.S. and 23.5% in 1996. With the onset of the Asian financial crisis in Thailand, the percentage plummeted first and then gradually rose again, eventually recapturing 1996 levels in 2007. If Thailand had been able to maintain its pace of catching up with the U.S. during 1990–1996, it would have reached the ranks of high-income countries in 2012 (Fig. 1.4).

Another Southeast Asian country worthy of note is the Philippines, whose population surpassed 100 million in 2015. In 1960, the per capita GDP of the Philippines stood at 1059 US dollars, roughly twice that of Thailand. However, the Philippines is particularly representative of countries that have experienced low growth for an extended period of time,

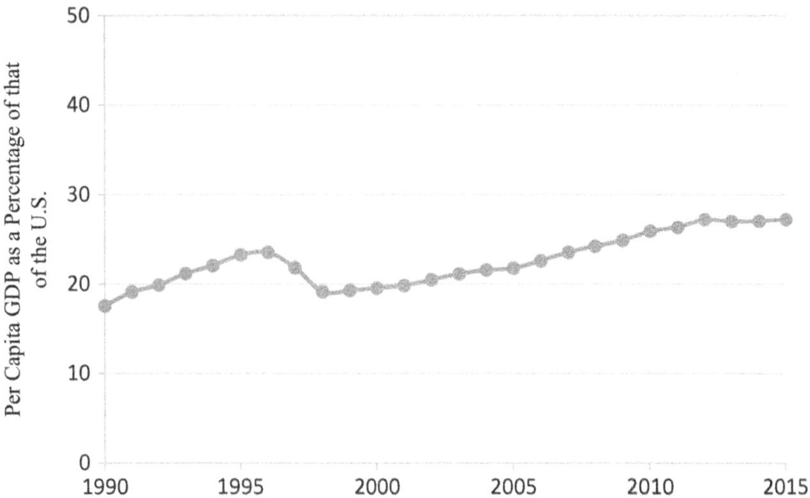

Fig. 1.4 Thailand's per capita GDP relative to the U.S. level (1990–2015). (Source: The World Bank, 2017 World Development Index. Note: per capita GDP percentage in PPP terms on the basis of 2011 constant prices is used)

registering a growth rate of approximately 1% during the period 1960–1986 and a mere 2.2% during 1986–2015. It claimed a per capita GDP of 2640 US dollars (in constant 2010 US dollar prices) in 2015, equivalent to only 40% of that of China. In 1960, the per capita GDP of the Philippines was more than five times that of China.

Why did the Southeast Asian countries, which had sustained rapid growth for two decades, faltered into an economic and social quagmire in the face of the financial crisis? A fundamental reason is that these countries did not investigate the objective reality of their own economic development and took for granted the notion that the neoliberal economic model could serve as the optimal recipe for their own economic development instead of proactively seeking solutions to the structural contradictions of their economies through deepening reforms and applying remedies accordingly. As a result, this led to the continual accretion of various fragilities in their economies, and eventually evolved into the drastic devaluation of currencies, turmoil in the capital markets, massive bankruptcy of enterprises and sharp deterioration of unemployment and inflation, which all constituted triggers for social instability.

In addition, before the financial crisis swept through these countries, there already existed severe social problems and conflicts. However, the governments of the said countries neglected the importance of social progress and overlooked the development of a social safety net in the process of promoting economic growth, leading to an increasing level of vulnerabilities in terms of social stability. Therefore, once the financial crisis plunged the economies into recession, the poor were hit first and the standard of living of the underprivileged deteriorated markedly, resulting in social discontent, questioning of the state leaders' ability to govern and even of the governments' political legitimacy. Eventually, widespread social discontent would continue to gather steam, and the economic crisis would transform into social turmoil and riots. The original political system would collapse and political power would exchange hands frequently, resulting in a vicious cycle of political instability and economic crisis.

The Southeast Asian financial crisis in 1997, generally speaking, resulted in such Southeast Asian countries as Thailand and Malaysia losing their opportunity to overcome the "middle income trap". We can see in Fig. 1.5

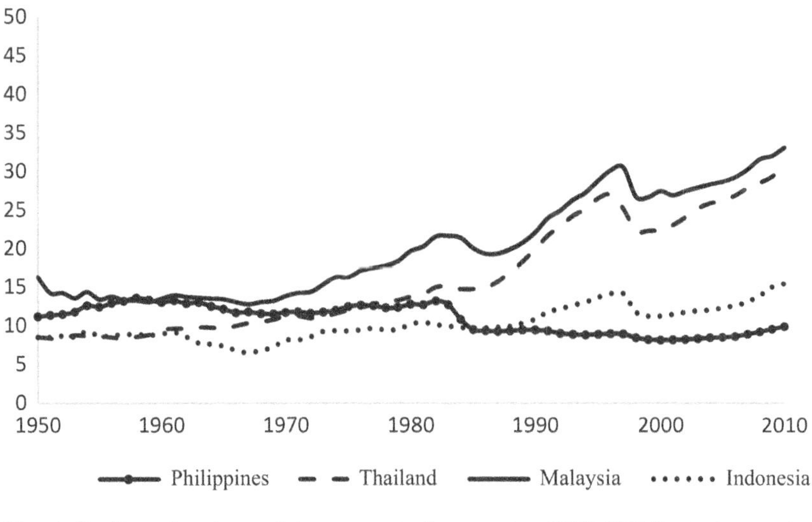

Fig. 1.5 Four Southeast Asian countries' per capita GDP (PPP) relative to the U.S. level (1950–2010). (Source: The Maddison-Project, http://www.ggdc.net/maddison/maddison-project/home.htm, 2013 version)

that the per capita income levels of these Southeast Asian countries had already exceeded 8% of that of the U.S. in 1950, but in the following six decades from 1950–2010, they were not able to follow in the footsteps of South Korea to overcome the "middle income trap". The relative level of economic development in South Korea in 1950 was comparable to that of the Southeast Asian countries.

1.3.2 Latin American Countries Ensnared by the "Middle Income Trap"

Latin American countries are also representative of those caught in the "middle income trap" and stand in stark contrast to the above-mentioned East Asian countries. Historically speaking, Argentina's per capita GDP already reached to 52.2% of that of the U.S. in 1950, landing it firmly in the category of high-income countries by the relative criteria. However, during the 1950–1980 period, not only did Argentina fail to catch up with the U.S. in terms of per capita GDP, the gap between the two actually widened, with Argentina's per capita GDP only equating to 44.2% of that of the U.S. by 1980. After the 1980s, the per capita GDP of Argentina slid rapidly against that of the U.S. to 27.7% in 1990 and has hovered around that level thereafter. It should be noted that Argentina was once one of the wealthiest countries in the world. Calculated on the basis of the constant dollar price of 2010, the per capita GDP of Argentina already reached 5620 US dollars in 1960, but only witnessed a slight increase to 5956 US dollars in 1990 during a 30-year span. Since then, per capita income in Argentina has reached $8205 in 2000 and $10,514 in 2015, but still falling short of the rank of high-income countries. Argentina's average per capita GDP growth rate stood at a mere 1.1% during the period of 1960–2015 at constant dollar prices. When viewed within the entire time frame, this rate of growth could only be characterized as a low rate of growth that resulted in Argentina's failure to escape the "middle income trap".

Argentina's overall low economic growth has been characterized by wide fluctuations in growth rate. During the period of 1960–2015, the country experienced 21 years of negative growth in per capita GDP. There were 12 years that the economic growth of Argentina exceeded 7% and there were 11 years that the economic growth was lower than −3%,

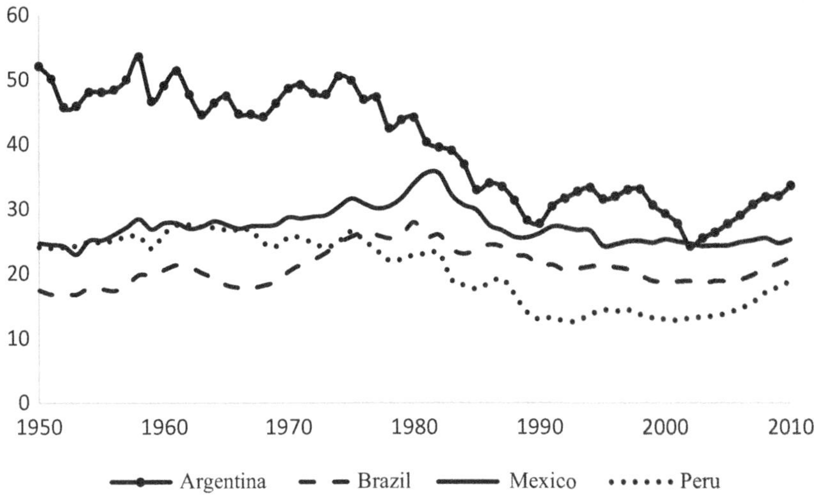

Fig. 1.6 Four Latin American countries' per capita GDP relative to the U.S. average (1950–2010). (Source: The Maddison-Project, http://www.ggdc.net/maddison/maddison-project/home.htm, 2013 version)

exhibiting a lack of stability in the country's economic growth. Although the country experienced periods of rapid growth, they often could not be sustained. The example of Argentina indicates to us that developing countries need not only relatively high rates of economic growth but also stable economic growth in order to overcome the "middle income trap". In this sense, only when "walking steadily" can one "walk far" (Fig. 1.6).

According to the World Bank's classification of countries by income, Argentina remained an upper-middle-income country in 2015. According to the country's average per capita GDP (PPP) as that of the U.S., Argentina's average per capita GDP fluctuated between 35%–37% of that of the U.S. from 2010 to 2015 and declined further in the recent two years, resembling a typical country caught in the "middle income trap". In the same vein, Brazil, Peru and Mexico have long remained in the ranks of middle-income countries and their per capita GDP also exhibited sharp declines relative to that of the U.S. in the 1980s. To date, no Latin American country has succeeded in making the leap from a middle-income to a high-income country.

1.3.3 A Comparison of the Two Groups of Countries

Fundamentally speaking, the promise of entering into the ranks of high-income countries from middle-income countries is the sustained and rapid economic growth. According to the method of economic growth accounting, economic growth rates are the results of growth in factor input (including labor and capital), growth of human capital and growth of total factor productivity (TFP). A close examination of the growth accounting for the East Asian economies reveals that the growth of total factor productivity constituted a crucial factor in their ability to maintain relatively high rates of economic growth since 1970. According to estimates by the International Monetary Fund, China claimed the highest average economic growth rate and total factor productivity growth rate in this period, and half of the growth experienced in the former could be attributed to growth in the latter. The same could be said about South Korea. Hong Kong, Taiwan and Singapore also observed their total factor productivity growth contributing to more than one third of the growth in the economic growth rate. In contrast, India witnessed much less contribution to economic growth from TFP growth (see Fig. 1.7).

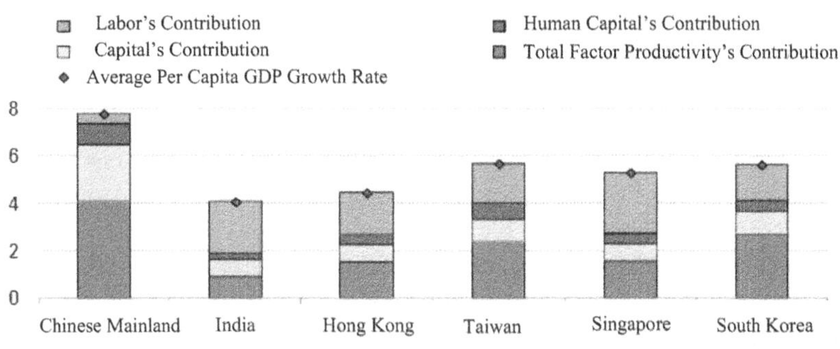

Fig. 1.7 Growth accounting for six Asian countries and regions (1970–2009). (Source: Shekhar Aiyar, Romain Duval, Damien Puy, Yiqun Wu and Longmei Zhang, Growth Slowdowns and the Middle-Income Trap, *IMF working paper*, WP/13/71, 2013. Note: The estimates for the Chinese mainland, Hong Kong, Taiwan, Singapore and South Korea are sourced from the period between 1970 and 2009; the estimates for India are sourced from the period between 1980 and 2009)

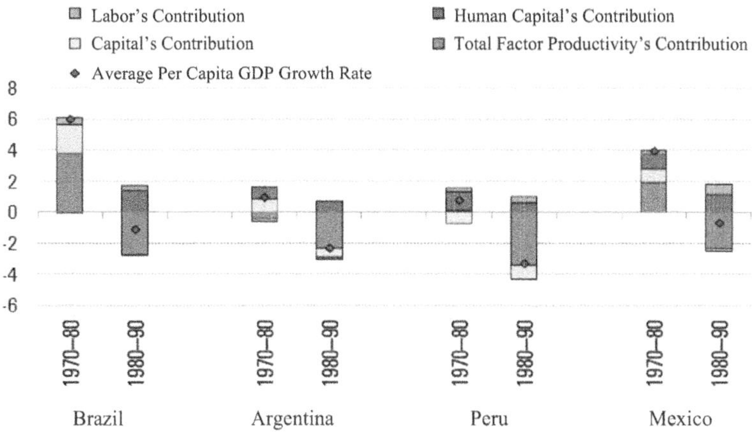

Fig. 1.8 Growth accounting for four Latin American countries (1970–1990). (Source: Shekhar Aiyar, Romain Duval, Damien Puy, Yiqun Wu and Longmei Zhang, Growth Slowdowns and the Middle-Income Trap, *IMF working paper*, WP/13/71, 2013)

Figure 1.8 depicts the economic growth rates of the four Latin American countries during the 1970s and 1980s and corresponding contributions by the four growth factors. A comparison of the two periods reveals that economic growth in the four countries observed drastic declines. In the 1970s, all four countries experienced positive per capita GDP growth, with an average growth rate of 6% in Brazil, 4% in Mexico and less than 2% in Argentina and Peru. By the 1980s, economic growth in the four countries all fell into the negative territory, with Peru's economy diminishing at a rate of 3.5% in size. An examination of the various contributing factors that determine economic growth reveals that all four countries experienced a significant diminution in total factor productivity, indicating that the decline in total factor productivity constituted a major factor in the decline of economic growth in the four countries. In addition, we can also see that the contribution of capital to economic growth in the four Latin American countries in the 1980s also dipped into the negative territory. The reason for this is that the decline in total factor productivity dampened investment and led to a negative growth in capital stock. By contrast, the contribution of capital to economic growth has remained positive in the six Asian countries and regions mentioned above which demonstrates that growth in total factor productivity can bolster investment, which in turn leads to the continuous growth of capital stock.

In comparing the aforementioned two groups of countries, we can draw the following conclusions: concerning economic growth accounting, *the sustained growth of total factor productivity represents the key to maintaining economic growth and creates the major impetus for middle-income countries to develop into high-income countries.* We could go one step further by stating that for middle-income countries, eventually navigating over the "middle income trap" is the inevitable result of long-term, stable and high-quality growth, which is evident in the contribution and importance of total factor productivity to economic growth.

1.4 Why Does the "Middle Income Trap" Emerge?

The above statistical and comparative study of the "middle income trap" raises a major theoretical and practical question: why is it that after 250 years of global industrialization, only a handful of more than 200 countries and regions in the world have achieved the status of developed economies? Why weren't many developing countries able to further progress into developed economies? Alternatively, why have many middle-income countries lingered in the middle-income phase for so long without joining the ranks of high-income countries with some even slipping into economic stagnation or regression? For instance, Latin America and Southeast Asia are two such representative cases. Countries in these regions failed to extricate themselves from the "middle income trap" for decades while, on the other hand, a number of East Asian countries and regions successfully overcame the trap and attained high-income status.

International experience indicates that the transformation of the economic growth model of a region typically undergoes three stages of development. The first phase involves the progression from low-income to lower-middle or middle-income status and can be characterized as the stage of "economic take-off". Generally speaking, a traditional model of economic development, which manifests as high factor input, low clustering of industries, low value-added trade, high consumption of natural resources and environmental pollution, dominates this phase. The second phase involves the progression from lower-middle to upper-middle-income status and can be characterized as a period of transition (see Fig. 1.9). Three possibilities exist during this time: if the transition proves to be successful, the economy will continue to grow or take off, landing it

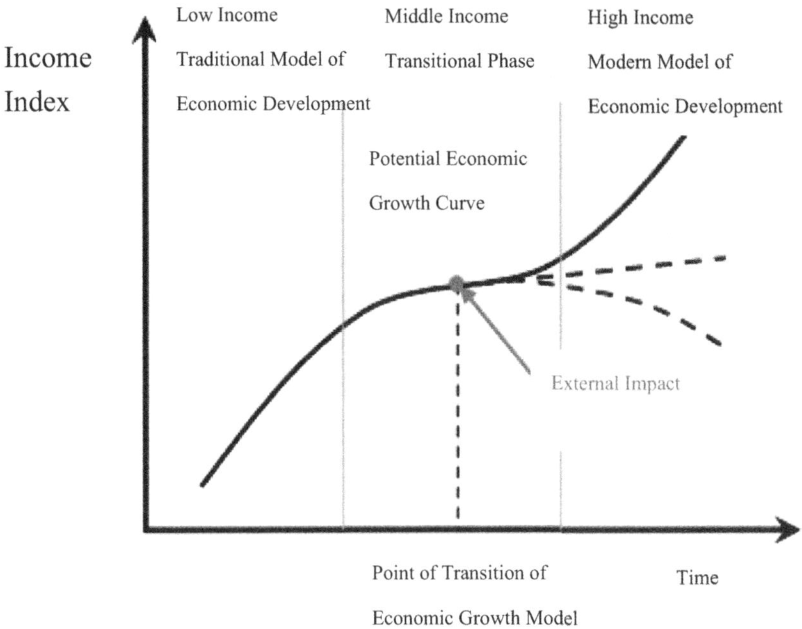

Fig. 1.9 The theoretical model for the "Middle Income Trap". (Note: formulated by the authors)

in the category of middle-income countries; if the transition does not prove to be successful, stasis ensues; or if the transition fails, the economic "take-off" is interrupted and the economy falls into the "middle income trap", resulting in a sharp dive in potential economic growth rate and stagnation. This period marks a time of anguish for economic restructuring, but also a time of strategic opportunity for the transformation of the economic growth model.

The third phase of development depends on the outcomes of the second phase of economic restructuring. If the second phase of transition proves to be successful, the country in question will proceed further to obtain the high-income or developed economy status. This phase of development is characterized by innovation, high spatial agglomeration, high value-added trade, harmonious development between man and nature, and social harmony. If the second phase of transformation fails, the country will then remain in the middle-income stage and fall into the "middle income trap". In addition, the stagnation of economic growth will inevitably compound various conflicts and lead to the exacerbation of political instability, rendering it impossible for the country to rise above the "vicious cycle" of development.

Generally speaking, total factor productivity growth constitutes a necessary condition for developing countries to overcome the "middle income trap" if their economic development does not depend upon the export of resources (some Middle Eastern countries for instance). The contribution rate of total factor productivity to economic growth or, to put it differently, whether or not total factor productivity can undergo sustained growth, to a great extent, can reflect the efficiency of resource allocation and the degree of contribution of innovation to economic growth. In the empirical study of economic growth, total factor productivity can generally be bifurcated into technical efficiency and technological progress. Technological progress refers to the progress of a country's technological frontier and can be regarded as the crystallization of innovation. Technical efficiency refers to efficiency displayed by a country in allocating input factors under given technological conditions and can be considered an outcome of market mechanisms. Both economic and non-economic factors may affect the two components mentioned above. We can conduct analysis from the economic, political, social and international dimensions.

From an economic point of view, the efficiency of a country's resource allocation is often predicated on its economic system. For instance, the former Soviet Union began implementing a planned economic system when Stalin came to power which was later referred to as the "Stalin model" or "Soviet model". This planned economic system is actually a product of the highly centralized political system of the former Soviet Union. Under the single ownership system, the Soviet model essentially represents a command economy. During a given period, this model promoted the industrialization of the Soviet Union and made it the linchpin of the anti-fascist campaign in World War II. After World War II, as the world entered into the Cold War era characterized by proxy conflicts between the U.S. and the Soviet Union, the latter poured its resources into developing heavy industries and neglected the development of agriculture and light industries, eventually resulting in severe imbalances in its industrial structure and the faltering living standards of its citizens, and in turn served as a key factor in galvanizing social discontent and ultimately leading to the dissolution of the Soviet Union. In a sense, a fundamental problem with the former Soviet Union's economic system is that it was designed principally for seeking world hegemony instead of raising people's living standards. This stands in stark contrast to the phase of development experienced in China after the implementation of reform and opening-up.

The failures in economic development strategization also constitute a crucial factor in the stagnation of total factor productivity growth. For example, Argentina used to belong to the rank of high-income countries, and according to Maddison's estimates, the country's per capita GDP (PPP, 1990 international dollars) was higher than that of the U.S. in 1896. Since then, Argentina's per capita GDP as a percentage of that of the U.S. had been on a downward trend and fell to 52% in 1950 despite Argentina still being considered as a high-income country according to the relative criteria. However, after 1950, Argentina failed to seize the opportunity for industrialized development following World War II. The country had long relied on the export of primary products and failed to effectively reconfigure its industrial structure and enhance its competitive edge. At the same time, against the backdrop of domestic political instability, it introduced neoliberal economic policies that led to macroeconomic instability, debt crisis and hyperinflation, which in turn undermined the foundation for economic growth. By 2002, Argentina's per capita GDP relative to that of the U.S. fell to a record low of 24.3%. It can be said that Argentina is representative of countries that have stumbled back into the middle-income group from the high-income one and would remain ensnared in the "middle income trap" for a long time. According to World Bank statistics (PPP, 2011 international dollars), Argentina's per capita GDP equated to 35% of that of the U.S. in 2015, even lower than the level in 2011. It can be argued that the country still faces tremendous challenges in overcoming the "middle income trap". In fact, other Latin American countries also share Argentina's experience. In the past six decades, the Latin American economies vacillated between the import substitution strategy and the neoliberal strategy. By contrast, the East Asian countries adapted themselves to the objective demands of economic globalization and succeeded in implementing export-oriented economic policies, responding effectively to new trends and challenges brought by globalization, continuously nurturing new competitive advantages and enhancing their global competitiveness.

In the long run, technological progress serves as the fundamental engine for the continuous growth of total factor productivity. Without technological progress, total factor productivity growth will eventually enter into stasis as resource allocation becomes optimized. The technological progress of a country either relies on the introduction of foreign technology with the purpose of promoting domestic technological advancement or its own capacity for independent indigenous innovation. Innovation plays a critical role in the growth of total factor productivity especially when a country's technological capabilities already lead the rest of the world. Among the world's high-income countries, excluding those that had established themselves as capitalist developed economies early on and the resource-exporting countries, innovation has been the key ingredient of success for those that joined the ranks of high-income countries later on.

The capacity for innovation of a country or region depends on two aspects of innovation investment, one being capital investment and the other being talent supply. In terms of capital investment, the intensity of a nation's investment in innovation is generally measured through the ratio of R&D expenditure to GDP. Let us compare South Korea with countries that have fallen into the "middle income trap". For example, in terms of investment in innovation (R&D expenditure as a percentage of GDP), South Korea registered at 2.64% in 2003, ranking seventh globally, compared to 0.69% and 0.41% in Malaysia and Argentina, respectively, both of which failed to enter the top 40 ranks. With respect to the supply of innovation talents, in 2006, the number of R&D personnel per 1000 people in South Korea stood at 4.8, while that of Malaysia and Argentina stood at a mere 0.42 and 1.1, respectively. The pool of innovation talents South Korea could tap into was 11.4 times and 4.4 times that of Malaysia and Argentina, respectively. As for the quality of their labor force, 35% of the workforce in South Korea claimed an undergraduate or higher education background in 2007, compared with 20.3% and 29.5% in Malaysia and Argentina, respectively. South Korea also displayed a clear advantage in this regard.

From another point of view, when a country has entered the middle-income stage, maintaining sustained total factor productivity growth can prove to be challenging without the capacity for innovation. This is due to the fact that during the middle-income stage of development (especially the upper-middle-income stage), with the growth of per capita income comes the rising costs of a variety of factors of production, diminishing marginal returns on capital investment and waning comparative advantages in the labor-intensive economy. These developments also actively and objectively call for economic restructuring, that is, realizing the transformation of the economic growth model through innovation. If this transformation cannot be attained, the economic growth will lose its momentum and the potential growth rate may plunge and even remain in a dismal state, making entry into the ranks of high-income countries a distant reality.

From international experience, the middle-income stage of development is also characterized by a polarization of the social structure. As the social structure is transformed in a dramatic fashion, the interests of each social stratum grow entrenched and social problems are exacerbated as a result. For example, at the turn of the nineteenth and early twentieth centuries, the U.S. economic take-off was both coined a "progressive era" and the "worst era", during which economic crises happened in a cyclical manner, the gap between the rich and poor grew ever wider, political corruption became widespread and class conflicts worsened. An examination of the history of earlier capitalist countries such as the U.K., France and Germany reveals similar developments.

The surge in social instability is both a product of and an impact on a country's economic development. This is because in the process of economic development and especially during the period of rapid development, wide arrays of imbalances tend to emerge, inevitably resulting in a widening income gap among different groups of people and thereby causing social conflicts. Countries in the middle-income stage of development will also see their chances of overcoming the "middle income gap" diminish if the issue of unfair distribution of income is not addressed. Existing empirical studies reveal that income inequality hinders economic growth, especially for countries that have yet to enter the stage of high-income development.[14] Income inequality will negatively affect the economic growth of middle-income countries in at least two regards and further diminish their chances of navigating over the "middle income trap".

On the one hand, as a country enters the middle-income stage, the demand for human capital investment of its citizens will undoubtedly increase correspondingly, resulting in an upsurge in the demand for quality education across society and further hiking up the cost of education. However, due to the relatively slower income growth experienced by

[14] Relevant literature can be found: Robert J. Barro (2000). Inequality and Growth in a Panel of Countries, *Journal of Economic Growth*, 5: 5–32; Dierk Herzer, Sebastian Vollmer (2012). Inequality and Growth: Evidence from Panel Cointegration, *The Journal of Economic Inequality*, 10: 489–503.

low-income families, their ability to invest in their children's human capital is diminished which in turn constrains the possibilities for future development and ultimately results in the real human capital growth rate falling behind the potential growth rate. Consequently, the limited growth proves unable to effectively meet the demand by this stage of economic development on human capital.

On the other hand, during the middle-income stage, the widening of income gap will inevitably aggravate social polarization and put social cohesion at risk. This is due to the fact that interest groups that benefit from the existing paradigm of income distribution will seek to obstruct reform measures aiming at achieving a fairer distribution of income in order to protect their vested interests, which would eventually lead to the entrenchment of interest groups, lower inter-generational social mobility, hostility among the vested interests and ordinary folks as well as escalating social conflicts. Furthermore, the decrease in inter-generational social mobility also means that economically disadvantaged people cannot gain fair access to opportunities for development. In a sense, the degradation of the income distribution structure is often a result of the lack of institutional arrangements that can effectively contain unfair development in income structure and the alliance between power and capital.

Many Latin American countries experienced long-term stagnation or even negative growth during the 1970s and 1990s, and have yet to overcome the "middle income trap" to date. Their economic stagnation occurred in tandem with widening income gaps and severe social polarization, with the Gini coefficient reaching as high as 0.5–0.6. All these countries had endured periods of military dictatorship when crony capitalism prevailed and power and capital conspired together in plundering the society for wealth which then led to ever-widening income gaps, social conflicts and regime changes. At other times, left-wing governments took power and overcorrected the course of development by instituting egalitarianism and diminishing the role of the market. This flip-flopping in development and social unrest severely affected the countries' economic development.

Income inequality tends to work in unison with a series of other factors in threatening social stability. These factors are both causes for and products of income inequality. For instance, one critical factor that contributed to many middle-income countries' inability to overcome the "middle income gap" after the 1960s was a gridlock in social progress, manifested through such social problems as corruption, nepotism and injustices in the administrative and judicial realms, which were in and of themselves causes for an unfair distribution of income. In addition, an unfair distribution of income will in turn diminish the government's capacity for redistribution, which is necessary for maintaining social stability. For example, a sharp rise in income disparity leads to an increase in the demand for government public service expenditures, but with a given amount of available budgetary revenue, the ever-expanding public service demand will result in a shortage of public services. The direct consequence of leaving such issues as growing polarization between the rich and the poor, lack of social mobility and shortage of public services unaddressed is a growing sense of distrust in society toward the government, absence of faith, distorted public sentiment, build-up of social discontent, the spread of populism and various radical ideologies (religious or secular). These issues will evolve into direct triggers for the eruption of social conflicts. Without sound social policies designed to resolve these issues, the problems will further aggravate the vulnerabilities of social development and lead to social or even political crises. Eventually, investment will be negatively affected, leading to economic stagnation or even regression, which could intertwine and interact with each other in a vicious cycle to eventually plunge the economy into the "middle income trap".

As the widening gap between the rich and the poor intensifies existing social polarization and conflicts, the aggravation of social conflicts in turn provokes social unrest, political division and confrontations between governments and ordinary people. Ultimately, initial rallies and protests on the streets transform into violent anti-government movements, resulting in regime change or even collapse. In fact, not only does a widening income gap pose a threat to the social stability and political structure of middle-income countries, it also produces the same effect on developed economies. As a matter of fact, one important factor that contributed to Donald Trump's winning the U.S. presidency was the dissatisfaction with the long-term deterioration of income inequality within the country's low-income populations (especially Caucasian blue-collar workers), who threw their support behind a candidate that advocated anti-illegal immigration and anti-free-trade policies.

From a political point of view, the middle-income stage is not only characterized by drastic changes in various economic variables and social structures, but also by drastic changes in the reorganization of political structures. A complex mechanism dictates the interactions among the three. Long-term economic stagnation leads to a buildup of discontent among the people and results in political instability, which in turn contributes to the exacerbation of economic and social problems. Conversely, if political stability is maintained, governments will have a better chance of addressing economic and social problems; while political disarray could only lead to the exacerbation of existing challenges. In this sense, a stable political environment constitutes the single most important public good, which in itself is the most crucial prerequisite for countries in overcoming the "middle income trap". According to the International Country Risk Guide (ICRG) database, in 1990 among the East Asian economies, Japan, Taiwan, Singapore and South Korea scored 7.25, 8.92, 8.08 and 8.67 respectively on Government Stability, significantly higher than the Latin American economies beset by the "middle income trap" (Ex. Argentina 6.58, Peru 4.00). *A stable political structure sets the cornerstone for overcoming the "middle income trap".*

The extreme form of political instability is manifested in a change of government or national disintegration. Generally speaking, the consequences of a change of government or national disintegration are not limited to short-term setbacks in economic growth and can lead to a direct fall into the "middle income trap". In the late 1980s and early 1990s, following the dissolution of the Soviet Union, socialist countries in Eastern Europe reverted to adopting a capitalist market economic model, which led to economic stagnation or even negative growth of their economies. Russia's per capita GDP (PPP, 2011 international dollars) amounted to 55.1% of that of the U.S. before the collapse of the Soviet Union in 1990, commensurate with other high-income countries by the relative criteria. After the disintegration of the Soviet Union, the ratio continued to decline and fell to the lowest level (26.4%) in 1998. Afterward, it saw gradual increases and surpassed 40% for the first time in 2007 after being in the "middle income trap" for more than 20 years (1993–2006). Furthermore, the ratio fluctuated between 43%–47% during the period of 2007–2015, with no apparent signs of a further upward trend. The country's per capita GDP relative to that of the U.S. experienced a steep decline after 2012 as a result of its economic performance being highly dependent on energy price movements. The global commodities crunch since 2012 has also caused sluggish economic growth in Russia. The above data indicate that from the end of 1991 when the Soviet Union dissolved up to the current time, Russia has yet to recover to its pre-dissolution levels in terms of economic development relative to that of the U.S.

A recent example of a country downgrading to the middle-income status from high-income is Libya. Toward the end of 2010, the wave of revolutions termed the "Arab Spring" had swept across the Middle East, resulting in civil wars and change of governments in countries such as Tunisia, Egypt, Libya and Syria. Among them, the wars in Libya and Syria have persisted to this day and led to a severe erosion of economic development and the standard of living of their people. Libya, for instance, claimed a per capita GDP (PPP, 2011 international dollars) that amounted to 49% of that of the U.S. in 2003, landing it in the category of high-income countries. Moreover, with the lifting of the 11-year sanctions in 2003 that had been imposed on Libya by the United Nations due to the Lockerbie plane crash in 1988 and the 1989 UTA Flight 772 bombing, the country's economy experienced some degree of growth during the 2003–2010 period, with its per capita GDP reaching 58% of that of the U.S. in 2010. However, the Libyan civil war that broke out in 2011 directly led to the collapse of the country's economy and its per capita GDP as a percentage of that of the U.S., plummeting to 21.8% in 2011. On the whole, as Libya entered a so-called post-Qaddafi era after 2011, the country has remained divided and spawned, together with Syria, a massive refugee crisis in Europe.

In addition to the aforementioned economic, social and political issues, external factors also figure substantially in whether or not a country may fall into the "middle income trap". One typical example is the impact of the 1997 Asian financial crisis on emerging economies in Southeast Asia. We can see in Fig. 1.5 that the financial crisis derailed the Southeast Asian economies from their path of economic growth and cost them the opportunity to overcome the "middle income trap". Moreover, the financial crisis evolved directly into an economic crisis, which in turn led to serious social and political upheavals that manifested as soaring unemployment, surge in the number of impoverished people, considerable declines in personal income, surge in crimes and violence and compromised confidence in society's prospects and in government.

In this sense, economic globalization, in and of itself, is a double-edged sword. The crisis in one country will affect its neighbors and the crisis in a major economy will have global implications. The 2008 global financial crisis triggered by the sub-prime mortgage crisis in the U.S. was considered a "once-in-a-century" event with repercussions for the global economic and financial systems. Its negative impact spread to all corners of the world. For many developing and emerging economies, the financial

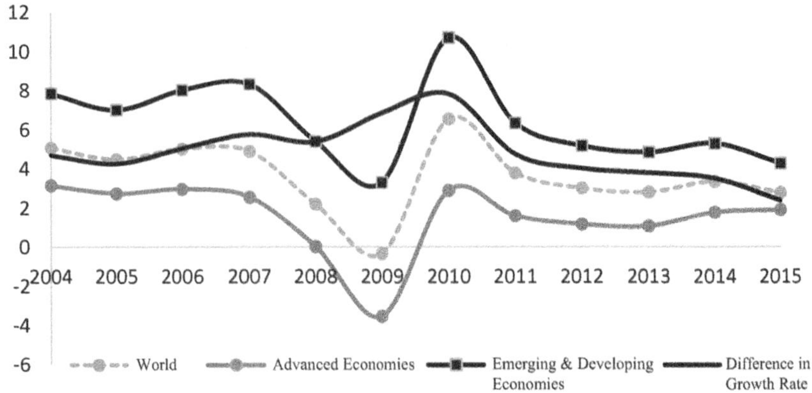

Fig. 1.10 Global economic growth before and after the global financial crisis (2004–2015). (Source: IMF)

crisis triggered by the sub-prime mortgage in the U.S. created massive negative externalities and delivered an external shock to the economic development of these countries. As the Chinese saying goes, "when the city gate catches fire, the fish in the moat suffer from it". When the U.S. sub-prime mortgage disaster evolved into a global financial crisis, it ended the momentum of rapid economic growth for some emerging economies. According to the relative criteria, a middle-income country will not be able to overcome the "middle income trap" as long as its per capita GDP growth rate falls short of that of the U.S. Since 2004, the world economy has dropped from a growth rate of nearly 5% during the pre-crisis period (2006–2007) to roughly 3% in recent years (2014–2015). Among the world's economies, the average growth rate of emerging and developing economies declined from 8% to 4.3% in 2015, while the difference in the rate of economic growth between developing and developed economies slid from 5.76% in 2007 to 2.37% in 2015. Although the momentum of catch-up with the developed world remained, it has weakened significantly (Fig. 1.10).[15]

Although nearly ten years have passed since the global financial crisis broke out in 2008, its impact has yet to run its full course and the global

[15] Among them, Brazil and Russia suffered heavy economic losses, with growth rates dipping into the negative territory in a number of years during the 2009–2015 period.

economy remains in a process of profound adjustment. In particular, in response to the financial crisis, the U.S. Federal Reserve implemented four rounds of "quantitative easing" from November 2008 to the end of 2012 which helped stabilize the U.S. financial system and stimulate the country's economic growth. However, as the U.S. economy recovered ahead of other advanced economies, the Federal Reserve began to gradually roll back its "quantitative easing" policies in early 2014 which delivered a substantial impact to the global financial market and aggravated capital market volatilities in the emerging economies. This, to a certain extent, also led to the pressure of capital flight, which has evolved into a hidden danger to the global economy in the post-crisis era. In this sense, the U.S. first brought on the global financial crisis of 2008 with its subprime mortgage crisis and then recovered its economic growth through "quantitative easing". As the country withdraws from quantitative easing policies and the Federal Reserve introduces benchmark interest rate hikes, uncertainties in the global financial market and especially the capital markets of developing countries will grow which in turn will affect the economic recovery of emerging economies.

We can draw the following conclusions based on previous discussions: a country does not necessarily or naturally enter the high-income ranks from the middle-income ranks. The "middle income trap" occurs as the combined result of a series of economic, social, political and international factors. Judging from the economic growth in developing countries after World War II, no country was able to maintain long-term and stable growth with a single unchanging economic growth model. The models of economic growth are characterized by the peculiarities of various stages of development. During the different stages of income, their basic conditions for economic development (including advantages and constraints) vary, and so do the opportunities and challenges. Therefore, the model of economic development should be adjusted accordingly. For developing countries mired in the "middle income trap", if they are not able to adapt their models of economic development to changing internal and external conditions, the latent risks existing in the original model will accrue and escalate, eventually leading to economic, political and social crises and even a vicious cycle of the three, plunging the economy into permanent stagnation and recession.

Alternatively, even if a country is in a period of rapid economic growth, without properly addressing the social problems that may arise in the course of economic development and maintaining political stability, its internal political and social crises may very well put the brakes on its economic development. In this sense, overcoming the "middle income trap" is not merely an economic issue, as non-economic factors often constitute the direct causes of a country's entrapment in the "middle income trap". In other words, economic downturns merely reflect the surface under which lie such fundamental issues as how to tackle the various internal and external challenges that hamper growth and cause economic instability.

The above analysis and summaries of international experiences and lessons provide us with critical information and reference in understanding such questions as what the "middle income trap" is, why countries fall into the trap and how countries can avoid and overcome the trap. Valuable lessons can be learned from the experiences of other countries particularly through studying their setbacks and mistakes. The crucial issue is, of course, how China can innovate and create its own path of development. By following Deng Xiaoping's strategic concept of modernizing China in "three steps", the country has not only succeeded in overcoming the "poverty trap", but will also be able to avoid the "middle income trap" in the future, move toward high-income status and achieve its "two centenary goals".

CHAPTER 2

How Did China Overcome the "Poverty Trap"?

Throughout the development cycle of a country, major tasks and challenges may arise during various stages of development and the possibility of a period of stagnation exists in each stage. In the low-income stage, anemic economic growth, lagging human development, political instability and social unrest often lead to a vicious cycle in national development. For instance, many countries in Africa have so far failed to fight poverty effectively and remain mired in the "poverty trap". In the middle-income stage, many countries fall into the "middle income trap". Even if countries succeed in overcoming the "middle income trap", their economic growth may still be plagued by the "high income trap", with Japan being one such example.

In order to understand whether China can effectively address the challenges of the middle-income stage and overcome the "middle income trap", we need to know how China has successfully escaped the "poverty trap". Throughout the history of the world economy, China's overcoming of the "poverty trap" and the rapid growth it has experienced since the country initiated the reform and opening-up policy, which has been described as an "economic miracle", both constitute major milestones in the history of world economic development. Understanding how China overcame the "poverty trap" is of great significance for us to gain insight into how the country should address the challenge of the "middle income trap".

S. Zhou, A. Hu, *China: Surpassing the "Middle Income Trap"*,
Contemporary China Studies,
https://doi.org/10.1007/978-981-15-6540-3_2

The passages below provide a multidimensional analytical framework for poverty and an introduction of China's achievements in poverty reduction before and after the implementation of the reform and opening-up policy, and on the basis of which, we further explicate how China was able to create a poverty reduction miracle by looking at economic development and the implementation of poverty alleviation policies. Finally, we elaborate on China's achievements in poverty reduction and its contribution to the cause of global poverty reduction with international comparisons.

2.1 The Analytical Framework of Multidimensional Poverty

Poverty is a chronic illness in civilized societies. In 1970, human beings completed their first journey to the moon, but at the same time, the vast majority of developing countries remained in abject poverty. In a sense, the technological advancements achieved by mankind and the global resource environment should prove sufficient in lifting everyone out of poverty. However, according to figures released by the World Bank, by the end of 2015, roughly 10% of the world's population (around 700 million people) remained in poverty. It is precisely due to the intractable nature of poverty that poverty reduction has become a common cause for all humanity. In September 2000, 189 countries adopted the United Nations Millennium Declaration following a three-day Millennium Summit of world leaders at the headquarters of the United Nations, and proposed eight Millennium Development Goals, which have been celebrated as a global convention to eliminate poverty.[1]

There is no doubt that an in-depth understanding of poverty is of great significance to development. Society's understanding of the concept of poverty is ever evolving and deepening. Amartya K. Sen, winner of the 1998 Nobel Prize in Economics, believes that poverty should be conceptualized as capability inadequacy instead of low income. In this sense, the root cause of poverty is the deprivation of capabilities, rights and welfare. Therefore, low income merely reflects the appearance of poverty while the

[1] The MDG proposed that countries should be committed to achieving the following goals by 2015: to eradicate extreme poverty and hunger; to achieve universal primary education; to promote gender equality and empower women; to reduce child mortality; to improve maternal health; to combat HIV/AIDS, malaria, and other diseases; to ensure environmental sustainability; to develop a global partnership for development.

lack of capabilities and the injustices caused by institutional factors constitute the deeper causes of poverty.

Based on his multidimensional understanding of poverty, Hu Angang (2009) proposed a four-dimensional poverty model, which[2] comprised income poverty, human poverty, knowledge poverty and ecological poverty. Among them, income poverty refers to the lack of material resources, meaning the lack of minimally sufficient income and expenditure which make it difficult to maintain basic living standards. Income poverty is the most commonly used measure of poverty. Internationally, the World Bank uses the international poverty line to define absolute poverty.

Human poverty refers to the lack of basic capabilities such as literacy, access to nutrition, sanitation, low average life expectancy and so on. This concept was proposed by the UNDP in the 1997 Human Development Report, which introduced the Human Poverty Index (HPI).[3]

Knowledge poverty refers to the lack of the ability to generate, acquire, exchange and apply knowledge, or the lack of access to knowledge, that is, the deprivation of people's ability and means to acquire, absorb and exchange knowledge. The knowledge here is broadly defined, including science and technology, education and training, information and network. Knowledge poverty encompasses the lack of ability to acquire, absorb and exchange knowledge.

Ecological poverty refers to extremely limited access to basic survival needs as a result of poor basic living environment that entraps people in poverty. On top of that, individual poverty may exacerbate the resource strain because of the impoverished population's increasing demand on its living environment which in turn further degrades an area's ecological integrity and increases its ecological vulnerabilities. Eventually, the carrying capacity of the environment will degrade to a level insufficient for meeting the basic survival and production needs of residents in the area.

As a chronic disease, the causes of poverty are often multifaceted and accompanied by other traits, which together manifest as a poverty

[2] Hu Angang (2009) "From a Large Poverty-Stricken Economy to a Moderately Prosperous Society: The Way China Eradicates Four Types of Poverty 1949–2020", compiled in: Pan Wei (ed.) (2009), "China Model: A New Developmental Model from the Sixty Years of the People's Republic", China Compilation and Translation Press.

[3] According to the 1997 Human Development Report, the human poverty index comprises the following: probability at birth of not surviving to age 40; adult illiteracy rate; unweighted average of population without sustainable access to an improved water source; proportion of people without access to health services; and children underweight for age.

syndrome. In the World Development Report 2000/2001, the World Bank stated three dynamic traits shared by the impoverished: first, lack of opportunities to participate in economic activities; second, no say in major decisions concerning their own destiny; third, vulnerable in the face of economic and other shocks such as illness, food crisis, recession and so on (World Bank, 2001). This demonstrates that poverty is not simply a matter of low income, but is also embodied in a multitude of aspects such as development opportunities, social equality and political participation.

Indian economist Abhijit Banerjee and French economist Esther Duflo conducted an in-depth research for 15 years on the impoverished populations in 18 countries and regions across five continents on the subject matters of their daily lives, education, health, entrepreneurship, aid, government and non-governmental organizations. In their co-authored work entitled *Poor Economics*, the two distilled the causes of poverty into four main factors: turbulent social situations, harsh natural environment, backward education and the absence of social assistance programs. Their research in fact corroborates Hu Angang's multidimensional perspective on poverty. Both agree that there is no single root cause of poverty (Fig. 2.1).

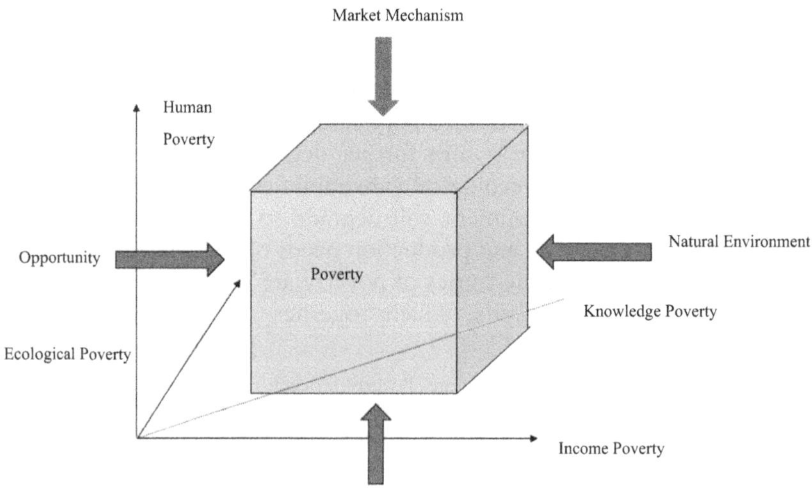

Fig. 2.1 The multidimensional analytical framework for poverty. (Note: Formulated by the authors)

2.2 Stagnant Development in China's Contemporary History Plunged the Country into Poverty

The eradication of poverty ultimately depends upon development, and poverty reduction itself is part and parcel to development. Judging from history, the economic development of countries in the world has undergone enormous changes in the past 200 years. Since the eighteenth century, and with the rise of capitalism and the spread of the industrial revolution, the world economy has entered a period of modern economic growth while disparity has become an important feature of development during this period. With the industrial revolution's remodeling of the world economy, the gradual formation of the global market and the world order yet to be brought to full fruition, in a contemporary world characterized by enormously unbalanced development, poverty often meant subjugation, and subjugation then led to worsening poverty.

Historically speaking, China gradually became the "left behind" in the global drive for modernization during the 1820–1950 period. The country faced the most egregious cases of external aggression during this period from the Western powers (including Japan). Not only was China not a participant in the global modernization process, it became a victim of aggression of the Western powers. According to Maddison's calculations, the world's average per capita GDP increased by 2.16 times during the 1820–1950 period while the per capita GDP of the U.S. rose eight-fold, the per capita GDP of Japan increased by 1.88 times and that of Western Europe grew 2.73 times. During this period, overall, China reverted from being a global economic powerhouse to a period of decline and from being a country with the world's most powerful economy to an economically weak nation. Its per capita GDP fell to a historical low of less than one-fourth of the world average, placing it at the bottom of the ladder globally. In 1820, China's per capita GDP was slightly below that of Japan and the world average, but by 1950, China's per capita GDP (1990 international dollars) had dropped to 439 US dollars, 27% lower than in 1820.[4] According to the Maddison Project Database, the average per capita GDP of China remained in the negative territory for more than 250 years

[4] Hu Angang, 2008, "The Political and Economic History of China (1949–1976)" (2nd edition), pp. 24–32, Tsinghua University Press.

Table 2.1 A comparison of per capita GDP growth among the major economies (1700–2015) (Unit: %)

	1700–1820	*1820–1952*	*1952–1978*	*1978–2003*	*2003–2015*
China	0	−0.08	2.34	6.57 (8.31)	9.15
India	0	0.1	1.81	3.27	6.11
Japan	0.1	0.95	6.66	2.11	0.82
Europe	0.22	1.03	3.56	1.79	
U.S.	0.62	1.63	2.1	1.85	0.91
Soviet Union/Russia	0.19	1.04	3.15	−0.78	3.05
Global average	0.09	0.92	2.56	1.55	2.58

Source: Maddison Project Database, 2008, "Chinese Economic Performance in the Long Run", p. 37 (data for 1700–2003 period); China National Bureau of Statistics data in parentheses; 2003–2015 data sourced from the World Bank database: http://data.worldbank.org/indicator/NY.GDP.PCAP.PP.KD?

during the 1700–1952 period. China commenced its industrialization in this historical context (Table 2.1).

One of the fundamental causes of China's backwardness and subjugation in its contemporary history lies in the lack of a strong and modern state leadership, which also constitutes an important reason for China's ineffectiveness in dealing with the global industrial revolution and the root cause for China's inability to launch its own industrialization and modernization.

2.3 Achievements in Development During China's Planned Economy Era

In 1949, following the founding of the People's Republic of China under the leadership of the CPC, China began its industrialization process to "catch up" with modernization. China's commencement of industrialization lagged 100–200 years behind that of developed countries. At the beginning of the founding of the People's Republic of China, the state of affairs concerning development in the country can be characterized as "poor and blank".[5] Therefore, such issues as how to promote economic

[5] Mao Zedong pointed out in the "Relationship between China and Foreign Countries" segment in his article "On the Ten Major Relationships" in 1956 that "we are firstly 'poor' and secondly 'blank'. 'Poor' refers to the fact that there is not much industry and our agriculture is underdeveloped, while 'blank' means blank slate. We are deficient in both literacy and science".

development, raise people's income and promote the quality of citizens through the development of science, education and health programs became the imperative and primary goals of national development after the country's founding.

Generally speaking, after the founding of the People's Republic of China up until the beginning of China's reform and opening-up, China's socialist construction had been by no means smooth sailing and had undergone several major setbacks, the Great Leap Forward and the Cultural Revolution being two examples. Nevertheless, China's socialist construction still witnessed unprecedented achievements. In terms of per capita income, according to Maddison's estimates, the country's annual per capita GDP growth rate stood at 2.34% during 1952–1978, significantly higher than before the founding of the People's Republic. China's per capita GDP in 1982 was significantly higher than in 1950 in 1990 international dollars, reaching 1186 US dollars. However, the same period also saw rapid development of capitalist and some developing countries in the post-war era, with global average per capita GDP growth reaching 2.56%. Therefore, although China did register remarkable achievements in development during this period, it failed to take full advantage of the historical opportunities to achieve better development.

With regard to poverty, China remained largely in extreme poverty during the early days of the country's founding. In the dimension of human poverty, China suffered from an exceedingly low level of human development during its initial days. During the planned economy era, it could be said that poverty was alleviated most markedly, especially in terms of human poverty. For instance, China made great strides in the domains of education and health: average life expectancy rose from 35 years in 1950 to 67.77 years in 1982; infant and maternal mortality rates also dropped significantly over the same period; the average years of schooling per person rose to 4.6 years.

Achievements in the area of health are largely the result of the development of public health infrastructure in China. For instance, following the founding of the People's Republic of China, the country conducted a long-running patriotic health campaign that covered all parts of its urban and rural areas through the mobilization of its people under the leadership of the CPC and the government. As a result, numerous epidemic diseases such as smallpox and cholera have been mostly brought under control. In addition, in spite of an extremely low per capita income, China has established a primary public health infrastructure. From the 1960s to 1980s, the "barefoot doctors" program and the rural cooperative medical system provided basic, accessible and affordable healthcare services for rural residents and coverage that became a crucial factor in raising people's average life expectancy.

China's achievements in the domain of health can be further confirmed through international comparison. In 1977, the average life expectancy in China stood at 65, much the same as that of Mexico, and significantly higher than that of India (53). According to Maddison's data, Mexico's per capita GDP was six times that of China in 1977, while India's per capita GDP was also higher than China's. In this sense, China's achievements in the domain of health in the era of planned economy with an exceedingly low average per capita income level constituted a historical miracle. In this regard, the World Bank praised China's accomplishments in the 1993 World Development Report, which stated that by the late 1970s, nearly all of China's urban population and 85% of the rural population were covered by health insurance in the country, marking an unparalleled achievement among the low-income countries.

Similarly, during the planned economy era, China also realized remarkable accomplishments in education development, mainly reflected in the elimination of illiteracy among young and midlife adults and the universal provision of primary education. In the early days of the People's Republic, the illiteracy rate stood at 80%, and the illiteracy rate in rural areas surpassed 90%. The People's Republic of China launched a large-scale literacy campaign immediately following its founding, which succeeded in greatly reducing the illiteracy rate among young adults while disseminated knowledge in the fields of production, daily life and health. By 1981, China had transformed 140 million illiterate people into literate citizens. Another important factor that led to the significant drop in illiteracy rates was the development of primary education in China. Before 1949, China's primary school enrollment rate stood at a mere 25%. However, in 1952, the enrollment rate of primary school-age children in China increased to 49.2% and subsequently reached 96.8% in 1975.[6] At the same time, the rates of graduates of primary and junior secondary schools also depicted a rising trend before China's reform and opening-up. What needs to be pointed out here is that the "Great Leap Forward" and the "Cultural

[6] Li Ling (2009): "Human Capital, Economic Miracle and the Chinese Model", compiled in: Pan Wei (ed.) (2009), "China Model: A New Developmental Model from the Sixty Years of the People's Republic", China Compilation and Translation Press.

Revolution" exerted a clear negative impact on China's education development. For example, the enrollment rate of primary school children and the rate of graduates of junior secondary schools in 1962 were significantly lower than in 1957, while the rates of graduates of primary schools and junior secondary schools were significantly lower than in 1965. However, on the whole, China had witnessed remarkable progress in the domain of primary education before the reform and opening-up.

According to data from the World Bank's World Development Report in 1983 and 1984, the adult literacy rate in China had already reached 69% in 1980 and its secondary school enrollment rate had hit 44% in 1981, both significantly higher than the majority of low-income countries, ahead of many middle-income countries at the time. Compared with the level of economic development at the beginning of China's founding, this undoubtedly constituted a tremendous achievement in development (Table 2.2).

Taking into account the economic, educational and health development since the founding of the People's Republic, development during the 1950–2015 period can be bifurcated into two stages, that is, 1950–1982 and 1982–2015, roughly corresponding to the planned economy period and the period following the implementation of the reform and opening-up. We can see from Table 2.3 that China's per capita GDP

Table 2.2 The development of China's primary education (1952–1985): Percentage of graduates entering higher level schools (Unit: %)

Year	*Junior secondary schools*	*Primary schools*	*Net enrollment rate of primary school-age children*
1952	168.6	96	49.2
1957	39.7	44.2	61.7
1962	30	45.3	56.1
1965	70	82.5	84.7
1970	38.6	71.2	
1975	60.4	90.6	96.8
1978	40.9	87.7	95.5
1979	37.6	82.8	93
1980	45.9	75.9	93.9
1985	41.7	68.4	96

Source: Comprehensive statistical materials on 60 years of the new China

Unit: %

Table 2.3 China's development through its economic, education and health indicators (1950–2015)

	1950	*1982*	*2015*
Per capita GDP (2011 international dollars)	172	802	13,572
Average years of education (years)	1.0	4.6	10.23
Life expectancy (years)	41	67.77	76.34
Infant mortality rate (‰)	200	37.61	8.1
Maternal mortality rate (per 100,000 people)	1500	100	20.1
Human Development Index	0.145	0.423 (1980)	0.738 UNDP

Sources: Per capita GDP (PPP, 2011 international dollars), 2015 data source: World Bank Database, 1950 and 1982 data calculated on the basis of 2011 international dollars; source of average life expectancy data: National Bureau of Statistics of China: China Statistical Abstract (2016), p.18; The average years of education for the working-age population are calculated by the authors on the basis of previous national census data; source of infant and maternal mortality data: National Bureau of Statistics of China: China Statistical Yearbook (2016), p. 725; source of Human Development Index (HDI) data: 2016 UNDP Human Development Report, Table 2, 1950 and 1982 figures are calculated by the authors

growth took a "small step forward" in the planned economy era whereas it took a "big step forward" in the domains of education and healthcare. This indicates that although China experienced major setbacks during the Great Leap Forward and the Cultural Revolution, the planned economy laid the groundwork for the rapid economic growth after the reform and opening-up through human capital investment. In addition, we can also see that between 1982 and 2015, the development of economy and education took a further "big step forward" while health outcomes also witnessed improvements.

2.4 Economic Development and Poverty Reduction

Economic development is a necessary condition for poverty reduction. Without economic development, it is more difficult for the poor to access opportunities that can improve their incomes and living standards. Fundamentally speaking, the substantial progress in China's poverty reduction was largely achieved after the reform and opening-up, which was closely related to the rapid economic growth thereafter. People often describe China's process of reform and opening-up as being like a person crossing a river by feeling his way over the stones. At the beginning of the reform and opening-up, China did not have a prescriptive "blueprint for development"; the implementation of various reform measures essentially was to meet the objective needs of economic and social development at the time, and adjustments were made accordingly as problems arose during the implementation process. In other words, the economic reforms after the reform and opening-up are largely adaptive in nature. The goal of China's economic reform is clear: to develop the economy and constantly raise the living standards of the people. Overall, the process of China's economic reform since 1978 has been methodical and can be characterized by a series of stages with differing priorities of reform at each stage. However, fundamentally speaking, the one common feature across the stages is creating economic opportunities for the people.

2.4.1 Rural Economic Reform and Poverty Reduction

China's economic reform began with the implementation of the household responsibility system in rural areas. The measure, which played a crucial role in alleviating poverty in China in the early days of the reform and opening-up, represented a typical example of institutional changes made on account of the development of farmers, or in other words, it was an induced institutional change. It should be noted that although China significantly reduced human poverty in the era of planned economy, progress was mainly found in the fields of education and health while the issue of income poverty remained outstanding. At the beginning of its reform and opening-up, China had stayed as a country with extremely low per capita income. According to Maddison's data, China's per capita GDP in 1978 stood at 979 US dollars (PPP, 1990 international dollars), comparable to that of India, but significantly lower than the average of 57 African countries (1439 international dollars).[7] According to the international poverty line, there were still 730 million impoverished people in China in 1978, equivalent to roughly 76% of its total population. The fundamental issue of food security remained unresolved. In April 1979, then Vice Premier of the State Council, Li Xiannian, admitted for the first time that per capita grain possession in 1978 was only slightly higher than in 1957. The import of agricultural products accounted for about one fifth of the total value of imports. Farmers in considerable parts of the country did

[7]Angus Maddison, 2003, Shi Jie Jing Ji Qian Nian Shi, p. 302 & 325, Peking University Press.

not have adequate food rations or in some cases severely lacked food supplies.[8] Therefore, the development of agricultural production for the purpose of eradicating hunger and alleviating poverty became the primary task during the early days of the reform and opening-up.

The collective agricultural system based on rural communes curbed farmers' enthusiasm for agricultural production. In the early 1980s, the household responsibility system gradually gained policy recognition through voluntary practices by farmers and was then implemented throughout the country. It evolved to become the basic economic system for rural economic development, reversed the trend of faltering agricultural development before the reform and opening-up, promoted greatly the overall development of agriculture, and raised the living standards of farmers. As a result, hunger in rural areas had been largely eliminated in the mid-1980s. During the 1978–1985 period, China's total grain output increased by 24%, while the actual per capita net income of rural residents rose by 169% with an average annual growth rate of 15.1%. Based on China's own poverty line, within just seven years from 1978 to 1985, the number of China's rural poor dropped by half from 250 million to 125 million. In the same period, the incidence of rural poverty fell from 31% to 15%, marking it a "miracle of poverty reduction" in human history. There is no doubt that the reform of the agricultural economic system, with the institution of the household responsibility system as its pillar, served as the key to achieving this triumph (Fig. 2.2).

Township and village enterprises represent another highlight of rural economic development after the 1980s. The predecessor of township and village enterprises was the commune and brigade enterprises under the system of people's communes in the early 1970s. Since the reform and opening-up, the township and village enterprises have not only evolved into prominence in rural economic development, but also become a bright spot in China's economy. In the planned economy era, township and village enterprises remained external to the planned economy, and the development of which followed the principles of market economy to a large extent, that is, operating independently, assuming sole responsibility for profits and losses with flexible operating mechanisms. When China remained a shortage economy, the rise of township

[8] Li Xiannian: Speech at the Central Work Conference, published in *Selected Works of Li Xiannian*, People's Publishing House, 1989 edition, p. 346.

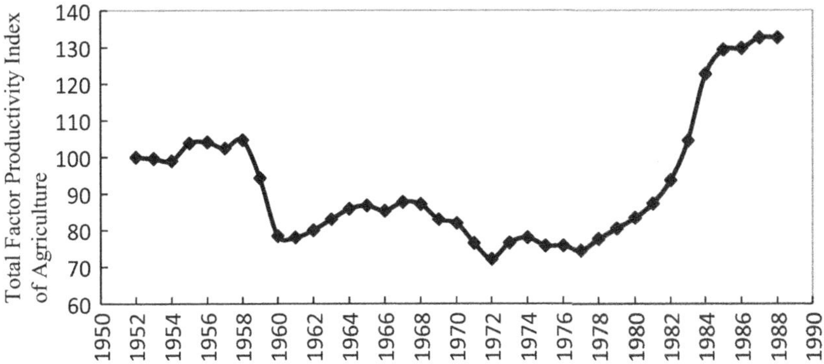

Fig. 2.2 Changes in the total factor productivity index of agriculture (1952–1989). (Source: Lin Yifu, "Institutions, Technology, and Agricultural Development in China", Truth & Wisdom Press, 2008 First Edition, p. 19)

and village enterprises created a large number of employment opportunities. In 1990, the number of people employed by township and village enterprises reached 92.62 million, comparable to the number of employees in China's state-owned enterprises in urban areas in 1990 (103.46 million). This sufficiently shows the importance of the development of township and village enterprises in the Chinese economy during the 1980s and the 1990s.

With the recovery and development of agricultural production and the rapid development of township and village enterprises, the income of farmers witnessed substantial growth. We can see from the distribution of rural families by income during 1980–1990 (see Fig. 2.3) that the income of rural households increased significantly in the 1980s. With the development of the rural economy, the number of rural poor continued to decline, falling to 85 million by 1990 and the incidence of poverty dropped to 9.4%.

2.4.2 *SOE Reform and Development of Private Sector Economy*

The economic miracle experienced by China since the reform and opening-up was a product of China's constant explorations in the establishment of a socialist market economic system instead of clinging to the

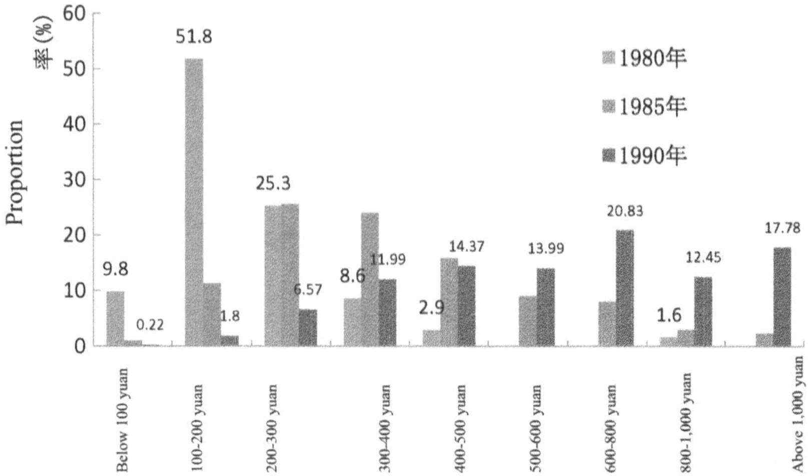

Fig. 2.3 Proportion of rural residents by income (1980–1990). (Source: National Bureau of Statistics, China Statistical Yearbook (1998), Beijing: China Statistics Press, p. 344. Note: This table is a sample survey of rural households)

planned economy. Although China did not specify a direction for economic restructuring at the beginning of the reform and opening-up, in terms of institutional arrangements, the country stayed on the path of liberating and developing the productive forces. *The Resolution on Certain Questions in the History of Our Party Since the Founding of the People's Republic of China* approved in June 1981 pointed out that "there is no rigid pattern for the development of the socialist means of production. At every stage, our task is to create those specific forms of the means of production which correspond to the needs of the growing productive forces and facilitate their continued advance". In addition, in the process of advancing economic restructuring, the role of the market in resource allocation has been constantly amplified. For example, during the drafting process of *The Resolution*, the following line was added to the document in light of Chen Yun's suggestion: "it is necessary to have planned economy and simultaneously give play to the supplementary, regulatory role of the market on the basis of public ownership".[9]

At the beginning of the reform and opening-up, China's economy was entirely dominated by the state. In 1978, state-owned enterprises and collective enterprises contributed to 97.8% of the total industrial output, of which state-owned enterprises alone accounted for 77.6%.[10] After the reform and opening-up, China began actively implementing the reform of state-owned enterprises, attracting foreign direct investment, and vigorously developing various types of self-employed and privately owned businesses. Development of the non-state-owned sector gradually evolved into a key driver for the Chinese economy. Together with the reform of state-owned enterprises, the development of the non-state-owned sector has nurtured the small companies for the construction of China's market economy.

The earliest reform of state-owned enterprises focused on the "decentralization of power and transfer of profits" in order to create incentives for state-owned enterprises.[11] By 1984, the central government began to

[9] In 1981, during the Fourth Session of the Fifth National People's Congress, the Report on the Work of the Government, in its elaboration on "actively and prudently reforming the economic system", stated that the basic direction of China's economic structural reform should be: to give play to the supplementary, regulatory role of the market on the basis of implementing the socialist planned economy, and the state should also give full consideration to and apply the law of value in the formulation of plans; the centralized and unified leadership of the state should be strengthened in regard to economic activities that affect the national economy and people's livelihood while with regard to the economic activities of enterprises, varying degrees of decision-making power should be delegated and the democratic rights of employees in managing enterprises should be expanded; the practice of simply relying on administrative means to manage the economy should be modified to combine both economic and administrative approaches and one should also pay attention to the use of economic leverages, laws and regulations in managing the economy.

[10] Calculated based on data from Comprehensive Statistical Materials on 60 Years of the New China.

[11] China began to carry out power decentralization pilot reforms in state-owned enterprises in Sichuan and Beijing as early as 1978–1979. In December 1981, the State Council approved and forwarded the Opinions on Several Issues Concerning the Implementation of the Economic Responsibility System in Industrial Enterprises formulated by the State Economic Commission with the goal of promoting the implementation of the production responsibility system of enterprises. In April 1983, the State Council approved and forwarded the Circular on the Measures for the Implementation of Replacement of Profit Delivery by Taxes from the Ministry of Finance with the aim of implementing the replacement policy and further advance the power decentralization and transfer of profits reform of SOEs.

treat the vitality of the state-owned large and medium-sized enterprises as the centerpiece of China's economic reform. The country began the pilot implementation of the "Enterprise Bankruptcy Law" draft in 1985. Subsequently, shareholding reform became a centerpiece in the country's SOE reform. In terms of reform design, the goal of state-owned enterprise reform during 1984–1992 was to gradually promote the separation of government from enterprises in accordance with the principle of the separation of ownership and management rights of state-owned enterprises, so as to further transform state-owned enterprises into independently operated and self-financed commercial producers and operators. In 1992, the 14th National Congress of the Communist Party of China made it clear that the goal of China's economic restructuring was to establish a socialist market economy. *The Decision on Issues Concerning the Establishment of a Socialist Market Economic System* adopted in the Third Plenary Session of the 14th Central Committee of the Communist Party of China in November 1993 clearly stated that the direction for the reform of state-owned enterprises in China was to establish a modern enterprise system that "meets the requirements of a market economy and socialist large-scale production, defines property and other rights and responsibilities clearly, and entails a separation of government and enterprises and scientific management".[12]

The report of the 15th National Party Congress of the CPC further demanded the strategic readjustment of the state-owned economy and stated that the dominant role of the state-owned economy lay mainly in its strength of control. The report mandated that the state-owned economy must assume the dominant role in key industries and fields related to the lifeline of the national economy. After the 16th National Congress of the

[12] In 1994, the Company Law of the People's Republic of China was promulgated to promote the establishment of a modern enterprise system. In September 1995, the Fifth Plenary Session of the 14th CPC Central Committee further proposed that "the reform of state-owned enterprises should focus on the revitalization of the entire state-owned economy and bring about strategic reorganization of SOEs through the flow and reorganization of existing assets. Such reorganization should be guided by the market and industrial policies. 'Grasp the large, release the small.' The optimization of the state-owned assets structure, corporate structure and investment structure should be organically integrated to allow for merit-based support and survival of the fittest".

CPC, changes in the way in which state-owned assets are managed and reforms in the capital market further advanced the reform of SOEs.[13]

The Report of the 17th National Congress of the Communist Party of China put forward the following proposal: "deepen the reform to introduce the corporate and shareholding systems in state-owned enterprises, improve the modern corporate structure and optimize the distribution and structure of the state sector of the economy to enhance its dynamism, dominance and influence". The 18th CPC National Congress explicitly proposed that "all kinds of state-owned assets management systems should be improved". In general, since the 16th National Congress of the Communist Party of China, the reform of the state-owned assets management system has seen positive progress and tangible results. The country has established three levels of state-owned assets supervision and administration entities, including the State Council, provinces (autonomous regions and municipalities) and cities (prefectures). The majority of non-financial state-owned assets have been incorporated into the supervisory and regulatory architecture, and a system of state-owned assets supervision and management laws and regulations has taken shape.[14]

After more than 30 years of state-owned enterprise reform, state-owned enterprises, together with various other types of economic entities, have become the primary players in the market and assume pivotal roles in such major areas as infrastructure construction, national defense and prominent science and technology projects in China. Meanwhile, the reform of state-owned enterprises has bolstered the development of the non-state-owned

[13]In 2003, the central and local governments established the State-owned Assets Supervision and Administration Commission with a vision of establishing and perfecting the state-owned assets management and supervision system, encouraging large state-owned enterprises to attract foreign investment and private capital, and implementing the diversification of ownership.

[14]Among them, 299 regulatory documents were issued by the State-owned Assets Supervision and Administration Commission of the State Council while more than 2800 laws and regulations on state-owned assets were promulgated by the local governments in conjunction with SASAC; supervision over the state-owned assets of enterprises was strengthened, mechanisms for performance appraisal, incentivization and restraint were developed and continuously improved, mechanisms for financial supervision, auditing and Board of Supervisors witnessed steady improvements as did the management of property rights, and the state-owned capital budget management system and revenue management mechanism gradually materialized. (See: Wang Yong, "Interpretation of the 18th National Congress of the CPC on the Improvement of Various State-owned Assets Management Systems by Wang Yong, Economic Daily, November 19, 2012.)

economy by relinquishing more room for latter's growth. Judging from the history of development, the state-owned enterprise reform has happened in tandem with the development of the non-state-owned economy. China began to develop its private sector economy and township and village enterprises as early as the early 1980s.[15] At the same time, China also began to actively attract foreign capital, cultivate market players in the development of the market economy and offer them policy support through the Party congresses.[16]

The development of the non-public economy is an important manifestation of expanding economic freedom. It has created tremendous employment opportunities for a large number of urban and rural workers and provided impetus for the transfer of the labor force of the agricultural sector to non-agricultural employment. At the beginning of the reform and opening-up, the agricultural sector employed approximately 70% of the entire labor force. With the development of the economy and the non-public economy in particular, the share of agricultural employment declined gradually from 58.5% in 1992 to 50% in 2002, and then diminished significantly further to 28.3% after joining the WTO (see Fig. 2.4).

[15] In August 1980, the CPC Central Committee's Circular on Forwarding the National Labor and Employment Conference Documents (Document No. 64) affirmed the policy of "combining together the three employment channels of labor administration, volunteer partnership and self-employment", and demanded the "encouragement and support of the development of urban individual economy". On October 17, 1981, the CPC Central Committee and the State Council released the "Decisions on Opening Up Employment Channels, Invigorating the Economy and Resolving Urban Employment". In 1981, the number of individual industrial and commercial households registered in urban and rural areas nationwide numbered 1.83 million, employing 2.27 million people.

[16] In 1982, the report of the 12th CPC National Congress stated that "China is still in the primary stage of socialism" and proposed the "leading role of the planned economy and supplementary role of market regulation" as the principle for reform. In October 1987, the report of the 13th CPC National Congress stated that "domestic-foreign joint ventures, cooperative enterprises and wholly foreign-owned enterprises are a necessity and a beneficial supplement for China's socialist economy". On April 12, 1988, the 7th National People's Congress passed the "Constitution of the People's Republic of China (Amendment)" to which the following clause was added: "the state allows the private economy to exist and develop within the scope of the law. The private economy is a supplement to public ownership. The state protects the lawful rights and interests of individual and private economies and guides, supervises and administers individual and private economies". By 1991, the number of individual workers in cities and towns had rapidly risen from 150,000 in 1978 to 760,000, accounting for 5.24% of the total workforce. From the perspective of gross industrial output, individual industrial output in urban and rural areas as a share of the total industrial output soared from almost non-existent to 4.83% in 1991.

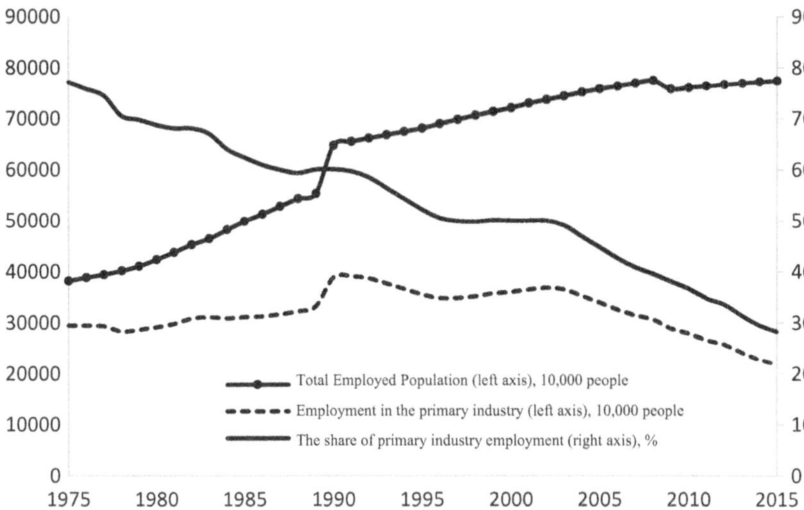

Fig. 2.4 Changes in China's employment structure (1950–2015). (Original data source: China Statistical Abstract 2016, p. 40)

The development of the non-public sector of the Chinese economy has provided enormous employment opportunities for the country's urbanization drive. In terms of the distribution of urban-rural employment, the share of the labor force employed in rural areas shrank from 76.3% in 1978 to 47.8% in 2015. In absolute terms, starting from 1998, the size of the rural workforce fell from 490.21 million to 370.41 million in 2015, representing a decline of 220 million people, equivalent to the combined population of Japan and Germany (see Fig. 2.5).

Urban employment has been expanding since 1978, from 105.25 million in 1978 to 404.1 million in 2015. The increase in urban employment was close to the total population of the U.S. (320 million in 2015). Concerning the ownership structure of employment, with the reform of state-owned enterprises and the development of the non-public sector of the economy, the share of employment in state-owned enterprises plunged from 78.3% in 1978 to 59.1% in 1995. In particular, the employment share of state-owned enterprises declined significantly after the mid-1990s and fell to 15.4% in 2015 (see Fig. 2.6). In the meantime, the share of

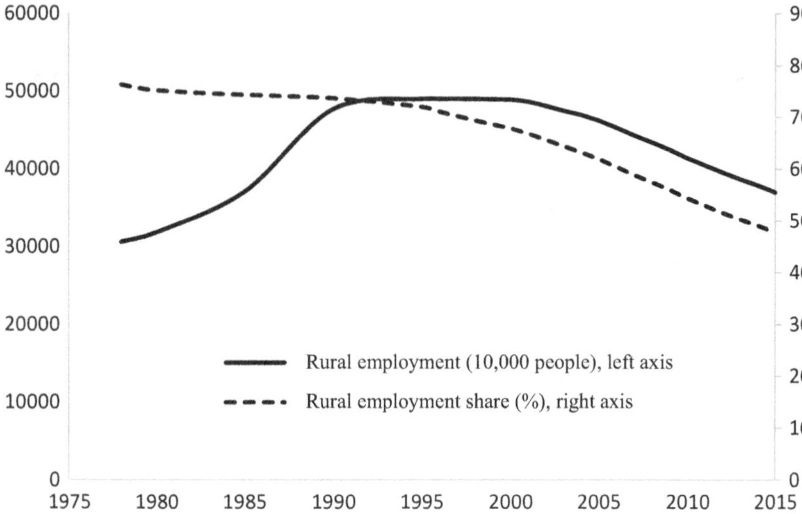

Fig. 2.5 Rural employment in China (1978–2015). (Original data source: China Statistical Abstract 2016, pp. 41–42)

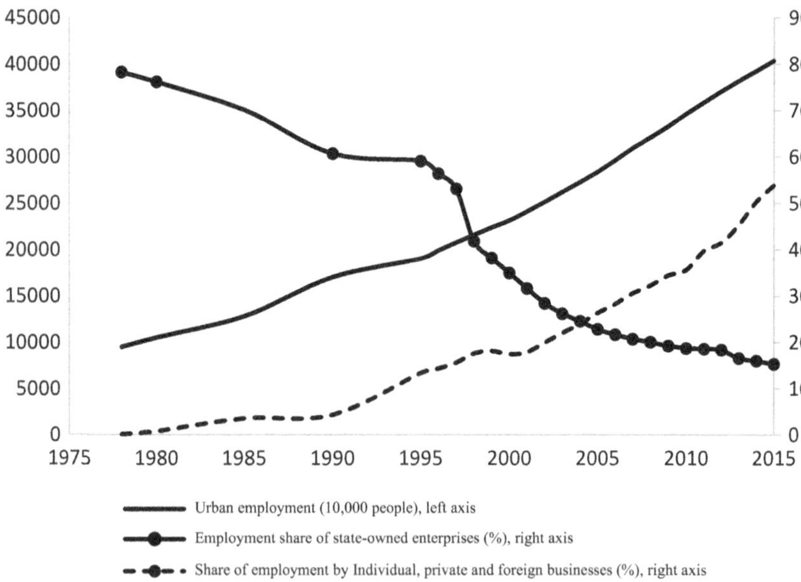

Fig. 2.6 Urban employment in China (1978–2015). (Original data source: China Statistical Abstract 2016, p. 41)

employment in individual, private businesses and foreign-funded enterprises grew from next to nothing to 53.9% in 2015, roughly equivalent to three times the employment in SOEs. In a sense, the reform of state-owned enterprises could not have been executed effectively without the rapid development of non-public-owned enterprises while the former has also objectively bolstered the development of the non-public economy.

As China gradually shifted from a planned economic system to a market economy, the per capita income of urban and rural residents in China has continuously risen. The per capita income of urban and rural residents in 2016 was 15 times and 16 times that of 1978, respectively; and the per capita income of urban and rural residents in 2016 was 3.9 times and 3.4 times that of 2000, respectively. Measuring the living standard of urban and rural residents by the Engel coefficient, China's urban residents had mostly reached affluent status in 2000 while its rural residents became moderately prosperous in 2010. In 2016, the Engel coefficient for urban residents dipped below 30%, suggesting that urban residents became even more affluent while that of rural residents dropped to 32.2% (see Table 2.4), suggesting that they moved closer to the affluent status.

Table 2.4 Per capita income of urban and rural residents and Engel coefficient (1978–2016)

Year	*Urban resident income index (1978 = 100)*	*Rural resident income index (1978 = 100)*	*Engel coefficient of urban residents (%)*	*Engel coefficient of rural residents (%)*
1978	100.0	100.0	57.5	67.7
1980	127.0	139.0	56.9	61.8
1985	160.4	268.9	53.3	57.8
1990	198.1	311.2	54.2	58.8
1995	290.3	383.6	50.1	58.6
2000	383.7	483.4	39.4	49.1
2005	607.4	624.5	36.7	45.5
2010	965.2	954.4	35.7	41.1
2013	1227.0	1286.4	35.0	37.7
2015	1396.9	1510.1	29.7	33.0
2016	1505.9	1638.9	29.3	32.2

Sources: China Statistical Yearbook 2014, China Statistical Abstract 2017, p. 56, p. 60

Note: The Engel coefficient refers to the proportion of food expenditure to household expenditure, which reflects the living standards of residents. The richer the households, the lower the proportion of food expenditure. According to FAO's criteria, an Engel coefficient of above 60% suggests an impoverished society; 50–59% suggests that people are able to meet their basic needs; 40%–49% suggests people are comparatively well-off; 30%–39% suggests an affluent society while below 30% indicates a very wealthy society

The establishment of special economic zones constitutes a major institutional innovation by China as a socialist country, which fully demonstrates its firm commitment to economic development. The establishment of special economic zones, open coastal cities, open economic zones and active participation in economic globalization emerged as important factors in the miracle of China's economic growth since 1978. Opening up to the outside world has become the external driving force for China's economic growth, given full play to its comparative advantage of abundant labor resources and at the same time played a critical role in refining China's socialist market economic system. Generally speaking, China's opening-up can be roughly divided into three stages. During the first phase, from 1979 to 1992, China's opening to the outside world mainly occurred through trade ventures involving processing and assembly with supplied materials and parts and compensation trade. The industrial transfer from Hong Kong and Taiwan to the coastal provinces of the Chinese mainland established the regions as active participants in global trade. During 1992–2001, with the clear delineation of the socialist market economic system reform, China gradually established and improved its market-based and outward-oriented economy. Through deepening reforms in the realms of exchange rate, foreign investment, foreign trade and finance, China's economy entered a new stage in its opening-up. After 2001, China's opening-up turned a fresh page with its accession to the WTO. Its economic opening-up witnessed positive changes in terms of scope, fields, depth and form. On the whole, China's opening-up has narrowed the gaps in technology and managerial experience between China and the developed countries, and promoted the institutional building of its socialist market economic system. Not only has it brought external impetus for deepening of the state-owned enterprise reform, but it has also expanded market opportunities for the development of various types of non-state-owned economic entities.

2.5 Poverty Alleviation and Development Serve as a Powerful Tool for Overcoming the "Poverty Trap"

2.5.1 Poverty Alleviation Policies During Different Development Stages

For developing countries, economic development is an essential condition for reducing poverty in the early stages of development. As economic development enters the middle-income stage, a sustained decline in the number of impoverished population hinges on the effective implementation of poverty reduction policies. China has always regarded poverty reduction as a priority for national development and implemented phased poverty alleviation and development projects at different stages of development, constituting an important element in China's poverty reduction campaign. Before the reform and opening-up, although China did not formulate an integrated poverty reduction strategy, its progress in the fields of education and health objectively promoted poverty reduction and markedly reduced the incidence of human poverty.

To tackle poverty, in the early 1980s, China began to pursue regionalized poverty alleviation and development policies in regions with concentrated poverty and lagged far behind in economic development. For example, in 1983, in light of the hardships caused by the serious destruction of vegetation in Gansu and Ningxia and the deterioration of the ecological environment, the government initiated a campaign to support agricultural development in "sanxi", or three impoverished areas in western China.[17] To this end, the State Council set up a leading group for the "sanxi" agricultural development campaign, which preluded China's regional poverty alleviation and development efforts.[18] While advancing its poverty alleviation work, China has established a series of designated funds for poverty alleviation since 1980, including the Development Capital Funds for Supporting Underdeveloped Areas created in 1980, loans for old revolutionary base areas, ethnic minority and remote areas, cash-for-work relief programs in 1984 and so on.

In the mid-1980s, imbalanced development of China's rural areas grew increasingly prominent. According to China's national poverty line, there were still 125 million rural poor who lived under the poverty line in 1985 in mostly former revolutionary base areas, areas inhabited by minority nationalities, remote and border areas and poverty-stricken areas. In 1986, China established the State Council Economic Development in Poor Areas Leading Group (renamed the State Council Leading Group of Poverty Alleviation and Development in 1993) and began to pursue an organized, planned and large-scale poverty alleviation and development

[17] The three western regions include the arid region of central China, with Dingxi in Gansu as a prime example, the Hexi Corridor region and the Xihaigu region in Ningxia.

[18] Zhang Lei, ed., The Evolution of Chinese Poverty Alleviation Policy (1949–2005), China Financial and Economic Publishing House, 2007.

strategy. In the 1986–1993 period, 331 counties were identified as impoverished counties and received special funding through loans, work-relief programs and fiscal development channels. From 1986 to 1993, cash-for-work and fiscal development funds as a share of central government expenditures averaged 2.73%. After eight years of hard work, according to the national poverty line, the number of impoverished fell from 131 million in 1986 to 86.6 million in 1993 while the incidence of poverty was reduced from 15.5% to 8.8%.

In 1994, China promulgated and implemented the "Eight-Seven Poverty Reduction Plan", which explicitly proposed to solve the problem of adequate food and clothing for the rural poor in about seven years by the end of 2000. The Plan became the first program of action with a clear set of objectives, targets, well-defined measures and a definite deadline in China's history. The plan covered 592 counties across the country, or 72.6% of the country's impoverished citizens and set out the following targets for poverty alleviation: (1) the annual net income per capita of the vast majority of the poor households should reach over 500 yuan (at constant 1990 prices); (2) helping poor households to create the basic conditions for sustainable solutions to attaining adequate food and clothing; (3) strengthening infrastructure construction; (4) addressing the backwardness in education, culture and hygiene.

In terms of capital investment, during the implementation of the plan, the cumulative investment in fiscal poverty reduction funds (cash-for-work relief and fiscal development funds) accounted for on average 2.94% of the central government's fiscal expenditures in the same period. With respect to the efficacy of poverty alleviation efforts, the number of rural poor dropped from 80 million in 1993 to 32.09 million in 2000 while the incidence of poverty declined from 8.8% to 3.4%. It should be pointed out that if the World Bank's poverty line were adopted, the incidence of poverty in China would be significantly higher than that if based on China's poverty line. However, even when judged based on the World Bank's poverty line, the incidence of poverty also witnessed a substantial decrease in the 1994–2000 period from 25.9% to 11.9%, while 116 million were lifted out of poverty, which still constituted a remarkable achievement. Meanwhile, China successfully achieved the strategic objectives of the first two phases of its modernization drive, and witnessed comprehensive economic and social development as its citizens generally became moderately prosperous. It is worthy of note that judging on the basis of the World

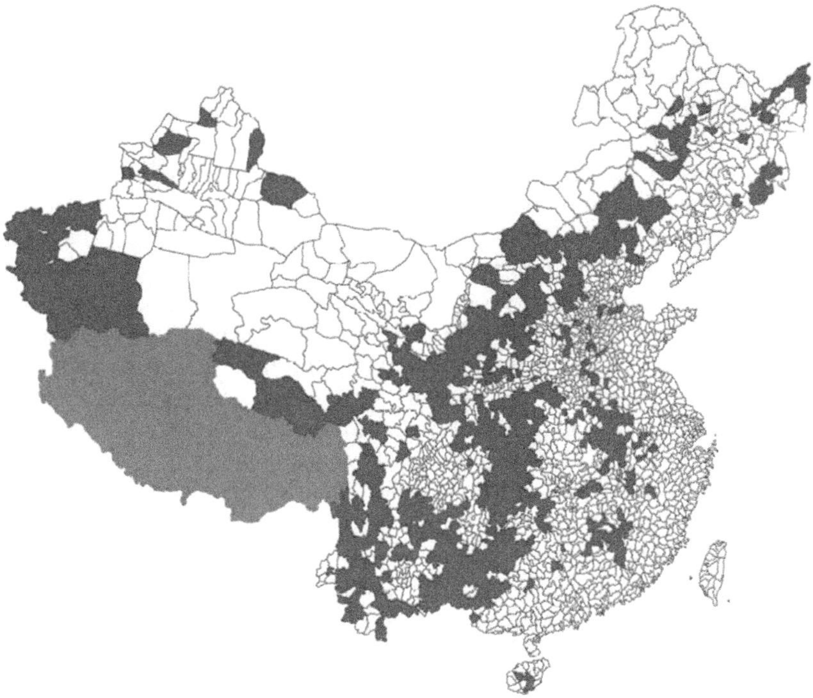

Fig. 2.7 Geographical distribution of impoverished counties in China. (Source: Heilig, G.K., Zhang, M., Long, H., Li, X., Wu, X., 2006. Poverty Alleviation in China: A Lesson for the Developing World? Geographische Rundschau (International Edition) 2 (2), 4–13. Notes: National Poor Counties designated in 1994 are denoted by regions shaded in red)

Bank's poverty line, there were still 116 million impoverished people in China in 2000, so poverty alleviation remains an arduous task (Fig. 2.7).

Since the twenty-first century, China's economic development has entered a new phase. Both its domestic economic structure and the external economic environment have furnished favorable conditions for the country's economic development. China has accelerated its urbanization drive, and its efforts in opening-up turned to a new chapter with the accession to the WTO in 2001. After the implementation of the "Eight-Seven Poverty Reduction Plan", the rural poor in central and western China became increasingly dispersed in impoverished villages rather than counties. As a result, the task of alleviating poverty has grown ever more challenging. In 2001, China formulated the Outline for Poverty Reduction and Development of China's Rural Areas (2001–2010),[19] which identified 148,000 poverty-stricken villages across the country; developed village-specific poverty alleviation programs encompassing the areas of farmland, drinking water for people and livestock, roads, incomes of poor farmers and social services; integrated the various funds designated for supporting and benefiting the development of agriculture in order to realize the goals of raising the incomes of impoverished people, upgrading infrastructure, developing public welfare programs, and improving the production and living conditions of the people. By the end of 2010, whole-village advancement programs had been implemented in 126,000 impoverished villages. Among them, the old revolutionary base areas, concentrated areas of minorities with a small population and impoverished villages in the frontier areas saw the basic completion of the programs.[20]

According to the white paper titled New Progress in Development-Oriented Poverty Reduction Program for Rural China released by the Information Office of the State Council on November 16, 2011, the national poverty line was gradually raised from 865 yuan in 2000 to 1274 yuan in 2010, an increase of 47%. The number of rural poor as measured by this criterion dropped from 94.22 million at the end of 2000 to 26.88 million by the end of 2010, a decrease of 72%; the share of rural poor in the total rural population fell from 10.2% in 2000 to 2.8% in 2010. In addition, China has strengthened rural infrastructure construction. As a result, 99% of Chinese villages enjoyed access to electricity, highways, telephones and televisions, marking the basic completion of rural infrastructure construction.

In the second decade of the twenty-first century, China has further prioritized poverty alleviation as part of its efforts in comprehensively building a moderately prosperous society. In 2011, China formulated the

[19] The objective is to promptly solve the problem of adequate food and clothing for people still living in poverty; further improve basic production and living conditions in poverty-stricken areas; consolidate the achievements in poverty alleviation; improve the quality of life and comprehensive capabilities of the poor; strengthen infrastructure construction in impoverished rural areas; improve the ecological environment; and exact progressive changes to address the backwardness of the economy, society and culture in impoverished areas so as to create the conditions for attaining moderately prosperous status. Poverty alleviation at this stage was characterized by whole-village advancement.

[20] Refer to http://www.china.com.cn/ch-book/2011-11/16/content_23934389.htm

Outline for Poverty Reduction and Development of China's Rural Areas (2011–2020), which ushered in the second decade of poverty alleviation and development since the Millennium. The overall goal of the program is the provision of adequate food and clothing, compulsory education, basic medical care and housing to the impoverished. The Outline also stated that the per capita net income of farmers in impoverished areas should increase at a rate higher than the national average, and that the indicators for the main areas of basic public services should prove comparable to the national average while the trend of a widening development gap should be reversed. It also set out specific and quantifiable targets in the areas of basic farmland and farmland water conservancy, special advantage industries, drinking water safety, electricity in production and living, transport, rural dangerous housing reform, education, health care, public culture, social security, population and family planning, forestry and ecology.

In particular, the new Central Committee of the Communist Party of China has continued to prioritize poverty alleviation. In 2012, General Secretary Xi Jinping traveled to Fuping County in Hebei Province, an impoverished and former revolutionary base area, to visit those living in poverty. During the trip, he stated that the most arduous task in comprehensively building a moderately prosperous society remained in the countryside and that a society neglecting its rural areas and especially impoverished areas would not constitute a proper one. In November 2013, when Xi stopped at the Xiangxi Tujia-Miao autonomous prefecture, he remarked that efficient measures for targeted poverty alleviation should be adopted on the basis of the village's specific situation, an occasion that marked his first use of the strategy of "targeted poverty alleviation". In 2014, the country declared October 17 as its Poverty Alleviation Day. In the same year, a nationwide poverty reduction strategy combining "targeted poverty alleviation", "regional development" and "social security" was implemented. From 2000 to 2014, the average annual increase in the central government's designated funds for poverty alleviation registered at 11.6%, which largely corresponded with the economic growth of the same period.

Toward the end of November 2015, the central government's Conference on Poverty Alleviation and Development promulgated the "Decision of the CPC Central Committee and the State Council on Winning the Tough Battle against Poverty", which demanded that the strategy of targeted poverty alleviation be fully implemented; its working mechanisms be improved; and the key tasks of accurate identification and the creation of poverty alleviation files be administered correctly so as to lay a solid foundation for winning the crucial battle against poverty and create conditions conducive to integrated urban-rural development and achieving equality in basic public services between urban and rural areas. Targeted measures shall be implemented in terms of funding, projects and recipients. Every impoverished household should be guaranteed help, every village has designated officials to carry out poverty eradication measures and goals are met within the defined standards. All social resources should be mobilized and a comprehensive strategy for poverty alleviation and development should be adopted so that by 2020 the rural population living below the current poverty threshold and impoverished counties are all lifted out of poverty, so that the problems of regional poverty are solved.

Generally speaking, China has instituted a poverty alleviation work mechanism under the Party leadership with extensive government engagement at all levels and the participation and accountability of Party secretaries from each of the five levels of government, that is, provincial, city, county, town and village. Twenty-two provinces and municipalities in the central and western regions have signed letters of responsibility for tackling poverty with the central government. Governments at all levels have taken a slew of measures and mobilized all social resources in the poverty alleviation campaign. The State Council Leading Group Office of Poverty Alleviation and Development has proposed a total of 16 related work items and facilitated the formation of an all-around work mechanism through a synergy of various policies and measures.[21]

In the process of the rural poverty reduction campaign, urban poverty has emerged as a new phenomenon in China with the reform of state-owned enterprises. In response to the issue, China began to implement the policy of "subsistence allowance" in 1993, which was basically extended to all cities by 1999. In the initial stage of its implementation, the policy played an important role in mitigating the impact of lay-offs brought about by the reform of the state-owned enterprises and provided basic relief to urban residents who were unable to work. Beginning in 2003, after a major breakthrough in the urban subsistence allowance

[21] The 16 work items refer to the creation of poverty alleviation documents, stationing officials in villages, concentrated efforts in areas, development of former revolutionary base areas, poverty alleviation by industial development, assistance by industrial organizations, relocation of the impoverished, whole-village advancement, talent training, innovation, performance evaluation, financial cooperation, international exchanges and cooperation, targeted poverty alleviation, enhancing regional collaboration and social support.

Table 2.5 Social assistance in China (2007–2015)

Year	*Number of urban residents receiving subsistence*	*Number of rural residents receiving subsistence*	*Number of centralized persons receiving livelihood guaranteed in five aspects in rural areas*	*Number of decentralized persons receiving livelihood guaranteed in five aspects in rural areas*
2007	2272.1	3566.3	138.0	393.3
2008	2334.8	4305.5	155.6	393.0
2009	2345.6	4760.0	171.8	381.6
2010	2310.5	5214.0	177.4	378.9
2011	2276.8	5305.7	184.5	366.5
2012	2143.5	5344.5	185.3	360.3
2013	2064.2	5388.0	183.5	353.8
2014	1877.0	5207.2	174.3	354.8
2015	1701.1	4903.6	162.3	354.4

Source: China Statistical Yearbook 2016, p. 731

program, China began to introduce subsistence allowances to its rural areas, which by now have achieved universal coverage. With the establishment of the system of subsistence allowance in both urban and rural areas, China has continuously improved its management and developed auditing and eligibility assessment mechanisms. In 2015, the total number of people receiving social assistance reached 71.21 million (see Table 2.5), of which 54.2 million were rural residents, a figure higher than the total number of rural poor in 2015. In this sense, although China has yet to fully eradicate poverty, the basic living needs of the vast majority of the impoverished have been met through the social assistance system. The main goal of China's campaign to eradicate poverty by 2020 is to ensure that individuals capable of working can overcome income poverty.

2.5.2 *Performance Evaluation of China's Poverty Alleviation Efforts*

The national poverty line is a measure of poverty reduction performance. At the beginning of the reform and opening-up, China set its national poverty line at a relatively low level. For instance, according to China's national poverty line in 1978, the number of rural poor stood at 250 million compared to a substantially higher 720 million when measured according to the international poverty line. Since the reform and opening-up, the Chinese government has routinely adjusted the national poverty criteria. Before 2008, two poverty reduction criteria existed in parallel in China, that is, the criteria for absolute poverty and for low-income. For example, the absolute poverty threshold was set at 206 yuan in 1986 and 785 yuan in 2007; the low-income threshold in 2000 was 865 yuan and 1067 yuan at the end of 2007. In 2008, the threshold for absolute poverty was combined with that for low-income to form one unified standard. 1067 yuan was first applied as the national threshold for poverty alleviation and later raised to 1196 yuan in 2009 (as the 2008 standard). At the end of 2011, the central government decided to set a per capita net income of 2300 yuan for farmers as the new national threshold for poverty alleviation (as the 2010 standard). Even after taking into account the changes in prices, the 2010 standard witnessed a tremendous increase of roughly 90% over the 2008 standard.[22]

The Chinese government's adjustments of the national poverty line show that it does not attempt to sidestep the issue of poverty in the country and underscores its determination to eradicate poverty. For example, according to the 2010 threshold, the size of the rural poor in China topped 166 million in 2010, much higher than that of 2008 (i.e. 26.88 million people). By 2015, according to the threshold, the number of rural poor has been reduced to 55.75 million and the country's poverty rate has dropped to 5.7% (see Table 2.6). China's 13th Five-Year Plan explicitly sets forth the goal of lifting its entire population out of poverty by 2020, and places it on the top of the Plan's agenda, which fully demonstrates the Chinese government's determination in promoting fair and inclusive development.

As the discussions above show, the achievements in poverty reduction since China's reform and opening-up have resulted from comprehensive development and governance programs, which include the enhancement

[22] According to an article by the U.K.-based Economist published on October 20, 2014, the number of rural poor in China stood at 81.7 million in 2011, accounting for 12.3% of its total rural population when measured based on the $1.25 global poverty line as set by the World Bank. On the other hand, according to the 2010 poverty line released by the Chinese government in 2011, the number of impoverished people in the country stood at 122.38 million, significantly higher than when measured based on the global line, indicating that China's poverty line is higher than the World Bank's. (See: Economist, China's economy: Poverty elucidation day, October 20, 2014.)

Table 2.6 Poverty in rural China (1978–2015)

Year	*1978 threshold*		*2008 threshold*		*2010 threshold*	
	Impoverished population (10,000 people)	*Poverty incidence (%)*	*Impoverished population (10,000 people)*	*Poverty incidence (%)*	*Impoverished population (10,000 people)*	*Poverty incidence (%)*
1978	25,000	30.7			77,039	97.5
1980	22,000	26.8			76,542	96.2
1981	15,200	18.5				
1982	14,500	17.5				
1983	13,500	16.2				
1984	12,800	15.1				
1985	12,500	14.8			66,101	78.3
1986	13,100	15.5				
1987	12,200	14.3				
1988	9600	11.1				
1989	10,200	11.6				
1990	8500	9.4				
1991	9400	10.4				
1992	8000	8.8				
1994	7000	7.7				
1995	6540	7.1			55,463	60.5
1997	4962	5.4				
1998	4210	4.6				
1999	3412	3.7				
2000	3209	3.5	9422	10.2	46,224	49.8
2001	2927	3.2	9029	9.8		
2002	2820	3.0	8645	9.2		
2003	2900	3.1	8517	9.1		
2004	2610	2.8	7587	8.1		
2005	2365	2.5	6432	6.8	28,662	30.2
2006	2148	2.3	5698	6.0		
2007	1479	1.6	4320	4.6		
2008			4007	4.2		
2009			3597	3.8		
2010			2688	2.8	16,567	17.2
2011					12,238	12.7
2012					9899	10.2
2013					8249	8.5
2014					7017	7.2
2015					5575	5.7
2016					4335	4.5

Data source: China Statistical Abstract 2017, p. 67

Note: 1. 1978 threshold: 1978–1999 termed rural poverty threshold, 2000–2007 termed rural absolute poverty threshold

2. 2008 threshold: 2000–2007 termed rural low-income threshold, 2008–2010 termed rural poverty rural threshold

3. 2010 threshold: the current rural poverty threshold, that is, 2300 yuan per person per year (at 2010 constant price)

Table 2.7 Policies in dealing with extreme and long-term poverty

Policies	*Content*
Education and health	Eliminate illiteracy among young and midlife adults and universalize primary education; Significantly improve accessibility to public health services;
Economic growth benefiting the poor	Household contract responsibility system; the development of township and village enterprises; Establish and improve market mechanisms, actively implement the policy of opening to the outside world, vigorously develop non-state-owned economy and promote employment and entrepreneurship;
Improve social policies	State-led and broad-based social participation in poverty alleviation policies; The gradual establishment of a social security system; Urban and rural subsistence allowance system; Social assistance system;

in human capital through developing basic education and health-care services before the reform and opening-up when China was economically backward, and the effective campaign against extreme poverty through economic and social policies that benefit the poor after the reform and opening-up (see Table 2.7).

2.6 The Global Effect of China's Poverty Alleviation Efforts

China's achievements in reducing the number of people living in extreme poverty have won global recognition. According to the World Bank's international poverty line, China's poverty-stricken population living under 1.90 US dollars per day (PPP, 2011 international dollar) declined from 884 million to 25.17 million between 1981 and 2013 while the incidence of poverty fell from 88.3% to 1.85%, a decrease of 86.47 percentage points; from 1981 to 2013, the number of people living below 3.10 US dollars a day decreased from 992 million to 151 million, a decrease of 841 million while the incidence of poverty fell from 99.14% to 11.09%, down 88.05 percentage points (see Table 2.8).

According to World Bank estimates, the rate of extreme poverty in China in 1981 stood at 84%, which was much higher than the average rate in developing countries (52%) and was significantly higher than that of

Table 2.8 Chinese population living below the international poverty line and its poverty rate (1990–2013)

Year	*Daily average of less than 1.90 US dollars per person (2011 international dollars)*		*Daily average of less than 3.10 US dollars per person (2011 international dollars)*	
	Number of poor (10,000 people)	*Poverty incidence (%)*	*Number of poor (10,000 people)*	*Poverty incidence (%)*
1981	88,383.59	88.3	99,211.38	99.14
1984	79,060.86	75.8	100,047.1	95.87
1987	66,498.12	60.8	97,440.95	89.15
1990	76,122.91	66.6	101,985	89.2
1993	67,554.69	57.0	97,551.34	82.31
1996	51,464.57	42.1	87,508.14	71.5
1999	50,993.64	40.5	84,503.03	67.18
2002	41,040.73	32.0	72,447.49	56.4
2005	24,516.75	18.8	54,603.71	41.75
2008	19,455.49	14.7	2517.332	32.96
2010	14,991.37	11.2	36,526.39	27.24
2013	2517.33	1.85	15,090.38	11.09
1981–2013 amount of change	−85,866.26	−86.47	−84,121	−88.05

Data source: World Bank database

1.90 US dollars: http://data.worldbank.org/indicator/SI.POV.GAPS?locations=CN

3.10 US dollars: http://data.worldbank.org/indicator/SI.POV.GAP2?locations=CN

India (60%), South Asian countries other than India (66%) and sub-Saharan African countries (52%).[23] However, the development of China since the 1980s has substantially reduced the rate of extreme poverty, which saw a tremendous decline every ten years. In other words, a paradigm shift is realized in the cause of poverty reduction. By the end of the last century, the rate of extreme poverty in China stood comparable to that of developing countries. By 2010, the rate of extreme poverty in China had declined to 12%, significantly lower than the average rate in developing countries (21%).

[23] World Bank: http://www.worldbank.org/content/dam/Worldbank/document/State_of_the_poor_paper_April17.pdf

China's achievements in poverty reduction have contributed tremendously to the cause of global poverty reduction. Based on the threshold of a per capita daily expenditure of less than 1.90 US dollars (PPP, 2011 international dollars), the proportion of China's poor to the world's total dropped from 46.4% to 3.28% from 1981 to 2013; in the same period, the world's impoverished population fell from 1.903 billion to 7.766 billion, marking a decrease of 1.137 billion. China's contribution to global poverty reduction registered at an impressive 75.55%. In this sense, such substantial progress in the global campaign against poverty could not have been made possible without the tremendous contribution of China's poverty reduction efforts. China's achievements in poverty reduction truly constituted a miracle in the global context.

International organizations have given due recognition and acknowledgment to China's achievements in poverty reduction. On the occasion of the 70th anniversary of the signing of the UN Charter, World Bank President Jim Yong Kim commented that "in the past 25 years, China has played the most significant role in eradicating extreme poverty in human history. China lifted some 600 million people out of poverty, so it is one of the most experienced countries globally in eradicating poverty".

By the end of 2016, the number of people living below the rural poverty line in China had dropped to 43.35 million and the rural poverty rate had fallen to 4.5%.[24] Overall, it took China around 40 years to successfully overcome the "poverty trap". In its 13th Five-Year Plan, China proposed to "comprehensively build a relatively prosperous society", and that poverty should be fully eradicated by 2020. Undoubtedly, this will constitute a continuation of China's "poverty reduction miracle" and set an example for the developing countries. Experiential evidence in China also proves that the "poverty trap" is not insurmountable.

Judging from the progress made by China in implementing the UN Millennium Development Goals (MDGs), China has either basically or fully achieved the goals (see Table 2.9) apart from the conservation of biological diversity. Of the 75 countries that participated in the assessment of progress toward the MDGs, only 25 achieved the MDG4 goal of reducing the under-five mortality rate by two thirds between 1990 and 2015, and China was one of the success stories; only China and a handful of

[24] National Bureau of Statistics, China Statistical Abstract 2017, p. 67.

Table 2.9 Progress by China in implementing the Millennium Development Goals

Specific goals	*Progress status*
Goal 1: Eradicate extreme poverty and hunger	
Target 1A: Halve, between 1990 and 2015, the proportion of people earning less than 1.25 US dollar a day	Achieved
Target 1B: Achieve full and productive employment, and decent work for all, including women and young people	Basically achieved[a]
Target 1C: Halve, between 1990 and 2015, the proportion of people who suffer from hunger	Achieved
Goal 2: Universal primary education	
Target 2A: Ensure all girls and boys complete a full course of primary education by 2015	Achieved
Goal 3: Promote gender equality and empower women	
Target 3A: Eliminate gender disparity in primary and secondary education, preferably by 2005, and in all levels of education no later than 2015	Achieved
Goal 4: Reduce child mortality	
Target 4A: Reduce by two thirds, between 1990 and 2015, the under-five mortality rate	Achieved
Goal 5: Improve maternal health	
Target 5A: Reduce by three quarters, between 1990 and 2015, the maternal mortality ratio	Achieved
Target 5B: Provide health services for all by 2015	Basically achieved[b]
Goal 6: Combat HIV/AIDS, malaria and other diseases	
Target 6A: Have halted by 2015 and begun to reverse the spread of HIV/AIDS	Basically achieved[c]
Target 6B: Achieve, by 2010, universal access to treatment for HIV/AIDS for all those who need it	Basically achieved[d]
Target 6C: Have halted by 2015 and begun to reverse the incidence of malaria and other major diseases	Basically achieved[e]
Goal 7: Ensure environmental sustainability	
Target 7A: Integrate the principles of sustainable development into country policies and programs and reverse the loss of environmental resources	Basically achieved[f]
Target 7B: Reduce biodiversity loss, achieving, by 2010, a significant reduction in the rate of loss	Not achieved
Target 7C: Halve, by 2015, the proportion of the population without sustainable access to safe drinking water and basic sanitation	Achieved

(*continued*)

Table 2.9 (continued)

Specific goals	*Progress status*
Target 7D: Achieve, by 2020, a significant improvement in the living conditions of around 100 million slum dwellers	Very likely
Goal 8: Develop global partnership for development	——

Source: Ministry of Foreign Affairs of the People's Republic of China, United Nations System in China: Report on China's Implementation of the Millennium Development Goals (2000–2015), July 2015

[a]By the end of 2014, the total number of employed people in the country stood at 772.25 million, and the registered unemployment rate in cities and towns was 4.09%. From 2003 to 2014, a total of 137 million new jobs were created in cities and towns throughout the country

[b]In 2013, the administration of free family planning technical services to China's household-registered population reached 100% coverage and to mobile population reached 96%. The systematic management rate of pregnant and lying-in women reached 89.5%

[c]China reported 104,000 new HIV/AIDS infections in 2014, up 14.8% from the previous year. The outbreak was generally contained at a low prevalence level and the rapid increase in incidence has been preliminarily contained. The death rate of AIDS patients that met the treatment standard dropped from 33.1% in 2003 to 6.6% in 2013

[d]Since 2004, China has implemented free HIV/AIDS voluntary counselling and testing. As of 2014, a HIV/AIDS prevention and treatment service network covering all urban and rural areas has been basically established

[e]The rising incidence of tuberculosis in China has been effectively checked, and the incidence of malaria has been significantly reduced. However, the incidence of chronic diseases has witnessed a steady rise in recent years

[f]Since 2000, China has fully integrated the principle of sustainable development into its plans for national economic and social development. The ecosystem of China has taken a turn for the better, and the trend of continued deterioration of the environment has been preliminarily contained

countries realized the MDG5 goal of reducing the maternal mortality ratio by three quarters between 1990 and 2015 (see Table 2.9).

Moving forward, as China takes center stage in global affairs, it will contribute to the cause of world poverty reduction through a different approach, that is, assisting the poverty reduction campaigns in developing countries through strengthening economic and trade cooperation and various types of development assistance. For instance, General Secretary Xi Jinping proposed the Belt and Road Initiative in 2013; in 2014, China announced the investment of 20 billion yuan in establishing the South-South Cooperation Fund on Climate Change in support of the poorest developing countries to combat climate change, and in particular improving their access to climate change funding provided by developed nations. At the end of 2015, China led the establishment of the Asian Infrastructure Investment Bank, the aim of which was to help the vast number of Asian and developing countries to promote investment in infrastructure so as to contribute to the economic growth and poverty reduction in the countries concerned.

CHAPTER 3

Will China Fall into the "Middle Income Trap"?

As the 2008 financial crisis unfurled with its impact on global trade and economy, China also saw a transition. The country's high (even super high) speed growth, which peaked at 14.2% in 2007, slackened to medium-to-high growth, thus entering the new normal era of economic development. In response, international organizations such as the International Monetary Fund and the World Bank began to adjust downward projections of Chinese economic growth. In some international media, the prevailing sentiment toward China's economic development was one of pessimism.

Prize-winning economist Paul Krugman wrote in his *New York Times* column in 2013 that China "is about to hit its Great Wall, and the only question now is just how bad the crash will be", which could be read as a theory of China's economic collapse. A *Washington Post* piece dated March 19, 2014, titled "China's Next Challenge", opined that China has already fallen into the "middle income trap" and this was "a significant event full of domestic and international implications".[1] Half a year later on August 30, Reuters cited a U.S. think tank study that claimed China has slipped into the "middle income trap". The study's author, Harry Wu, senior advisor at the Conference Board China Center for Economics and Business, concluded: the over-building, over-capacity and the "advance" of the less efficient state into private sector markets have increasingly

[1] *Reference News*, March 21, 2014.

S. Zhou, A. Hu, *China: Surpassing the "Middle Income Trap"*,
Contemporary China Studies,
https://doi.org/10.1007/978-981-15-6540-3_3

burdened China's growth. The study found that following the financial crisis, China's actual total factor productivity growth turned negative, dropping from an average of 3.3% in 2001–2007 to −0.9% in 2007–2012. This marked the first time that total factor productivity has weighed down growth since 1971–1977.[2] This study was considered a primary source of evidence that China had indeed been edging toward the "middle income trap".

It is fair to say, "middle income trap" has become the keyword for the media and both domestic and international economists when analyzing China's economic prospects. Nevertheless, how does China view the "middle income trap"? Will China, in fact, fall into the "middle income trap"?

3.1 Development Challenges During the Middle-Income Stage

Development challenges could arise for any country, at any developmental stage; so do opportunities. Long-term sustainable and stable development depends on seizing these opportunities whilst successfully handling the various problems that emerge during the development process. This is done by clearing the development obstacles as well as controlling risks. If the opportunities are missed and problems are allowed to exacerbate, development inevitably stalls. Generally, it appears that the leap for a country from middle income to high income marks a unique phase of economic development, with far more complexities than the move from low income to middle income.

In this development phase, opportunities still abound in part due to the notable gap that exists with developed countries. However, the former engines of development may well weaken, which would render ineffective the initial strategies of development that were adopted. This, coupled with the rise of new challenges, both internal and external, could make the development path ever more difficult to tread, even if it is paved with pitfalls. The "middle income trap" is not the result of one factor alone but rather multiple complicating elements at work together. Many countries have indeed fallen into this "middle income trap", and the reason is that they were unable to effectively counter the arising challenges along the development path.

[2] *Reference News*, September 1, 2014.

As China pushes ahead with its economic development and urbanization process, the country's socio-economic structure will shift accordingly to a great degree. This entails changes to public consumption in terms of its level, structure, perception and pattern; diversification of the social fabric; increase in public interest and participation in social agenda such as environmental protection and social progress; complication of governance; and the impact of external environments on China would be more direct and diversified. In a sense, discussions of the "middle income trap" serve as a warning bell to China, as it highlights the urgency for the country to proactively adjust its development model and scientifically deal with challenges. It is also a reminder that development must build upon sustainability, social harmony and a steady march toward democracy. Specifically, China faces the challenges below in its current development phase, and it is precisely these challenges that have given rise to the speculation of China slipping into the "middle income trap".

3.1.1 *The Challenge in the Transformation of the Economic Growth Model*

After the 2008 global financial crisis, the Chinese economy switched into a new phase and faced two principal development challenges. The first: economic growth has slackened from high growth to medium-to-high growth, perhaps will even abate to medium speed growth. During the 12th Five-Year Plan, China's GDP growth rate slowed from 9.5% in 2011 to 6.7% in 2016. In particular, economic growth in 2015 dipped below 7% for the first time since 1991. The slide in economic growth gained world's attention.

The second challenge: China's structural transformation has reached a phase that is both critical yet painful; the structural imbalances are glaring, further aggravating the pressure on growth. Since entering the 12th Five-Year Plan period, the structural imbalances have been particularly evident in the housing market with its excess inventory, and over-capacity in heavy industries like coal and steel. Equally, soaring leverage and growing costs of doing business in China are also fettering economic growth. We could say that the moderated growth is a consequence of structural transformations. Thus sustainable growth hinges on whether China can, in fact, transform its model of economic growth.

China's moderated growth since 2008 is in part due to the external impact of the financial crisis, and also the internal effects of economic

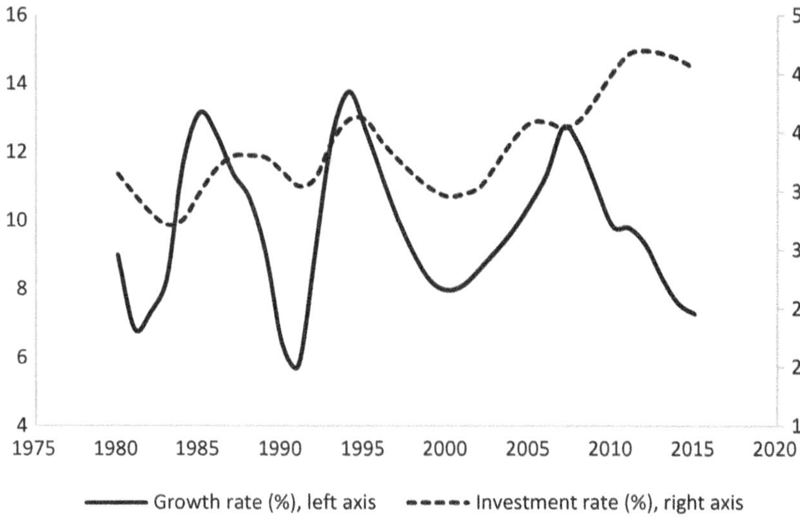

Fig. 3.1 Chinese economic growth and investment rates (1980–2015). Note: Growth Rate is the three-year compound annual growth rate; Investment Rate is the three-year geometric mean. (Source: *China Statistical Abstract 2016*)

restructuring. However, considering that in the 40 years after the Chinese economy took flight in 1978, GDP growth has maintained an annual average of 9.8%, the growth speed in itself is not the principal contradiction of economic development. Looking at the model of economic growth, we can see that the Chinese economy has long displayed the characteristics of investment-driven growth, but this model is clearly no longer sufficient to prop up high growth. Let us examine the correlation between economic growth and rate of investment from 1980–2015. Prior to 2007, the two largely moved in tandem, but after 2007, despite increasing investment sustained around 45% in the 12th Five-Year Plan period, growth took a downturn (see Fig. 3.1). This indicates that the efficiency of the investment-driven model has waned markedly since 2008.

We turn to the Incremental Capital-Output Ratio trend (see Fig. 3.2): it has been on an upward trajectory from 2007, indicating even more investment is required to support GDP growth. What this implies is the falling productivity of capital, thus influencing returns on investment. Lower investment returns in turn hampers investment growth, potentially

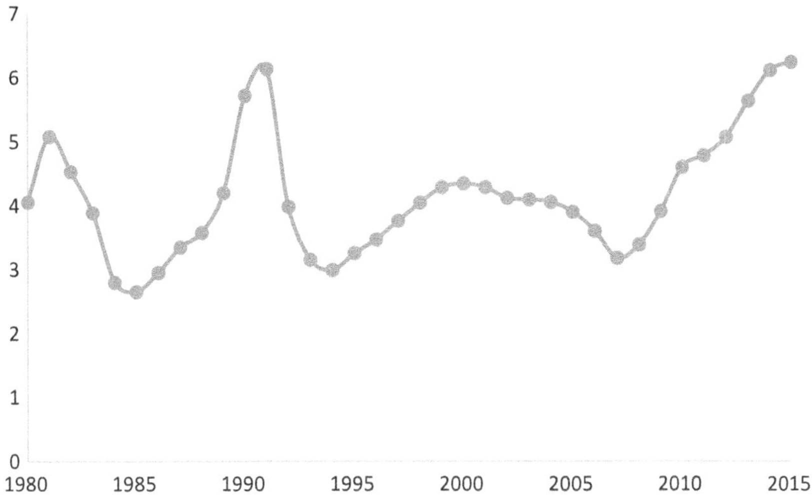

Fig. 3.2 The dynamic changes in Incremental Capital-Output Ratio (1980–2015). Note: Incremental Capital-Output Ratio (ICOR) = annual incremental investment (I)/annual GDP increase (ΔY). This gives the ratio of annual investment to annual incremental output. For computation purposes, three-year annual compound growth rates and three-year geometric mean of investment rates are used. (Compiled by the authors)

dragging down economic growth. Therefore, transforming China's economic growth model and gradually establishing new drivers of growth would help to improve investment returns and the quality of economic growth.

3.1.2 *The Environmental Resource Challenge*

In the long run, resources and the environment will present the biggest hindrance to China's economic growth. Soil erosion, land pollution and degradation, dwindling arable land, desertification, grassland degeneration, decline of biodiversity, pollution of water systems (rivers, oceans and groundwater), frequent natural disasters, poor city air quality, industrial waste discharge and household waste disposal management—to name but a few—are the current and future obstacles to quality economic development. The quandary lies in reconciling China's ecological environment with the long-time goal of "accelerated growth", and it forms one important feature of Chinese industrialization model, i.e., over-reliance on heavy industry, over reliance on exports, and over-reliance on investment.

The *2015 Report on the State of the Environment in China* did not paint a positive picture of China's ecological environment overall, as tough challenges lie ahead (see Table 3.1). If these problems are not addressed in time, they will exacerbate demands on environmental governance in the future and could potentially be a source of social conflict. Overall, the

Table 3.1 Status quo and challenges of ecological environment in China

Project	*Status quo and challenges*
Air pollution	In 2015, 73 out of the 338 cities at or above prefectural level attained air quality standards, just 21.6%; the remaining 265 cities did not, accounting for 78.4%. Air quality in the 338 cities met the standards on 76.7% of the days in the year; the days they did not account for 23.3%. Rainfall was monitored in 480 cities (districts, counties), and acid rain was recorded in 22.5% of them.
Water pollution	Surface water quality was monitored in 967 sites. 64.5% of those sites attained Grade I~III national standard, 26.7% attained Grade IV~V, and 8.8% failed Grade V standard. Out of the 5118 groundwater quality monitoring sites, 9.1% recorded excellent water quality, 25% good, 4.6% fairly good, 42.5% fairly poor and 18.8% extremely poor. Of the offshore seawater monitoring sites, 18.3% failed to attain Grade IV quality standard; the East China Sea was especially poor with 46.3% of test sites unable to attain Grade IV quality. Out of 195 river monitoring sites, 21.5% failed Grade V standard. They were monitored for COD, BOD5 and total phosphorus.
Ecological environment quality	In 2014, out of 2591 counties, 564 were found to have excellent ecological environment, 1034 good, 708 fairly good, 262 fairly poor and 23 extremely poor. Fairly poor and extremely poor counties account for 30.6%, the majority of which are in west Inner Mongolia, central-west Gansu, west Tibet and much of Xinjiang.
Coastal wetlands	Estuarine ecosystems monitored posted sub-health status; 80% were in a state of eutrophication, with high levels of phytoplankton.
Desertification and sandification	The fifth national monitoring survey of desertification and sandification results show, at the end of 2014, desertification affected 2.6116 million square kilometers of land, while sandification affected 1.7212 million square kilometers. Compared with the previous survey in 2009, that is a net reduction of 12,120 square kilometers of land converted to desert in five years. Since 2004, three monitoring surveys have shown a reduction in both desertification and sandification areas. This is a positive trend, but the situation facing prevention and control is still grim.

(*continued*)

Table 3.1 (continued)

Project	*Status quo and challenges*
Biodiversity	An evaluation of the threat to 4357 terrestrial vertebrates species show, 4 were extinct (EX), 3 extinct in the wild (EX), 10 regionally extinct (RE), 185 critically endangered (CR), 288 endangered (EN), 459 vulnerable (VV), 598 near threatened (NT), 1869 of least concern (LC).
Land resources and arable land	According to the *Bulletin of First National Water Census for Soil and Water Conservation* in 2013, soil erosion affected 2.9491 million square kilometers, accounting for 31.12% of surveyed land. Of this, water erosion accounted for 1.2932 million square kilometers, wind erosion 1.6559 million square kilometers. The quality of arable land nationwide in 2014 was overall low; excellent quality land accounted for 2.9%, high quality 26.5%, medium quality 52.9% and low quality 17.7%.
Agricultural non-point source pollution	In the production of three primary crops—rice, corn and wheat—fertilizer use covered 35.2%, pesticide use 35.6%.
Forests	Results of the eighth national forest inventory (2009–2013) show, there were 208 million hectares of forests in China, with a coverage of 21.63%. Compared to the seventh national inventory, forest coverage expanded by 12.23 million hectares, an increase of 1.27 percentage points. China is expanding the area and improving the quality of forests.
Grassland	In 2015, the area of grassland reached approximately 400 million hectares, taking up about 41.7% of the national territory; it is the largest land ecosystem safe zone. In 2015, China's grassland productivity increased, grassland disasters decreased. Rodent pests caused harm to 29.084 million hectares of grassland, accounting for 7.4% of the total, a decrease of 16.5% from 2014. Insect pest attacks affected 12.547 million hectares, accounting for 3.2% of total grassland, a decrease of 9.6% from 2014.
Pollutant emissions	A marked improvement was observed in monitoring of major pollutants in waste water. In 2015, COD emissions dropped 12.9% from 2010 levels, and anomia nitrate emissions dropped 13%. Nationwide, municipal waste water treatment rate reached 91.97%, meeting the goals of the 12th Five-Year Plan.

Source: Ministry of Environmental Protection of the People's Republic of China, *2015 Report on the State of the Environment in China*, May 20, 2016

ecological environment quandary has already become the biggest threat to China's sustainable development.

What is worth noting, though, is that the environment is by and large no longer deteriorating; the environmental deficit, in a manner of speaking, is easing. The 2015 Report shows that remedial environmental projects have all achieved some degree of results; certain indicators even posted notable improvements. This is the result of China's unceasing efforts to strengthen environmental governance. The government has made continuous organizational restructuring to this end. To cite an example: in 1988, the Environmental Protection Agency was established, being extracted from under the auspices of the Ministry of Construction; in 1998, the agency was elevated to Ministry of Environmental Protection; eventually in 2008, it became an organ under the State Council, thus affording it higher authority and independence to carry out environmental protection work.

3.1.3 *Challenge of an Aging Population*

An aging population denotes a shift in the country's demographic structure toward older ages and is the result of a declining birth rate and increasing life expectancy that accompany economic development. It is internationally recognized that a population is deemed aging, if the 60-plus group accounts for 10% of the total population, or if the 65-plus group makes up 7%. By this standard, China had already become an aging population in 2000. The United Nations projected in its 2015 revised report, that China's population will age even faster after 2015—by 2025, the 65-plus group will make up 20.4% of the population, an increase of 7.3 percentage points compared with 2015; and by 2035, that number will rise to 32.7%, increasing 12.3 percentage points from 2025. When compared with Japan, China's dependency ratio in 2015 was equivalent to Japan's in 1980, in 2020 it will be equivalent to Japan's in 1995, while in 2050 it will match Japan's between 2015 and 2020 (see Fig. 3.3).

Typically, an aging population curtails the growth of labor supply, leading to a rise in labor costs and weakening the competitiveness of a country's labor-intensive manufacturing, thus affecting economic growth. The reality in China is, since 2003, coastal areas have experienced difficulties in the labor market—labor costs were clearly on the increase. This has given rise to the viewpoint that China's economic growth will irreversibly decline as population aging speeds up. Japan is an important reference for those who adopt this view. Figure 3.4 is the United Nation's collation of China and Japan's total dependency ratio in 1950–2050. We can see that in the 1970s, Japan's dependency ratio began on an upward trajectory, increasing from 45.25% to 48.38%. At the same time, the urbanization rate rose from 72% to 76%, increasing 4 percentage points. In the 1980s, the dependency ratio

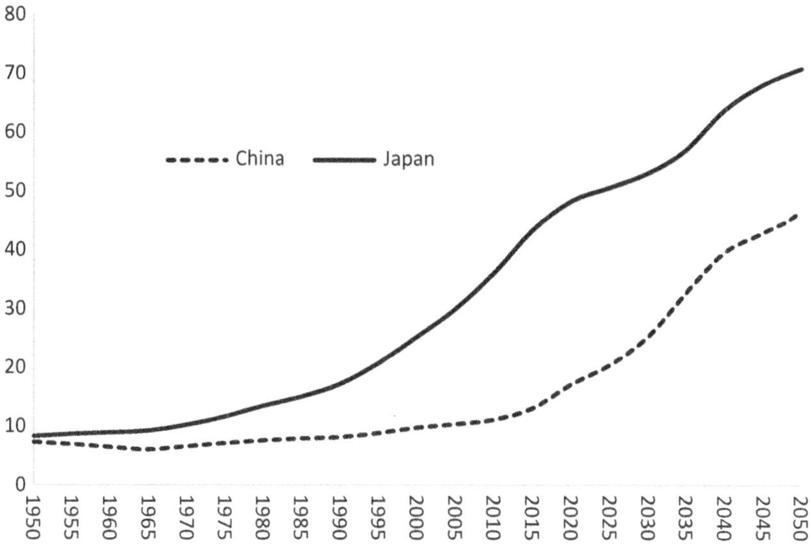

Fig. 3.3 The old-age dependency ratios in China and Japan (1950–2050). Note: Old-age dependency ratio = number of people aged 65 and over/number of people aged 15–64. There is a slight discrepancy in the data on the Chinese population with that of the Chinese National Bureau of Statistics. (Source: Population Division, Department of Economic and Social Affairs, United Nations, *World Population Prospects*, the 2015 Revision)

slipped from 48.38% to 43.40%, lower even than in 1970, while urbanization increased just 1 percentage point from 76% to 77%.[3] However, Japan's GDP growth in the two decades of 1970–1980 and 1980–1990 remained largely the same, at 4.46% and 4.64%, respectively. Additionally, in 1990–2000, Japan's dependency ratio rose from 43.6% to 46.6%, similar to the levels in the 1970s, while economic growth was only 1.13%. Judging by the correlation between growth and dependency ratio, it appears that Japan's economic growth decline cannot be attributed to population alone (Table 3.2). For example, Japan's economic growth fallen into a low growth rate in 1990s, when the dependence ratio only experienced a slight increase.

By this same reasoning, it is unnecessary to adopt an overly pessimistic outlook of an aging population's impact on China's economic growth.

[3] According to World Bank data, Japan's urbanization rate in 2015 reached 93%.

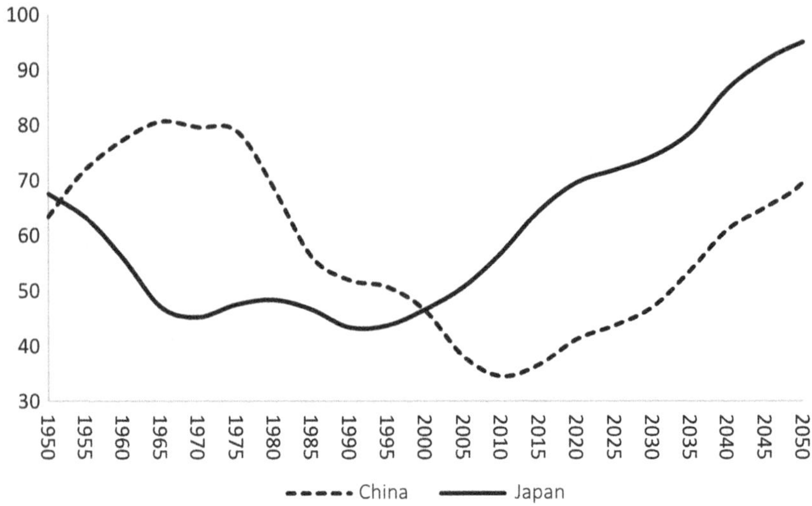

Fig. 3.4 The total dependency ratios in China and Japan (1950–2050). Note: Total dependency ratio = (number of people aged 0–14 + number of people aged 65 and over)/number of people aged 15–64. There is a slight discrepancy in the data on the Chinese population with that of the Chinese National Bureau of Statistics. (Source: Population Division, Department of Economic and Social Affairs, United Nations, *World Population Prospects*, the 2015 Revision)

Table 3.2 Japan's population, urbanization and economic growth (1960–2010) (Unit: %)

	1960–1970	*1970–1980*	*1980–1990*	*1990–2000*	*2000–2010*
Urbanization rate	63–72	72–76	76–77	77–79	79–91
Dependency ratio	56.0–45.3	45.3–48.4	48.4–43.4	43.4–46.6	46.6–56.8
Economic growth rate	9.22	4.46	4.64	1.13	0.77

Source: Calculations based on data from the World Bank's *World Development Indicators*

The aging population trend is just one feature of the population in China; the economy can draw benefits from others. For starters, Japan's urbanization rate reached 70% in the 1970s, which was a mature phase of urbanization development, while China's urbanization rate in 2015 was 56.1%, equivalent to Japan's levels in 1955. China still has room for urbanization, and these improvements in the future would be a key factor in propping up economic growth in the next 20 years. In particular, as the household registration system continues to reform, facilitating the movement of rural residents to towns and cities, the problems of labor shortage presented by an aging population will be alleviated.

Secondly, China's education development, specifically in higher education, will provide the human capital that supports economic growth. Bearing this in mind, despite the diminishing demographic dividend, the "education dividend" so to speak, will be conducive to labor productivity. Thirdly, even though there is no mistaking the trend displayed in the population, the working population will not substantially drop, as the decline of labor participation rate will be gradual. For example, the percentage of people aged 65 and over increased from 8.9% in 2010 to 10.5% in 2015, but even so, the labor participation rate only slipped from 56.8% to 56.3% in the same period. We estimate that as China implements its policy of late retirement and as more retirees opt to take up informal employment, the impact of an aging population on growth will be somewhat mitigated. Fourthly, China is already adjusting its family planning policy, and this will to some extent offset the pressure of an aging population post-2030. Finally, an aging population can in fact, be a booster to China's consumption-drive growth model.

3.1.4 The Income Gap Challenge

In the early days of China's reform and opening-up, the country's Gini coefficient was 0.28 and the distribution of income was near equal. However, as the market economy flourished, the Gini coefficient climbed to 0.4 in around 2000, indicating relative inequality in wealth, and then peaked in 2008 at 0.491. After 2008, the index began to slide, but China's income disparity remains relatively large (see Fig. 3.5). There is a pronounced discrepancy in development among regions as well as between urban and rural areas in China and these differences are a major reason for the overall income disparity. It is worth pointing out that the regional disparity has been noticeably narrowing since 2004. For urban and rural residents, the income gap spiked at 3.33-fold in 2009, but narrowed slightly to 2.95-fold in 2015. However, within cities and the countryside, inequality is immense. For example, in 2015, the disposable income of the top 20% of urban earners was 5.32 times that of the bottom 20% of urban earners, a small drop from the peak in 2008 of 5.77 times. Meanwhile, the disposable income of the top 20% of rural earners was 8.43 times that of

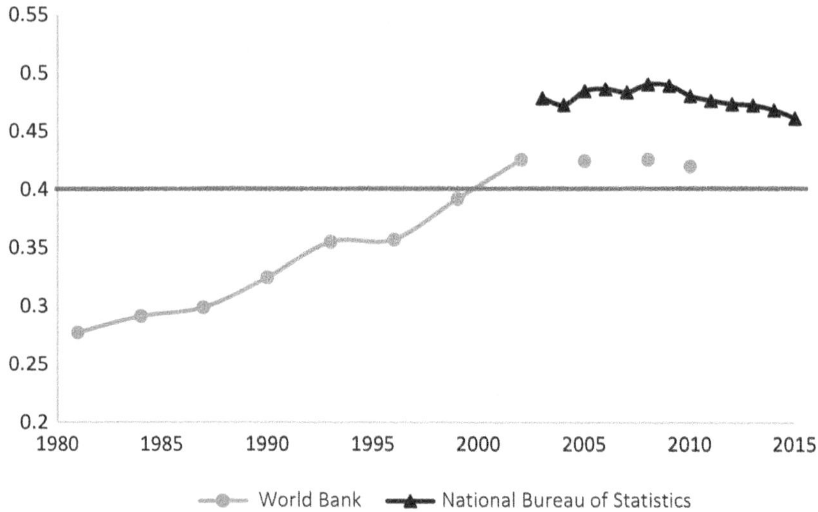

Fig. 3.5 China's Gini coefficient over time (1980–2015). Note: According to UN standards, a Gini coefficient lower than 0.2 expresses absolute equality; a range of 0.2–0.3 is relative equality; 0.3–0.4 is a relatively reasonable income gap; 0.4–0.5 is a relatively large income gap; and over 0.5 is considered dangerous. (Source: World Bank, China's National Bureau of Statistics)

the bottom 20% of rural earners, which was an increase from before. This goes to show that narrowing the income gap presents a formidable challenge.

The income gap problem is a matter in the public eye. The *Society of China Analysis and Forecast* blue book cites a 2015 nationwide general social survey asking people to rank 15 significant social matters. In that, income disparity and the poor-rich divide were the third most-voted-for problem, whereas most people see "serious or very serious conflict existing between the rich and poor". This result shows that despite the narrowing wealth gap in China, the situation does not yet allow for optimism.

An excessively large income gap would have multiple impacts on socio-economic development. First, it hinders the consumption power of the low-income group, thus the full potential of consumption-driven economic growth cannot be realized, leaving growth dependent on investment and trade. We have seen how dependency on investment and trade cannot guarantee sustainable growth. By effectively increasing incomes and harnessing the consumption power of the low-income group, China can move further toward a consumption-driven economic growth.

Secondly, a wide income gap threatens social cohesion. The rich-poor divide has various ramifications on social stability and development. Hu Lianhe and Hu Angang (2007) concluded that a wealth gap affects social advancement in four ways. The first is the spread of discontent, which is a hotbed for breeding social instability. Second, it is detrimental to social order; it could induce criminal behavior and threaten people and property, endangering public security. Third, it upsets the social balance and could cause imbalanced or even skewed development, trigger class conflicts, and thereby inciting social conflicts and confrontations. Fourth, it discredits a governing system's justice and authority, weakens a country's cohesiveness, and at its worst, is a menace to a nation's security and unity.[4]

Objectively speaking, the income gap arose from an uneven development of the market economy in urban and rural areas as well as across different regions in China. It is also a consequence of unequal opportunities in an imperfect system. Narrowing this gap is a task that takes time. Despite all this, we are able to see a trend of improvement, and as China persists in refining its social welfare system, we are bound to see some remedy of the inequality.

3.1.5 *The Social Stability Challenge*

Economic development and population shifts present challenges to social stability. At a forum on social governance and innovation for ministerial and provincial officials on February 19, 2011, General Secretary Hu Jintao said China is in a critical development phase where both strategic opportunities and social conflicts abound. Thus, if stability cannot be ensured, important development opportunities will slip by. Now, China is presented with a strategic opportunity to leap over the "middle income trap". The experiences of other countries show that social stability is essential to the middle-income development stage. This is because in this stage, economic development and social development are more intertwined than ever, with one relying on the other. If social stability is at risk, more expenditure

[4] Hu Lianhe and Hu Angang, "How Does the Rich-Poor Gap Influence Social Stability?" *Jiangxi Social Sciences*, Issue 9, 2007.

must be redirected to guarantee it, thereby leading to the crowding-out effect.

China is currently in the middle-income phase, and its social stability could see impact from the following aspects. First, there is large-scale social mobility. Prominent development gaps exist among regions and between urban and rural areas—a major incentive for migration. Since 2000, the country's transient population has been continuously expanding, from 121 million people in 2000 to a peak of 253 million in 2014. The number declined slightly to 245 million people in 2016,[5] which accounted for 17.7% of the total population. Generally, society's vulnerable groups make up some of this transient population—they are prone to the volatility of employment and physical ailments, which also make them a threat to social stability.

Second, the transition toward a steady social structure is complicated. China's social structure is in constant flux as the economy develops, urbanization expands, education advances and income distribution evolves. Professor Li Qiang of Tsinghua University referred to the International Socio-Economic Index of Occupational Status (ISEI) collated in the fifth and sixth census, to show China's overall social structure is shifting from the "inverted T" to the Chinese character "土"—akin to a pyramid structure. This indicates that China's social structure is still evolving, and will be a feature of development in the long run, until it reaches the stable "olive" shape.

An important feature of an olive-shaped social structure is the expansion of the middle-income group, which was pointed out in the 2013 *Guidelines on Deepening the Reform of Income Distribution System*. At the 13th meeting of the Central Leading Group on Financial and Economic Affairs on May 16, 2016, General Secretary Xi Jinping emphasized that enlarging the middle-income group is instrumental to realizing the goal of building a moderately prosperous society, attaining structural reforms, maintaining social peace, harmony and stability, and is necessary for the country's lasting wellbeing. Vital to the transition toward an olive-shaped social structure is a high quality, inclusive new type of urbanization, which will generate economic opportunities for all—an inclusive growth will prevent class solidification and allow for a virtuous circle of efficiency and justice.

[5] Source: *Statistical Communiqué of the People's Republic of China on the 2016 National Economic and Social Development*.

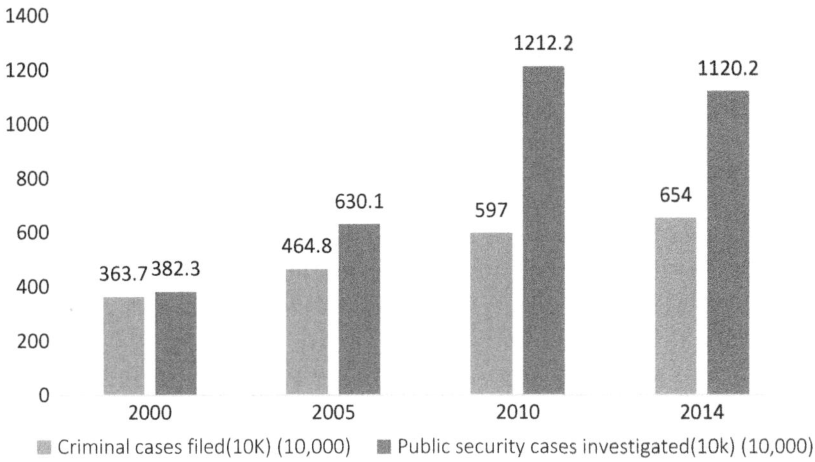

Fig. 3.6 Criminal and public security cases statistics (2000–2014). (Source: *China Statistical Yearbook 2015*)

Overall, Chinese society has been stable since the reform and opening-up, but threats to that stability have always existed, and incidents have erupted involving certain groups. Since 2000, the number of public security and criminal cases has notably increased (see Fig. 3.6), with the number of filed criminal cases rising steadily. Although there had been a downturn in the number of public security cases from 2010–2014, the number was still higher than that of 2000–2005. This suggests that we should view the stability of the Chinese society with concern rather than with complacency. In terms of the rate of increase of cases, in both categories it was slower in 2010–2014 than in 2000–2010. The rate of increase at which criminal cases were filed reduced from 5.1% in 2000–2010 to 2.3% in 2010–2014, while for public security cases, the rate of increase reduced from 12.2% to −2%. What this tells us is that even though social stability challenges remain, there is some assurance to be found. The CPC Central Committee's focus on "people-oriented" scientific development and building a harmonious socialist society is a contributing factor. As social governance strengthens, public services and basic social welfare coverage will only broaden, and that should alleviate social conflicts, particularly those arising during the course of development.[6]

[6] Hu Angang and Yan Yilong, *China: Towards 2015*, Zhejiang People's Press, 2010.

In China, it is said that "transformation is the absolute principle". This refers to the changes the country is experiencing—from accelerating development itself to accelerating transformation of the mode of development, and at the heart of this is social transformation, not just economic. This ought to be the principal mindset guiding China's development—accelerate socio-economic transformations, maximize net socio-economic welfare and minimize the cost of development. This requires us to liberate our thinking and move away from the dogmatic principles that dictate growth is the top priority, to not hinge everything on GDP figures and to do away with the tenet that economy is everything.

3.1.6 Political Development and Political Stability

Political stability is the premise of economic development; political development is the premise of social development; together, political stability and political development form the pre-conditions to enable a middle-income country to sidestep the "middle income trap". The relationship between political development and political stability is one of mutual support and mutual advancement. Without political stability, development cannot be safeguarded, and without political development, stability cannot be safeguarded in the long run. Since the reform and opening-up, China's rapid economic growth has fundamentally relied on the overall political stability, while political development made strides. To a large extent, this was possible because the Communist Party of China (CPC) did not cling to ideological doctrines, but rather adhered to the governance principle of "putting the people first", learned from experience during the course of development, improved its strategic planning capabilities and was pragmatic in handling internal and external challenges.

In the early days of the reform and opening-up, as the ruling party, the CPC returned to the mentality of seeking facts and pragmatism, setting out a path for the Party with "economic construction at the core" and "adhering to the four fundamental principles and reform and opening up". It applied the Constitution in practice and pushed economic reform forward. These are all significant political developments. Logically speaking, without such political development, China would not have been able to sustain nearly 40 years of high-speed economic growth since the reform and opening-up. We can go further and say, China's political development was, to a large extent, built upon the foundation of political stability.

Nonetheless, threats to China's political stability exist, both internal and external. On the external front, because of ideological prejudices, certain Western countries have disregarded China's achievements and choose instead to criticize, negate or even smear China for the problems that emerged during development. These countries are disapproving of issues such as democracy, human rights and ethnic minority rights, and often tout the "China collapse" theory. Now, nearly 40 years on since the reform and opening-up and as China moves into a prominent position on the world economic and political stage, we are hearing the "China threat" theory. This even descends into interference in China's core interests of sovereignty and territorial integrity, painting China as the saboteur of regional peace, thus negating China's actual efforts to safeguard peace internationally. It is undeniable that as China rises, its international standing has not simply become stronger; instead, it faces a somewhat deteriorating international environment.

While we cannot overlook the external impact on China's political stability, we must acknowledge that the bigger threat is internal. Now that China is in the middle-income stage, as society continues to open up and internet-use proliferates, views that are jeopardous to stability disseminate with more ease. One idea that has had a particular foothold is that, with China's increasingly globalized market economy, the natural next step is adopting a Western democratic system. It seems to uphold Western democracy as "divine". Some people see problems such as corruption and group unrest as attributable to the lack of a Western democratic system. Additionally, as urbanization progresses, destabilizing "black swan" events could occur more frequently with magnified reach. All these negative incidents combined with adverse social views would directly shake political stability.

The aforementioned idea is erroneous for the following reasons. Firstly, it excessively glorifies Western democracy. Take the U.S. for example, it holds itself up as the champion of democracy and human rights, yet it is not short of problems at home. Its human rights record is patchy at best—its out-of-control gun laws, police brutality, racial inequalities and inadequate protection for vulnerable groups. Let us look at the American democratic system in practice: during every presidential election, both Democrats and Republicans avidly make promises to voters, but how many of these promises are kept? On the surface, the system advocates equality of rights—"one person, one vote", but what it fails to disguise is the influence of money on votes. In a sense, money has become the "lubricant" in American politics. Vested interest groups make political donations that trickle through other media for their own gains—this is, in fact, grossly unjust. In 2010, the Supreme Court ruled to remove caps on corporate donations to campaigns, enabling financially powerful corporations to back candidates that will benefit their businesses, and in reverse, deter candidates whose policies do not work in their favor.

The influence exerted by interest groups and lobbyists not only distorts democracy, but also erodes the effective running of government and in practice, creating a "vetocracy", which results in a political system prone to the whims of the rich with their powerful finances, while bills beneficial to ordinary citizens are liable to being delayed or shelved. Case in point: healthcare. President Carter proposed universal healthcare coverage reforms in 1976 but ultimately failed to push them through. Reagan's attempt in 1989 to expand Medicare coverage in order to protect the elderly from "catastrophic" medical expenses, as well as Clinton's universal healthcare initiative in 1994 were both shot down by Congress. It was only in 2010 that Congress passed President Obama's Affordable Care Act. Reform of the healthcare system that concerns all Americans took 35 years from proposal to approval. In 2014, there were still 33 million people in the U.S. without medical insurance—that is more than 10% of the population.[7] Yet as soon as Donald Trump took the presidential post, he sought to repeal Obamacare, casting it down to just a short-lived bill. The U.S. remains the only developed country that does not provide universal medical care. In contrast, China, despite being a developing country, has in place a system of basic insurance coverage for all.

Secondly, the view in question reflects an incomplete understanding of China's political development. Since the reform and opening-up, China has been working to perfect its systems of the National People's Congress and People's Political Consultative Conference, in order to form a socialist consultative democracy. As early as 1981, at the Sixth Plenary Session of the 11th CPC Central Committee, the Party laid out its central tenet of "all is for the people, all depends on the people, from the people, to the people". This was the path followed by the CPC in governance. We can see from the annual "Two Sessions" that the delegates of the National People's Congress and CPPCC members exercise their democratic rights to put forward motions and proposals related to people's livelihoods. In

[7] Source: https://www.census.gov/content/dam/Census/library/publications/2015/demo/p60-253.pdf.

2015, the CPC Central Committee issued *The Opinions on Strengthening the Construction of a Socialist Consultative Democracy*, which discussed the arrangements of consultations at various levels, such as party, congress, government, political, public organizations, grassroots and social organizations. Overall, democracy in China manifests itself in the government's widely collecting people's opinions on development, and responding to those through active policy-making.

For China, political stability and social order are the highest priority for the people, and are the premise for continued economic development. As the country looks to stride past the "middle income trap", it must cautiously choose its direction for social reforms and political development, in order to achieve advancements, while avoiding social and political upheavals. Having experienced 40 years of reform and opening-up, both the CPC and the public are becoming ever more rational, mature and smart in seeking a democratic system that meets Chinese circumstances, has Chinese characteristics and is beneficial to the country's political development, stability and overall advancement.

There are challenges facing China's political development, one root cause being the current critical stage that the reforms have reached. Deepening reform is a formidable and complex task, and it is further complicated by the reshuffling of interests, which could lead to entities with vested interests to obstruct reform under the guise of safeguarding political stability. Without question, a halt to deepening reforms is a halt to political development, which ultimately would rock political stability. The fundamental purpose of political development, after all, is to lay the groundwork for and to safeguard reform.

In this sense, the "middle income trap" is essentially a political trap. Therefore, building a stable political environment is key to avoiding the "middle income trap". This is what the Chinese mean by "universal order"; it is also the ultimate public service product that guarantees a country's long-term, sustainable and stable modern economic growth. And who is the public service provider? The Communist Party of China and the Chinese government—this is their obligation and a momentous task. In order to achieve this task, it is necessary to modernize the governance system and governance capability. How complete that system is and the strength of governance capability reflects more than a nation's competitive quality globally, as well as the overall strength of a nation. Without a modern governance system in place and fairly strong governance capability, the conflicts and problems that arise in the course of economic development cannot be effectively managed. That means an absence of the central force and unity required for building and developing the country, which will inevitably lead to social instability, stagnation of economic growth and more grave issues. Modernizing the governance system and governance capability depends on utilizing the Chinese system's advantages. The reality is, there is no one system that fits all. "Blindly copying another country's system and development path without regard for national circumstances will never succeed; it will not solve any practical problems, but will cause economic stagnation, political change, social upheaval, loss of sovereignty and other severe consequences".[8] Thus, modernization of the governance system and governance capability is an important means to overcome the political trap.

3.2 Favorable Conditions for China to Overcome the "Middle Income Trap"

From a perspective of public policy, which factors should we highlight which could cause growth to stagnate or even go into recession? The answer is many, but we believe these boil down to a few points. One, the implementation of the correct development strategy; two, the implementation of correct macroeconomic management; three, basic capacity for sustainable growth (e.g. infrastructure facilities, human capital); four, basic capacity for continued innovation; and five, capacity to counter external impact and risks. Judging from the above five points, China is entirely able to cross over the "middle income trap" and complete the transition from the middle-income to high-income phase.

3.2.1 Steady Transition of the Economic System and Maturing of Macroeconomic Management

Since the reform and opening-up, China's macroeconomic management system has matured and adapted to the needs of building a socialist market economy, while guaranteeing the overall stability of the macro economy and realizing high-speed economic growth. Collectively, the macroeconomic management system was suited to the key stages of economic reform, which included phasing in market mechanisms to the planned

[8] Wang Weiguang, "Pushing Forward Modernization of the National Governance System and Governance Capability", *Qiushi Journal*, Issue 12, 2014.

economy system, operating a planned commercial economy, establishing a socialist market economic system, and perfecting the socialist market economy.

From 1978 to 1984, China introduced market mechanisms within its planned economy system. On November 26, 1979, Deng Xiaoping voiced his epoch-making view that a market economy can be developed under socialism. At the 12th National Party Congress in 1982, the idea of "ensuring the leading role of the planned economy, supplemented by market regulations" was put forward. This not only endorsed market regulations, but also distinguished between mandatory and guidance planning. During this time, farmland was reformed to institute the household contract responsibility systems reforms, and certain industrial enterprises were given greater autonomy. At the Third Plenary Session of the 12th CPC Central Committee in October 1984, the *CPC Central Committee's Decision on the Reform of the Economic System* was passed, which formally raised the concept of a planned commodities economy as the basis of a socialist economy. In 1987, the 13th CPC National Congress report further pointed out that a socialist planned commodities economy should incorporate both planned and market systems. China also took steps to reform various macroeconomic control mechanisms, such as planning, investment, fiscal, finance, circulation, pricing, distribution and social welfare, in order to adapt to market changes and the ensuing economic reforms.

In 1992, Deng Xiaoping said in a speech whilst touring in southern China, that China has broken free of ideological tethers in its attempt to build a market economy system. He said, "the proportion of planning and that of market forces is not the essential difference between socialism and capitalism. A planned economy is not equivalent to socialism, because there is planning under capitalism too; a market economy is not capitalism, because there are markets under socialism too. Planning and market forces are both means of controlling economic activity". Based on Deng Xiaoping's assertion, the 14th National Party Congress Report clearly outlined that the goal of reforming China's economic system is to build a socialist market economic system. The Third Plenary of the 14th CPC Central Committee in 1993 unanimously passed the *Decisions of the CPC Central Committee on Issues of Building a Socialist Market Economy*, which laid out the framework for a socialist market economy. From here on, every third plenary session arranged for building and refining the market economy system.

The Third Plenary of the 12th CPC Central Committee, the Third Plenary of the 14th CPC Central Committee, the Third Plenary of the 16th CPC Central Committee, and the Third Plenary of the 18th CPC Central Committee all laid out top-down designs for China's economic reform, and deepened efforts to build a socialist market economy. In this process, the plenary sessions clarified the relationship between government and market, as well as government and society, and upon this basis continually improved macroeconomic management in order to adapt to the developing socialist market economy.

Once the goal of moving toward a market economy was set, China began a vigorous drive to reform state-owned enterprises with the core aim of establishing modern enterprise systems. At the same time, the country pushed for the development of the non-public sector to cultivate the micro-foundations of the market economy. China also continually made improvements to its macroeconomic regulations to complement the practical needs of the socialist market economy. In 1994, China began to reform its tax system, with tax distribution as the prime feature, and formally aligned the Renminbi's official exchange and swap market exchange rates, implementing a managed floating exchange rate system based on market supply and demand. At the 9th National People's Congress in 1998, Premier Zhu Rongji proposed what he termed the "one goal to ensure, three tasks to accomplish, and five areas to undergo reform". This included several reforms in areas of macroeconomic management, such as of the financial, grain circulation, investment and financing, housing, healthcare and fiscal and taxation systems. These reforms not only effectively allayed the adverse impact of the Asian financial crisis on the Chinese economy in the late 1990s, but also paved the way for China's membership of the WTO within the socialist market economy framework.

In the twenty-first century, China continued to work toward advancing its macroeconomic regulation and market economy. The Third Plenary Session of the 16th CPC Central Committee in 2003 approved the *Decisions of the CPC Central Committee on Issues of Completing the Socialist Economy System*, which laid out comprehensive plans to this end. This included continuing to build an economic system that has public ownership as its mainstay but with a diversified-ownership model as the basis. This also put forward the "five balances": balancing urban and rural development, development among regions, economic and social development, man and nature, and domestic development and opening-up to the outside world. It emphasized cultivating a unified and open market system with orderly competition, improving macroeconomic regulations, and perfecting employment and social security systems. In 2012, the Third Plenary Session of the 18th CPC Central Committee charted 336 reform measures needed for modernizing the country's governance system and governance capability. In particular, the session clarified: "Economic system reform is the focus of comprehensively deepening the reform. The underlying issue is how to strike a balance between the role of the government and that of the market, letting the market play the decisive role in allocating resources and the government play its functions better".

On the whole, China's macroeconomic management capability has been maturing steadily since the 1990s, and provided a solid foundation for continued economic growth. Looking at the four key macroeconomic performance indicators (economic growth, inflation, unemployment and balance of international payments), we could say that the overall picture for China after 1992 is rosy. When it comes to economic growth, the average annual growth rate in 1992–2016 was 9.6%. Per capita GDP in 2016 was 7.7 times than in 1992. There was an obvious slowdown in the growth rate after 2007—from 14.2% in 2007 to 6.7% in 2016. However, this was mostly due to falling external demand brought about by the global financial crisis combined with internal structural adjustments, not an indication of an underlying decline of productivity in the long run. It is worth noting that the slowdown in growth rate is not unprecedented since the reform and opening-up. Growth rate slipped from 15.2% to 8.8% in 1984–1986 (down 6.4 percentage points in two years); in 1987–1990 it slipped from 11.3% to 3.8% (down 8.5 percentage points in three years); and then in 1984–1986, it slipped from 14.2% to 7.8% (down 6.4 percentage points in six years).

In terms of inflation, since the reform and opening-up, China has never experienced the hyperinflation that Latin American countries went through. In those 20 years since the 1990s, aside from a bout of high inflation in 1994 and 1995 which reached around 20%, inflation was generally kept under 6% and in most years under 4%. Compared with most emerging economies, China's inflation record is exemplary. Inflation levels can reflect the competence of a macroeconomic regulator in making adjustments through fiscal and monetary policies, and give clues as to whether the government is taking the "helping hands" or "grabbing hands" approach in macroeconomic regulations. The "helping hands" approach not only acknowledges the "invisible hand" of the market in distributing resources, but also proactively extends "visible hands" to remedy areas where the market fails. An example would be intensifying infrastructure construction in order to provide a more efficient market environment for the private sector, or improving public services to boost social stability and eliminate risks, thereby creating a harmonious environment for economic development. In contrast, the "grabbing hands" behavior is destructive and impedes the market; it spawns unfair income distribution and is often accompanied by high inflation, which hinders investment activities and causes steep depreciation of the public's financial assets; the result is—the public suffers.

On the matter of unemployment, China's registered urban unemployment rate has always stayed below 5%, and from 2010 onward, the rate remained below 4.1%. China has not yet released its full surveyed unemployment rate. Nonetheless, because of the active employment policies implemented since the 1990s and the major drive to develop the private sector and encourage informal employment, the scale of urban employment has been continually expanding—from 190 million people in 1995 to 232 million people in 2010, and rising again to 404 million people in 2015. Non-state entities were the main source of newly created jobs in urban areas. To cite some examples, during the 11th Five-Year Plan (2006–2010), the number of employed people in urban areas increased by 62.98 million, while in state-owned enterprises it only increased by 280,000 people. During the 12th Five-Year Plan (2011–2015), the number of employed people in urban areas increased by 57.23 million people, while state-owned enterprises saw a drop in employment of 3.08 million people. Suffice to say, developing the private sector is bound to be the stabilizer for job creation in urban areas.

Turning to the balance of payments, since 1994, China's current account and capital and financial account have seen twin surpluses. This has built up a sizeable foreign exchange reserve and strengthened China's ability to weather global financial risks. Once China joined the WTO, its participation in the global economy expanded rapidly. Total import-export of goods rose from 509.7 billion US dollars in 2001 to 4.3015 trillion US dollars in 2015, and in terms of proportion of GDP, that is an increase from 38.5% to 41% (2006 saw a peak of 65%). In 2013, China became the biggest trading nation in the world and the biggest trading partner of more than 120 countries. In 2014–2016, feeling the impact of a global trade slowdown, China's foreign trade in goods saw negative growth, but its net export remained in the black.

3.2.2 Continual Improvement in National Capacity for Strategic Planning

China's national strategic planning is evident in both the CPC congresses and the "Five-Year Plans"; the latter is also a blueprint charting development at different stages. In the early days after the foundation of New China, the country began to implement the Five-Year Plans with the assistance of the Soviet Union. In those days of the planned economy, national plans were the main instrument to allocate resources. As China initiated the reform and opening-up however, the market increasingly took on this function, and China no longer stuck to the old ways of a planned economy. The 14th CPC National Congress Report expressly said the Chinese economy is transitioning toward a socialist market economy, and that is to give the market a fundamental role of distributing resources, under the nation's macro regulations.

The Ninth Five-Year Plan was the first five-year plan set after Deng Xiaoping's southern China tour. Its full title is "The Outline of the Ninth Five-Year Plan for National Economic and Social Development and the Long-range Objectives to the Year 2010 of the People's Republic of China". This was also China's first medium-to-long term plan after it switched to the path of a market economy, and was a cross-century development plan that gazed forward 15 years. Two all-encompassing fundamental changes comprised the main track of the Ninth Five-Year Plan. One is the transformation from a traditional planned economy, while the other is the transformation from an extensive to intensive mode of growth, which would enable a sustainable, fast, healthy development, and social progress. These two fundamental transformations affect both the economic system and the economic growth model, while economic reforms also facilitated the transformation to a more efficient growth model. These two fundamental transformations dictated the main track of China's development and reform: the need to advance productivity and to adjust the relations of production. This dynamic process requires reciprocal adaptation and continuous adjustments. Undoubtedly, this was not a task that could be completed within a five-year-plan period, but rather took 20 odd years. The Tenth Five-Year Plan (2001–2005) was the first five-year plan upon the turn of the twenty-first century; China had moved from a low-income stage to a middle-income stage and joined the World Trade Organization. The Tenth Five-Year Plan outlined important tasks, including correctly balance reform, development and stability, abide by the principle of aligning speed and efficiency to transform the growth model, maximize the market mechanism, stand by the strategy of sustainable development, and gradually reduce the development gap among regions. Overall, the Tenth Five-Year Plan puts a clearer emphasis on balanced development.

As China continued to build and complete its socialist market economy, it tweaked the name of its five-year plans to mean "five-year guidelines" from the 11th round of 2006–2010 and onward, and categorized the development goals into "binding" and "anticipated". The two categories of targets reflect on both the "invisible hand" of the market in allocating resources, and the "visible hand" of the guidelines in facilitating the process which is also the important function of the government in guiding development. In practice, macro-control by the government is indispensable because the market can fail, so guidelines are the starting point of macro-control which encapsulate the aspired goals. "Binding targets" were set mainly in the areas of energy conservation, environment protection and people's livelihoods, which goes to show that since the 11th Five-Year Guideline, national development has put special emphasis on the quality of development and the shared nature of the outcomes.

Since the 11th Five-Year Guideline, China has generally put the focus on managing the objectives of the guidelines. If we examine how these guidelines are set, we can see that it is a process that condenses all the understandings of social development and involves wide social participation; it is a display of democracy in a sense. Regarding development strategy, such guidelines have become the steering wheel of the nation's development. The very concept and objectives of the five-year guidelines increasingly reflect the adaptive quality, comprehensiveness, scientific and steering nature of the nation's development. They embody changes in the government's functions, the drive to strengthen social harmony, accelerate transformation of the mode of growth, make "green development" goals binding and push the transformation of the development model from a pure pursuit of economic growth speed to a "scientific" one—which is comprehensive, inclusive, balanced and sustainable.

The 11th Five-Year Guideline focused on accelerating the transformation of the economic growth model, making resource efficiency a national policy, accelerating the construction of a "resource-conserving, environmentally friendly society", balancing economic development with the population, resources and environment, advancing the informatization of society, and seeking a feasible new type of industrialization. The 12th

Five-Year Guidelines revolved around scientific development, and focused on transforming the economic development model based on economic structural adjustments. The 13th Five-Year Guidelines made supply-side structural reform the primary means to bring about economic structural adjustments, and touted the five development concepts of "innovation, coordination, greening, opening-up and sharing" to comprehensively realize a moderately prosperous society in 2020.

From the Ninth Five-Year Plan objective of accelerating the model of economic growth to the 13th Five-Year Guideline objective of supply-side structural reform, it appears that China's economic development path has been generally consistent. China identified the strategy of economic structural adjustment as its basic direction, and has expanded and enriched it. This required an economy that was sustainable and stable with high speed, persistent economic structural adjustments, improvements and upgrade, and with a focus on the quality of economic development.

From the 11th Five-Year Guideline onward, China's economic development moved gradually onto a scientific development track and realized the shift in development mode. The country saw an obvious dip in social cost, resource expenditure, and ecological cost, as well as an improvement in production safety. It saw the disparity in regional productivity narrow, better use of resources, reduction in environmental pollutant emissions, and a turnaround in the environment and ecological systems. The 13th Five-Year Guideline period is a critical period for scientific development. Guided by the five major development concepts, it requires comprehensive supply-side structural reform, adaptation to the economic new normal, realization of green, harmonious and sustainable development, in order to build a moderately prosperous society by 2020 and lay the developmental groundwork for the country to bypass the "middle income trap".

To date, China has already implemented 13 five-year plans or guidelines. These inclusive outlines, serving as a conscious control on development, have become the blueprint and program of action for Chinese development. In setting out clear objectives, tasks, strategies, policies and measures suited to each developmental phase, they are oriented toward the overall, balanced and long-term development of the country, and are based on goal-oriented governance. Looking at how strategies have been adjusted at each stage since the reform and opening-up, it is apparent that the development strategy has not followed any one dogmatic method, but rather continued to reform and yield results by utilizing the "invisible hand" of the market, exploring the government's "visible hand" in macro-control and planning, mobilizing proactiveness at both central and regional levels, and effectively incorporating an efficient market with a useful government. This explains how the Chinese economy has been able to sustain the relatively high-speed growth for so long.

It is necessary to note that China's development strategies do not simply revolve around the five-year periods. Longer-term objectives are set during CPC congresses. Take for example the 12th CPC National Congress Report in 1982, which stated that on the premise of increasing economic efficiency, in the two decades from 1981 to the end of the twentieth century, China's central economic objective was to double the annual national agricultural production value, and bring its citizens' material and cultural quality of life to a "moderately prosperous" level. This was the first mention of "moderately prosperous" as a long-term development target, though the notion then was limited to looking at the quality of life from an income angle. In the 15th CPC National Congress Report in 1997, it was stated as an objective, that the first decade of the twenty-first century should see gross national production double from the turn of the century, in order to enrich citizens' moderately prosperous living standards.

In 2002, the 16th CPC National Congress voiced for the first time the idea of building a "prosperous society"—a far more multi-faceted concept that goes beyond the initial "moderately prosperous living". The Congress report stated that the first two decades of the twenty-first century is an important period filled with strategic opportunities for China, one that must be seized and utilized. The CPC Central Committee clarified that in those two decades, it is necessary to concentrate strength and comprehensively build a better-off moderately prosperous society to benefit the billion-people population. The State Development Planning Commission Director at the time, Zeng Peiyan, listed three indicators to measure the moderately prosperous society by 2020. The first is a measure of wealth—with per capita GDP growing annually at 7.2%, and at more than 3000 US dollars by 2020. The second is a measure of urbanization—with the rate growing by one percentage point each year and exceeding 50% by 2020. The third is a measure of industrialization—seeing agriculture account for less than 30% of employment by 2020. The fact is, China has met these above targets ahead of plan: GDP in 2015 is 3.96 times more than that in the year 2000 and per capita GDP has reached 8000 US dollars (current rate); the urbanization rate is 56.19%; and agricultural employment has dropped to 28.3% of total employment. The country has smoothly stepped into the middle-income phase, and raised the bar for building a moderately prosperous society.[9]

The 18th CPC National Congress further clarified the development objective of "building a moderately prosperous society by 2020". General Secretary Xi Jinping views lifting the rural impoverished population out of poverty as the toughest task ahead in fulfilling this objective. The definition of "moderately prosperous" evolved once again. In the past, it was meant as raising the average standard of life for citizens—an "average" was enough. For example, going back to the 1997 15th CPC National Congress report, it was said the first decade of the twenty-first century should see GNP double from the number at the turn of the century, in order to enrich citizens' moderately prosperous living standards. However, making "lifting the rural impoverished population out of poverty" the gauge for attaining a moderately prosperous society establishes a "bottom line". In other words, it is more than just raising the average standard of life for citizens; more importantly, it is about lifting the most impoverished population out of poverty. Fully eradicating poverty goes beyond lifting income levels above the poverty line, but also guaranteeing that basic public services for the underprivileged population is close to the average national standards. What this also shows is that China has not only set the poverty bar higher than that of the World Bank, its poverty alleviation targets are also of a higher standard and are enshrined in its national development goals. In particular, the demand on public services to reach an average national standard is in practice a great safeguard, as it recognizes the vulnerability of families that have just been lifted out of poverty, and reduces the risk of them "returning to poverty" because they cannot afford hefty medical bills and such.

The phrase "moderately prosperous" has been associated with Chinese development goals for nearly 40 years now. From when the phrase was first raised in 1979, it has evolved many times, from the initial "moderately prosperous living" to "moderately prosperous levels" to "overall moderately prosperous" to "all-round moderately prosperous" and finally to the "comprehensive moderately prosperous society" we are familiar with today. This evolution reflects the ruling party's promise to the nation, as well as the consistency in the CPC's development goals and strategic phases.

[9] In 2014, per capital GNI (current rate) in China reached 7400 US dollars; even at a fixed rate, it would be close to 4000 US dollars, attaining the 2020 target ahead of time.

Another area where we can identify the CPC's strategic thinking on development is the "two centenary goals", which was first raised in 1997 in the 15th CPC National Congress report. The two goals stated: when the CPC completes 100 years of its founding, China will have built a more developed economy with well-rounded systems; and when the People's Republic of China turns 100, China will have realized modernization, and built a prosperous, democratic, civilized socialist country. In 2012, the "two centenary goals" were revised in the 18th CPC National Congress report to say: in the new century, the economic and social development strategic target is to consolidate and advance the moderately prosperous standards, which have been preliminarily met. When the CPC completes 100 years since its founding, a high standard moderately prosperous society that benefits the billion-people population will be built; and when the PRC turns 100, per capita GDP will meet the standards of developed countries, and the country will realize modernization. The "two centenary goals" will be the key phrase associated with China's development strategy post-2020.

Overall, the CPC, as the ruling party, has a mature system to thoroughly arrange and draw up development strategies in all fields. This is evident in all the CPC's National Congress reports and plenary sessions. Normally, the third plenary is primarily for setting economic and reform agenda, the fifth plenary discusses the next five-year guideline, while the fourth and sixth plenaries touch upon Party building, law and governance, cultural and social matters. The decisions made at these sessions are held up as the consensus with which the CPC will govern the country, as well as reflect the evolving duty and promises the CPC endeavors to fulfill for the nation.

Take the plenary sessions held since the 18th CPC National Congress as an example—the CPC Central Committee has clearly outlined the development goals and governing methods in the approved decisions. The Third Plenary Session of the 18th CPC Central Committee laid out the strategy for all-round deepening reform for 2013–2020. The plenary decision is referred to as the blueprint of development through deepening reform with General Secretary Xi Jinping at the core of the CPC, and reflects the firm political determination to push forward with reforms. It clearly states the grand goal of "modernizing the national governance system and governing capability", and has elevated the role of the market in resource allocation from "basic" to "decisive". Additionally, the decision drew up a clear and unequivocal list of tasks to complete by 2020, including 60 areas needing all-round deepening reform, and 336 detailed measures, all of which are up for assessment by 2020. This indicates that the CPC is endeavoring to meet its political promises of fulfilling long-term national development goals.

The Fourth Plenary Session of the 18th CPC Central Committee made important arrangements for strengthening the rule of law, and stressed it should be the basis for governance and politics. This was the first time that rule of law was made a central topic at a plenary session. The Fourth Plenary stated: law is a powerful tool of governance, and good law is the premise of good governance; justice is the lifeline of the rule of law, the authority of law derives from the people's heart and sincere belief; the vitality of law lies in implementation, as does the authority of law. The decision clarified the important task of advancing the rule of law, including perfecting a socialist legal system with Chinese characteristics with the Constitution at its core and strengthening implementation of the Constitution, enhancing administration according to the law and accelerating construction of a rule of law government, guaranteeing judicial justice and raising judicial credibility, strengthening public awareness of rule of law and advancing the construction of a rule of law society, strengthening construction of a rule of law working team, and strengthening and reforming the leadership of the CPC in advancing the rule of law. All in all, the Fourth Plenary of the 18th CPC Central Committee put forward a top-down design for comprehensively advancing the rule of law, and charted a new road map for the country to perfect its legal system and enhance modernization of its governance system and governing capacity.

The Fifth Plenary Session of the 18th CPC Central Committee proposed a new concept, new thinking and new measures in relation to the Chinese economy entering a new normal and the goal of building an all-round moderately prosperous society by 2020. The session assessed the development situation, and deemed the country to be facing major strategic opportunities, but also steep challenges and conflict. Thus, the session adopted the *CPC Central Committee's Proposal on Formulating the Thirteenth Five-year Plan (2016–2020) on National Economic and Social Development*, which set out the five major development concepts of innovation, coordination, greening, opening-up and sharing. This is both a highly concise extraction of past experiences in development, and is also a strategic mindset for solving the biggest problems in contemporary Chinese development.

The Fifth Plenary of the 18th CPC Central Committee also raised new objectives of building an all-round moderately prosperous society. It sought to keep a medium-to-high speed economic growth on the basis of enhancing the balance, inclusiveness and sustainability of development, and double 2010's GDP and urban rural incomes by 2020, move industry toward a medium-to-high level, make consumption a bigger contributor to growth and increase urbanization. Other objectives included more achievements in modernizing the agricultural sector, raise the standard and quality of living for citizens, lift the rural population living under the national poverty line out of poverty so there is no longer any impoverished counties and regions, raise the standard of a civilized society, improve the ecological environment, refine and mature all systems and go further in modernizing the national governance system and governing capacity. Furthermore, at the end of 2015, the CPC Central Committee proposed supply-side structural reforms and made these a top priority of development during the 13th Five-Year Guideline period, which will guide economic structural transformations and improve the quality and efficiency of growth in the new normal era.

In summary, since the 18th CPC National Congress, the CPC Central Committee has charted out key strategies for different phases, major focus areas and general direction of development. At the National Congress itself followed by the third and fourth plenary sessions, the CPC raised the "four comprehensives" strategy, which comprises of "comprehensively building a moderately prosperous society", "comprehensively deepening reform", "comprehensively advancing the rule of law" and "comprehensively running the Party strictly"—the last was raised on October 8, 2014, at a conference for party education. It sought to advance the five major areas stated in the 18th CPC National Congress report: the economy, politics, culture, society and ecological development. We believe that China is capable of realizing a basically modernized governance system and governing capability by 2020, which will lay the foundation for China's march toward a high-income nation.

3.2.3 Modernized Infrastructure Provides Essential Support for Economic Development

China is in the stage of accelerated modernization of infrastructure development. Since 2001, transportation, communication and energy, among other major infrastructural areas, have seen rapid advancements and function both as the foundation and engine for economic development.

In terms of transportation infrastructure, China had begun building highways since the late 1980s, and construction sped up in the 1990s. In

1995, the network of highways totaled a mere 2100 kilometers; in 2000, it increased to 16,300 kilometers, roughly eight times the length in 1995. In 2005, the highways spanned 41,000 kilometers, 2.5 times more than in 2000. Then in 2015, that number became 123,000 kilometers, tripling the 2005 length. Railway infrastructure entered a fast development phase in 2008. From 1980 to 2008, the operational mileage rose from 53,300 kilometers to 79,700 kilometers, an extension of 24,600 kilometers, which averages out to be 879 kilometers per year. However, from 2008 to 2015, the operational mileage expanded to 121,000 kilometers, a difference of 43,100 kilometers, which is an annual average extension of 6157 kilometers.

High-speed rail is a highlight in particular when it comes to China's transportation infrastructure expansion, and it is also an important symbol of China's infrastructure upgrade. High-speed rail went from non-existent in 2008 to an operation mileage network of 19,800 kilometers in 2015 (see Fig. 3.7), more than the total sum of other countries. It signified infrastructure development made in leaps and bounds. Together, high-speed rail and others comprise more than 40,000 kilometers of rapid transit network, and have basically covered all provinces and cities with a population of more

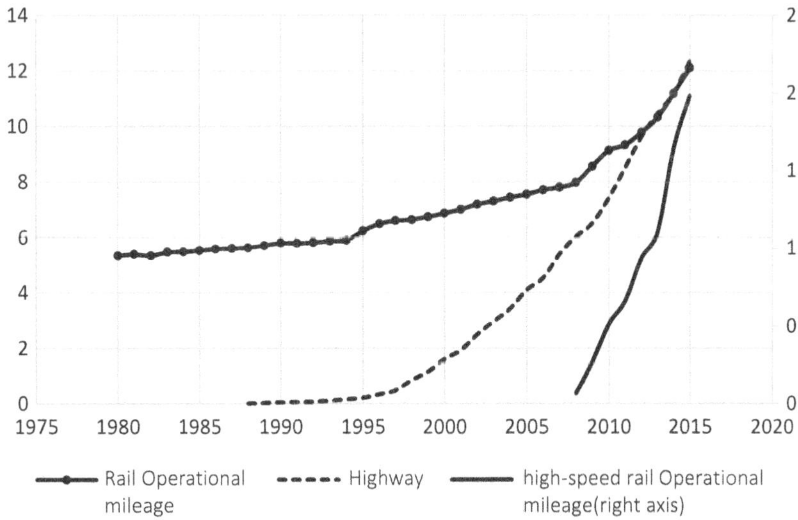

Fig. 3.7 Transport infrastructure (1980–2015, ten thousand kilometers). (Source: *China Statistical Yearbook 2016*)

than 500,000. In the 13th Five-Year Guideline, the goal was set for high-speed railways to operate across 30,000 kilometers of track by 2020 and cover 80% of the major cities. According to the *Medium and Long-term Railway Network Plan* issued in July 2016, the entire railway network aims to reach 175,000 kilometers by 2025, with high-speed railway to account for 38,000 kilometers. The plan aims to expand coverage and improve the road systems to play a key role in guaranteeing economic and social development. Looking ahead to 2030, it is expected that the transportation network will have extensive coverage, connecting areas with multiple travel options, linking up all provincial capitals with high-speed trains, enabling fast travel between cities, and covering most county areas.

Moving on to energy infrastructure: the main phase of development was after the year 2000. The installed power generating capacity increased from 3.19 gigawatts in 2000 to 15.25 gigawatts in 2015, averaging at around 11% year-on-year growth, which was sufficient for the high-speed economic development at the time. Pipeline transportation of gas rose from a mileage of 24,700 kilometers in 2000 to 108,700 kilometers in 2015 (see Fig. 3.8). Aside from the increasing scale of infrastructure construction, construction in various energy fields significantly improved

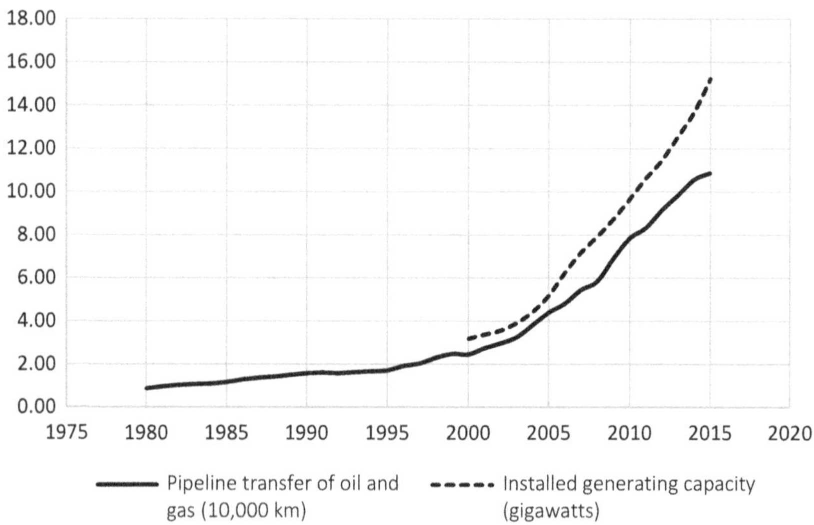

Fig. 3.8 Energy infrastructure (1980–2015). (Source: *China Statistical Yearbook 2016*)

cross-regional energy configuration. One feature of China is the uneven spread of the population, resource reserves and level of development across the country. Generally, the western regions have rich resources, but their population density and economic development lag behind that of eastern regions. In terms of the distribution of energy resources, coal reserves are mainly in the north, hydroelectric resources in the southwest, and gas reserves in the west. Meanwhile the east is the most economically developed and also where energy consumption is concentrated. In order to bridge the spatial difference between where energy is produced and where it is consumed, energy infrastructure construction provides instrumental support to economic development. Since China launched its "western development strategy" in 2000, projects such as the "west-east gas pipeline" and "west-east electricity transmission" have been made a priority in the development of western regions. The energy configuration structure was essentially settled in this manner, and this has helped to balance regional development. Post-2004, a trend of convergence could be seen in development among China's various regions.

The advancement in communication infrastructure could be viewed as the biggest highlight of China's twenty-first century development, especially in modernized communication facilities (mobile switch capacity and optical cable length); relative to China's economic development levels, it is progress made in huge strides. The optical cable length in 2015 was 20 times the length in 2000, while mobile switch capacity in 2015 was 15 times the capacity in 2000 (see Fig. 3.9). The extensive upgrade in communication infrastructure is a result of the nation's informatization strategy. The Tenth Five-Year Plan issued in 2001 raised for the first time the concept of "tri-networks integration", referring to the integration of telecommunications, television and internet. Following this, communication infrastructure saw rapid progress in both coverage and on a technological level, especially in mobile communication and the spread of broadband. China essentially attained universal access for its citizens to communication facilities, becoming a global power in mobile communication and internet. The rapid development in communication infrastructure building has provided much support to China's "new economy"—one that is characterized by advancements in internet and mobile communication.

The 13th Five-Year Guideline proposed "speed up the construction of a new generation of high-speed, mobile, secure, ubiquitous information

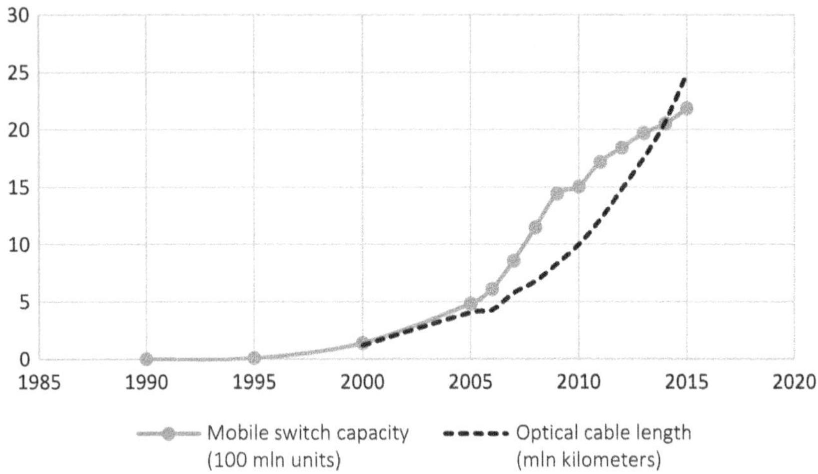

Fig. 3.9 Communication infrastructure (1990–2015). (Source: *China Statistical Yearbook 2016*)

infrastructure, promote the wide use of information network technology, and form a world of internet space where everything is interconnected, humans and computers interact, and space and ground integrate". The Guideline laid out the objective of fiber network coverage of all urban areas by 2020, realizing access for 98% of rural areas, optimizing the configuration of global communication network, and enhancing the construction of cross-border land and sea cables. In terms of communication technology, the Guideline encouraged research and development of 5G and super-broadband technology, promoted commercializing 5G use and laying the groundwork for the next generation of internet technology. We estimate that around 2020, China's information infrastructure coverage and technological levels will reach a new height, making it a leader in mobile communication and internet technology, and expanding the online economy. In particular, the "Internet Plus" plan raised in the 13th Five-Year Plan will boost China's "new economy" and become a source of support for the adjustment and upgrade of industrial structure under the economic new normal.

3.2.4 China Already Fulfills the Essential Preconditions for Innovation-Driven Development

As early as the 1980s, China began strategizing ways to improve its scientific and innovative capacity. In 1986, Deng Xiaoping endorsed the proposal of four scientists, Wang Daheng, Wang Ganchang, Yang Jiachi and Chen Fangyun, that China should develop its own advanced technologies in line with the world. After this, the State Council approved the *State High Tech Development Plan* (863 Program), which selected seven key technological development fields with impact on socio-economic progress, such as biotechnology and information technology. It circled 15 projects as priority areas to keep up with world standards. Deng Xiaoping made a series of science and technology related propositions. To cite a few examples: in September 1988, he made the notable remark at the National Science Conference that "science and technology are the primary productive forces". In October that same year, while inspecting the Beijing Electron Positron Collider project, Deng said, "China must develop its own high technology, so that it can take its place in this field".

Since the turn of the century, China's knowledge in science and technology has further prompted innovation-driven development. In 2002, the 16th CPC National Congress raised the strategy of "enhancing capacity for independent innovation and building an innovative country". In 2012, the 18th CPC National Congress underscored the "innovation-driven" development strategy, and insisted that China must stick to its own path of self-innovation with Chinese characteristics. With this innovation-driven development strategy in place, many medium- and long-term plans were set to this end, such as the *National Medium and Long-Term Program for Science and Technology Development (2006–2020)* in 2006; *National Outline for Medium and Long-Term Education Reform and Development (2010–2020)* in 2010; and *National Outline for Medium and Long-Term Talents Development (2010–2020)* in 2010. These three major plans essentially laid the foundation for the "holy trinity" of innovation-driven development—education, talent and science and technology—and set out clear development goals.[10] After this, China succes-

[10] For example, the *National Medium and Long-Term Program for Science and Technology Development (2006–2020)* stated that by 2020, the nation's gross expenditures on R&D (GERD) are expected to rise to 2.5% or above of the gross domestic product (GDP) with the rate of S&T contribution to the economy reaching 60% or above, dependence on imported technology reduced to 30% or below, and the annual invention patents granted to Chinese

sively issued multiple national innovation and development plans, such as the *11th Five-Year Plan on National Independent Innovation Capacity Building* from the State Council in January 2007; *12th Five-Year Plan on National Independent Innovation Capacity Building* also from the State Council in May 2013; and *13th Five-Year Plan on Scientific and Technological Innovation* in August 2016. These plans state clearly China must have its eye on the frontier of global science and technology; and integrate, digest and absorb imported innovation in order to recreate and improve its own capacity.

Aside from plans targeted at science and technology innovation, China also laid out guidelines for promoting the development of the high-tech industry. To cite a few examples, in 2007, China issued the *11th Five-Year Plan for Development of High-Tech Industries,* which covered high-tech manufacturing industries such as electronic information, biology, aerospace, new materials, new energy and marine, among others. It also covered high-tech service industries such as electronic communication, internet and data content. Then in 2012, the country issued the *12th Five-Year Plan for National Strategic Emerging Industries,* which accelerated incubation of the strategic emerging industries and integration of sci-tech innovation and economic development. It also outlined 20 major projects within the key industries of energy-saving and environmental

nationals and the international citations of scientific papers moving into the top five countries. The *National Outline for Medium and Long-term Education Reform and Development (2010–2020)* stated, the strategic goals to attain by 2020 are to basically modernize education, bring a learning society into shape and turn China into a country rich in human resources. The specific goals are to popularize senior middle school education with a 90% gross enrollment rate, and further popularize higher education with a gross enrollment rate of 40%; the average number of years of education received by newly added members of the workforce shall rise from 12.4 to 13.5 years; the average number of years of education received by the working-age population shall extend from 9.5 to 11.2 years; 20% of the working-age population shall have finished higher education, doubling that of 2009. The *National Outline for Medium and Long-term Talents Development (2010–2020)* stated the overall goals by 2020 are to cultivate and train a large team of talents that have optimum structure, rational distribution and good caliber, form comparable advantages for talent competition, make China a strong country rich in talents, and lay a foundation of talents for attaining socialist modernization in the middle of this century. The specific goals are to increase the total number of talent resources by 58% from the current 114 million to 180 million, and increase the proportion of talent resource in human resources to 16%; the proportion of human capital investment shall account for 15% of the total GDP, the contribution ratio of human capital to economic growth shall be 33% and the talent contribution ratio 35%.

protection, new generation information technology, biology, high-end equipment manufacturing, new energy, new material and new energy autos. In 2015, China proposed the "Made in China 2025" plan in line with the target of becoming a manufacturing powerhouse. There are three steps to this plan: elevate China's role in the global manufacturing industry by 2025, raise China to a mid-ranking position among the most powerful manufacturing nations by 2035 and finally, bring the overall strength of the manufacturing industry into the leading ranks of the world's most powerful manufacturing nations by 2049, one hundred years on from the founding of the People's Republic of China. The "Made in China 2025" plan clarified nine strategic tasks and focal points, and eight aspects needing strategic support and guarantee.[11] Additionally, also in 2015, China issued the *Guidance on Actively Promoting the Internet Plus Action Plan*.

Aside from the aforementioned strategies, the fast upgrade in China's human resources served as a base for innovation-driven development. Development of the education sector is a reason for the rapid accumulation of human capital, which entered a period of accelerated advancement from the end of the last century. The number of associate's and bachelor's degree holders rose from 950,000 in 2000 to 6.81 million in 2015, an average annual increase of 14%. The total accumulative number of such degree holders in 2000–2015 reached 60.83 million, equivalent to the population of Italy. In 2000, the number of holders of associate's degree and above was 45.71 million nationwide, and that expanded by 3.45 times to 158 million people in 2014 (see Fig. 3.10).

The number of master's degree holders increased from 58,800 in 2000 to 551,500 people in 2015. The total accumulative number of such degree holders in 2000–2015 reached 4.85 million, equivalent to the population of New Zealand. Returning overseas graduates increased from 9100 people in the year 2000 to 409,100 in 2015, while the cumulative number of returning overseas graduates in 2000–2015 was 2.1 million. If we examine the ratio of returning overseas graduates to students studying abroad, we can see that it fell from 1:4.27 in 2000 to 1:1.28 in 2015 (see Fig. 3.11), indicating that domestic development conditions have made China more appealing.

[11] On April 6, 2016, Premier of the State Council Li Keqiang hosted a State Council executive meeting, during which *Plans Regarding Equipment Manufacturing Industry Standards and Quality Improvement* was approved to facilitate the "Made in China 2025" plan.

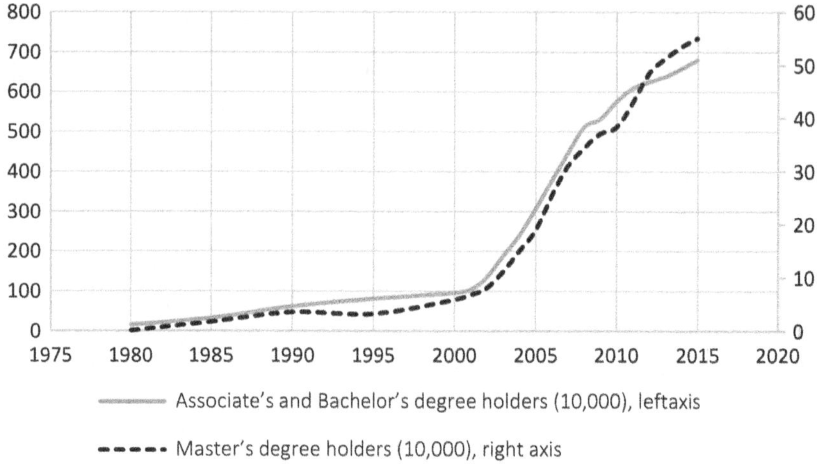

Fig. 3.10 The number of associate's, bachelor's and master's degree holders (1980–2015). (Source: *China Statistical Yearbook 2016*)

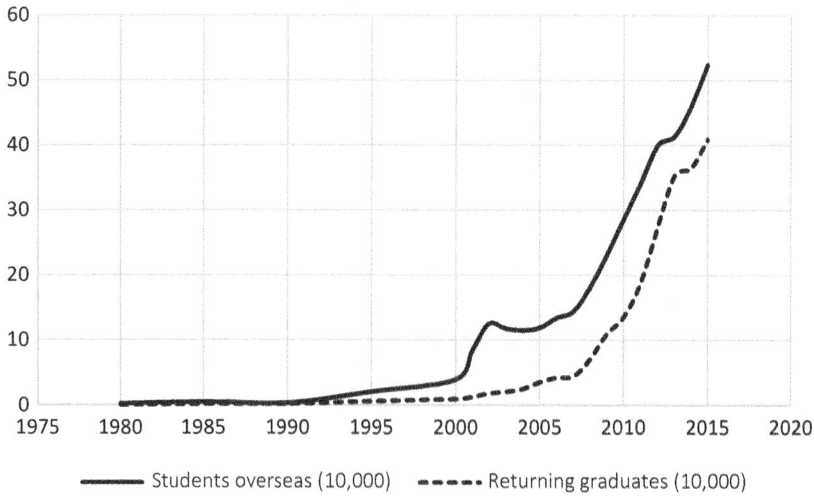

Fig. 3.11 The number of students studying abroad (1980–2015). (Source: *China Statistical Yearbook 2016*)

Owing to the innovation-driven development strategy and support of human capital, China has also expanded investment in innovation. Take for example research and development (R&D) expenditure, it rose from 1.76% of GDP in 2010 to 2.07% of GDP in 2015, closing in on the target of 2.2% set in the 13th Five-Year Guideline and already overtaking the average levels of 28 European Union countries. The 13th Five-Year Guideline expects gross national R&D expenditure to reach 2.5% of GDP, similar to U.S. levels. A look at the source of R&D expenditure: the bulk of R&D activities are carried out by enterprises, and the financial contribution of enterprises has firmly remained above 70%, even reaching 75% in 2015; this pattern is similar to that of the developed countries.[12] In terms of patents, in 2015, there were 6.3 patents owned among every 10,000 people, already significantly exceeding the objectives set in the 12th Five-Year Guideline of 3.3 patents. The 13th Five-Year Guideline went further to set a patent ownership target of 12 out of 10,000 (see Table 3.3), elevating China's sci-tech innovation capability to a new level.

With the advance of sci-tech innovation, we see the increasing application of the results yielded. The tech market turnover increased from 390.7 billion yuan in 2010 to 983.6 billion yuan in 2015.[13] Internationally, the global share of the added value of China's high-tech industry is gradually enlarging. Let us compare with the U.S.: in 2000, China's high-tech industry took only a 2.53% share of the world's total, while the U.S. accounted for 37.10%. But come 2015, China and the U.S. are

Table 3.3 Key indicators of China's innovation-driven development

	2010	*2015*	*2020 target*
R&D expenditure (100 million yuan)	7063	14,170	23,200
R&D expenditure as percentage of GDP (%)	1.73	2.07	2.5
Invention patents filed (10,000)	39.1	110	177
Invention patents granted (10,000)	13.5	35.9	55.2
Invention patent owned every 10,000 people (patent/10,000 people)	1.7	6.3	12
Invention patent owned (10,000)	22.8	118.9	168

Source: *China Statistical Yearbook 2015*, *China Statistical Yearbook 2016*

[12] Source: *China Statistical Yearbook 2016*.
[13] Source: *China Statistical Yearbook 2015*, *China Statistical Yearbook 2016*.

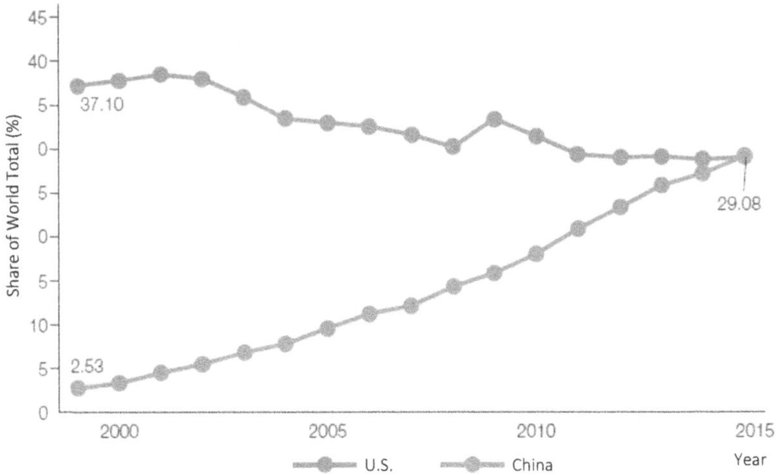

Fig. 3.12 The added value of high-tech industries in China and the U.S. as a share of the world's total (2000–2015). (Source: Hu Angang and Ren Hao, "How China's High-technology Industry Catches-up with United States", *Bulletin of Chinese Academy of Sciences*, Issue 12, 2016)

virtually tied. The two countries are both powerhouses in the global high-tech industry, and together hold a 60% share of the world's total value (see Fig. 3.12).

Another measure of competitiveness in the high-tech industry is export of high-tech products. This reflects the innovation capability of a country's high-tech industry, integrated manufacturing capability as well as its production cost advantages. If we compare again with the U.S., China's export of high-tech products is increasingly grabbing a bigger share of the world pie, surpassing the U.S. in 2004, and leaving the U.S. far behind in 2014 (Fig. 3.13). It is necessary to point out that China's increasing competitiveness in this sector is mostly owing to the country's integrated manufacturing capability as well as the relative advantage it has in labor costs. In terms of high-tech innovation capability, China is improving, but that element has not yet become the export driving force of high-tech products. However, we have reason to believe that China's independent innovation capability in the high-tech sector will eventually catch up with the developed world. Take a look at the data from the World Bank, which shows there were 1.519 million people working in R&D in China in 2014,

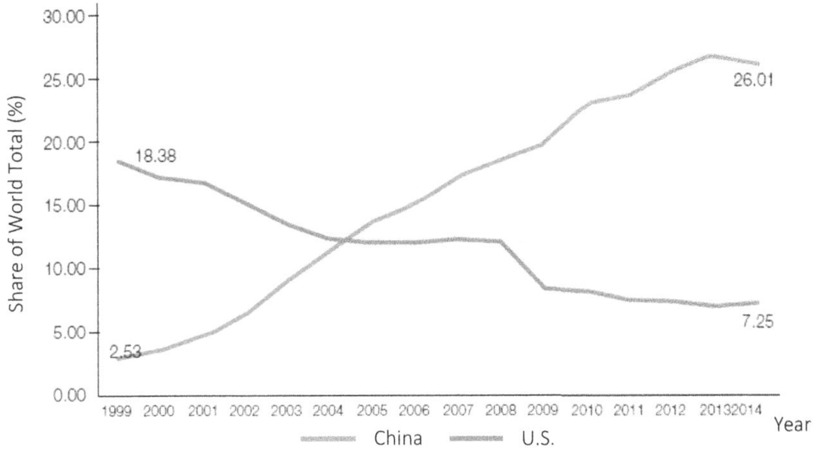

Fig. 3.13 The value of high-tech exports from China and the U.S. as a share of the world's total (2000–2014). (Source: Hu Angang and Ren Hao, "How China's High-Technology Industry Catches-up with United States", *Bulletin of Chinese Academy of Sciences*, Issue 12, 2016)

surpassing the number in the U.S. in 2012 (1.262 million people), but below the number in the EU in 2014 (1.769 million people). We project that around the year 2020, China's R&D sector employment will overtake the EU, and significantly exceed the U.S.

Overall, from the turn of the century, China has been gradually shaping the mechanisms for innovation-driven development. High-tech related industries are becoming the new force behind economic development, pushing the transition from "manufactured in China" to "created in China". The high-tech sector is moving from chasing innovation to being on the frontier of innovation on the global stage, already exceeding its initial strategic expectation of simply "having a foothold" in the sector. The 2014 Global Innovation Index released by Cornell University ranked China 29th out of 143 countries, earning it the title of an "innovation learner". But it also has the highest score out of the "learners", and is edging closer to innovation leaders.[14] In the 2016 Global Innovation Index,

[14] This study compares the Global Innovation Index with GDP (PPP) and ranks countries into three categories: leaders, learners and underperformers.

China climbed up to 25th out of 128 countries, the only upper-middle income country to join the ranks of highly developed economies.[15] It is remarkable that China graduated from learner in 2014 to a leader in innovation in 2016.

This is evidence that China's sci-tech innovation capability is transitioning from "chasing after" to a phase where it is "running alongside or even overtaking" leaders of the field. This is an important period of transition from quantity to quality, from breakthrough to systematic advancement. We expect innovation-driven development strategies will take an even more central position in the nation's bigger development picture, and China will become increasingly prominent on the global innovation map as it improves its innovative capabilities. China will be more than just an influential country in the sci-tech field, but also a leader in global innovation.

3.2.5 *China's Capacity for Green Development Continues to Grow*

Looking at the global picture, China is a country with relatively low ecological resources per capita and natural resources (water, land and minerals) per capita, and as urbanization continues and the economy develops, environmental deterioration will only become a bigger concern. We could say that ecology, resources and environment are the three big hurdles for development, and also three constraints. In terms of the ecological challenge, a large part of the national land space qualifies as extremely ecologically fragile areas, and its protection is laden with difficulties. Moderately ecologically fragile zones account for 55% of the land space, while severely ecologically fragile zones account for 19.8%.[16] Looking at the resource challenge, China's main resources, including water, arable land, forests, grasslands, petroleum, natural gas, coal, account for a far smaller share of the world's total compared to the proportion of its population.[17] It is clear from this that China is a natural-resource-poor per capita nation. Moving

[15] Specifically, China ranked 29th in the Innovation Input Sub-Index, 15th in the Innovation Output Sub-Index and 7th in the Innovation Efficiency Ratio, the highest ranking upper-middle income country.

[16] Refer to *National Functional Areas Planning – Building an Efficient, Coordinated, Sustainable Land Space Development*, December 21, 2010.

[17] For relevant data, refer to Hu Angang and Yan Yilong, *China's National Conditions and Development*, page 66, China Renmin University Press, 2016.

on to the environment challenge, atmospheric pollution, soil pollution and water pollution among others present a momentous task for environmental governance, and threaten industrial, agricultural production as well as the health of citizens. China remains in a development phase of accelerated industrialization and urbanization, when demand for resources is ever growing. This explains why resources and environment will pose a serious constraint on future economic development. If China wants to bypass the "middle income trap", it is imperative that the country does not disregard national conditions and pursue the traditional path of industrialization taken in the West of "pollute first, clean up later"; instead, it must implement green development as soon as possible.

China has been actively taking measures to address ecological concerns since the reform and opening-up, and has generally managed to contain ecological deterioration with its continued endeavors. In 1979, China initiated the "three-north" shelterbelt program to protect forests, planting large-scale forest strips in the north, northeast and northwest, eventually covering an area of 4.07 million square kilometers. To date, the "three-north" program has been in progress for nearly 40 years. It has had important impact on mitigating soil erosion, improving agricultural conditions and shoring up forestry resources in northern areas, and has contributed positively to ecological conditions there. From the end of the last century, China began to intensify ecological construction efforts. In 1999, it rolled out the "grain for green" policy—encouraging afforestation on fragile farmlands. This policy formed a crucial part of the western development strategy mentioned before, and has helped to turn around the ecological conditions in western regions by preventing soil erosion.[18]

From the 11th Five-Year Plan onward, China gradually rolled out and refined its green development strategy. For example, the 11th Five-Year Plan raised "building a resource-conserving, environmentally-friendly society"; the 12th Five-Year Plan proposed "green development and building a resource-conserving, environmentally-friendly society"; and the 13th Five-Year Plan set "green development" as one of the five major development concepts with which to guide economic development under the new normal. In particular, resource-related goals were classified as

[18]According to data from China's State Forestry Administration from 1999 to 2014, the "grain for green" project has acquired 9.0634 million hectares of farmland, 16.5676 million hectares of barren mountains and lands and closed off 2.9473 million hectares of hillsides for afforestation.

Table 3.4 Distribution of main indicators in the 13th Five-Year Plan

	Targets	*Proportion (%)*	*Actual targets*	*Proportion (%)*	*Binding targets*	*Actual binding targets*
Economic development	4	16	5	15.2		
Innovation	4	16	5	15.2		
People's livelihoods and wellbeing	7	28	7	21.2	3	3
Resource and environment	10	40	16	48.5	10	16
Total	25	100	33	100	13	19

Note: Compiled by authors with reference to the 13th Five-Year Plan

binding targets, and environmental protection was made a core objective of development. Both the 12th and 13th Five-Year Plans strengthened environmental targets. Take the 13th Plan as an example, actual targets related to resources and environment totaled 16, accounting for 48.5% of all targets in the Plan. Not only this, all 16 are binding targets (see Table 3.4).

If we assess the results, we can see that the main ecological and environmental targets were met. For example, energy consumption per unit of GDP dropped 19.1% during the 11th Five-Year Plan period, and further dropped by 18.2% during the 12th Five-Year Plan period. On the whole, as public awareness of environmental matters increases alongside economic development and urbanization, environmental management will become more complex, and is sure to pose a considerable challenge throughout China's middle-income development phase.

3.2.6 *China Actively Participates in Globalization and Global Governance*

With the end of World War II, globalization has become the irreversible trend of world development, propelled by technological and market forces. Participation in globalization is an important means for developing countries to advance their economy. The economic success of the "four Asian tigers" is an example of the importance of adapting to and maximizing the opportunities presented by globalization after World War

II. China's own economic development after the reform and opening-up goes to show participation in economic globalization provided the external driver of high-speed growth. However, economic globalization is also a "double-edged sword"; ineffective handling of external impact can drag a country into economic stagnation. The 1998 Asian financial crisis and its impact on Southeast Asian nations is a case in point, while the 2008 global financial crisis similarly dragged down many emerging economies to low or negative growth. The reality is, many middle-income countries end up falling into the "middle income trap" because, to a large extent, they were unable to shield their economies effectively against external impact.

With the advent of the reform and opening-up, China went from being on the periphery of the global economy to an active participant, beneficiary and contributor. Globalization not only provided the external push needed for China's economy, the global economy also benefited from China's participation. China's membership of the WTO propelled it into a new economic arena; its connection with the world grew ever closer, and as the largest import-export country, China also became the largest contributor to world trade. The 2008 financial crisis also signified a new phase of globalization for China. The country participated actively in a range of regional and international economic cooperation mechanisms, and is proactive in helping to build a fair and equitable international economic system. This is evident in the following ways.

First, China has a strategy of actively establishing bilateral and multilateral free trade agreements. The implementation of these FTAs enriches the mechanisms for China's economic relationship with foreign countries.[19] At the same time, China has set up multiple free trade pilot zones,[20] which are the focal points for institutional innovation, accelerating the changing role of the government, reforming the system of administrative approval, implementing the system of the negative list, opening-up investment fields, facilitating trade, further opening up the financial sector, exploring

[19] China has so far signed successive FTA deals with ASEAN, Iceland, Switzerland, completed negotiations with South Korea, Australia, initiated the second phase of negotiations with Sri Lanka, Pakistan, entered negotiations for upgraded FTA with ASEAN (10+1) and participated in the Regional Comprehensive Economic Partnership (RCEP) talks which incorporates 48% of the global population and 30% of GDP.

[20] The China (Shanghai) Pilot Free Trade Zone was set up in 2013, followed by the China (Guangdong) Pilot Free Trade Zone, China (Tianjin) Pilot Free Trade Zone, China (Fujian) Pilot Free Trade Zone in late 2014, as well as the expansion of the Shanghai Pilot Free Trade Zone.

importable and replicative systems and innovations and driving the overall upgrade of the system.

Second, China has been proactively building new mechanisms for international economic cooperation. In September and October of 2013, while visiting Central Asia and Southeast Asia, President Xi Jinping proposed respectively the concepts of the "Silk Road Economic Belt" and "Twenty-first Century Maritime Silk Road", garnering much international attention. In late 2015, the Asia Infrastructure Investment Bank (AIIB) was established, spearheaded by China, and with 57 founding members. This is an important multilateral organization to guarantee Asia's sustainable and stable economic development. The "One Belt, One Road" initiative will give impetus to cooperation between China and all the countries along the route in multiple aspects, such as infrastructure construction, trade and investment, energy, regional integration, and Renminbi internationalization. Aided by the Silk Road Foundation and AIIB's establishment, this has set up a new platform for China's opening-up. The 13th Five-Year Guideline also prioritized "open development" as the development concept, encouraging active participation in economic globalization, and building a fair, reasonable, win-win international economic order. In the present climate, against the backdrop of rising anti-globalization sentiments, China has become the champion of globalization. In 2017, President Xi Jinping delivered his keynote speech at the Davos World Economic Forum, titled "Jointly Shoulder the Responsibility of Our Times, and Promote Global Growth". He made a strong case of globalization as "win-win" for everyone, earning worldwide endorsement.[21]

China has been a stabilizing force for world trade in the last two rounds of financial crises during the past two decades. Amid the Asian financial crisis, in 1998, China made a commitment not to devalue the Renminbi, which was conducive to stabilizing Southeast Asian economies. When the global financial crisis erupted in 2008, China initially proposed a "Four Trillion Economic Stimulus Plan", then set itself to vigorous national economic restructuring, which was crucial in stabilizing the country's

[21] In President Xi Jinping's keynote speech, he advocated firmly promoting economic globalization, injecting vitality to growth, taking a win-win approach to cooperation, developing a fair and reasonable model of governance, a balanced and equitable model of development, and consolidating the goal of a shared future for mankind and common prosperity.

economic growth as well as the world's. The impact of the global environment post-2008 led to a slowdown in Chinese foreign trade from high-speed growth to medium-to-high, trade surplus as a proportion of GDP narrowed, the effect of net export as an engine of economic growth weakened, which in turn led to economic growth slowing. Nonetheless, China still managed to maintain its medium-to-high-speed growth, signaling that the Chinese economy is fairly sturdy and has the capacity to ward against external impact, particularly when compared with Southeast Asian and Latin American countries.

For a start, China has a number of world-class enterprises, which forms a safeguard against external risks. The Fortune Global 500 list is a reflection of a country's composite strength. In 2016, the revenues of Fortune Global 500 companies totaled 27.6 trillion US dollars, equivalent to 36% of the world's GDP. If we now look at the distribution of these companies in 2016, we will see that they are based in only 29 countries (Table 3.5). A total of 298 are based in highly developed European countries and the U.S., 110 in China, 67 in Japan and South Korea, and only 25 in other developing countries (excluding China). In addition, out of the 35 OECD countries, 13 do not have any companies that made the Fortune Global 500 list. As mentioned earlier, this list is an important indication of a country's strength.

Table 3.5 The distribution of Fortune Global 500 companies by countries (2016)

Country	*Number*	*Country*	*Number*	*Country*	*Number*
U.S.	134	Italy	9	Austria	1
China	110	Australia	8	Poland	1
Japan	52	Brazil	7	Denmark	1
France	29	India	7	Luxembourg	1
Germany	28	Russia	5	Malaysia	1
U.K.	25	Sweden	3	Norway	1
South Korea	15	Singapore	3	Saudi Arabia	1
Switzerland	15	Ireland	2	Thailand	1
Netherlands	12	Belgium	2	Turkey	1
Canada	11	Mexico	2	Indonesia	1
Spain	9	United Arab Emirates	1	U.K./Netherlands	1

Source: fortunechina.com, http://www.fortunechina.com/fortune500/c/2016-07/20/content_266955.htm

Table 3.6 Changes in the distribution of Fortune Global 500 companies by countries (1990–2016)

Country	*1990*	*1996*	*2000*	*2005*	*2008*	*2010*	*2016*
U.S.	164	153	179	177	162	140	134
Japan	111	141	108	81	67	71	52
U.K.	43	32	38	35	34	30	25
Germany	30	40	37	36	37	37	28
France	30	42	37	39	38	39	29
Canada	12	6	12	13	16	11	11
South Korea	11	12	11	11	14	10	15
India	6	1	1	5	6	8	7
Russia		1	2	3	4	6	5
China	1	2	11	18	30	54	110

Source: Fortune Global 500 database

There is a correlation between changes in the distribution of Fortune Global 500 companies across the world and the relative ranking of countries by economic scale. As seen in Table 3.6 Japanese companies made the Fortune Global 500 list in 1996, but as the growth of the Japanese economy faltered in the ensuing two decades, the number of Fortune Global 500 companies also dwindled to 52 in 2016. On the other hand, the number of Chinese companies has increased the most since 1990. In 1990, only one Chinese company made to the Fortune Global 500 list; in 2000, there were ten; then in 2008, there were 30; and eventually in 2016, 110 made the list—making China the country with the second most number of Fortune Global 500 companies. This increase is also in sync with the rise of the Chinese economy to become the world's second largest. It is estimated that by 2020, Chinese Fortune Global 500 companies will even exceed American companies.

Secondly, China has sizeable foreign exchange reserves, which means it is unlikely to experience the substantial currency depreciation Southeast Asian nations did in 1998 as a result of rapid outflow of short-term capital, nor the sovereign debt crisis some European nations underwent in recent years. By the end of 2016, China had 3 trillion US dollars in foreign currency reserves, slightly less than the peak of 3.84 trillion US dollars in 2014. Even though the amount of reserves has ebbed, it is still more than sufficient to cover all of China's debt as well as half a year's worth of foreign exchange needed for imports. This scale of fluctuation in foreign exchange reserves is normal in the long run, and there is no need to view it as a portent of a bleak economy to come.

Thirdly, China has already set in motion large-scale foreign direct investment (FDI). In 2016, Chinese non-financial FDI in 7961 overseas enterprises in 164 countries and regions totaled over 170 billion US dollars, 44.1% more than the previous year. A significant amount of investment by Chinese companies overseas is in resource-related projects, which provides a certain guarantee for future development of the Chinese economy. In addition, China is also actively accelerating its Renminbi internationalization process. The formal inclusion of the Renminbi in the International Monetary Fund's SDR currency basket on October 1, 2016, is sure to expand the Renminbi's circulation overseas and facilitate development of the domestic capital market. It will help the Renminbi gain favor internationally for settling cross-border trade and as a reserve currency.

3.2.7 *The Superiority of the Socialist System Provides the Political Foundation for Overcoming the "Middle Income Trap"*

China is a massive country of 1.38 billion people; the problems it confronts in the course of development are often the toughest in the world. The hurdles it has encountered thus far encompass practically all those predicaments faced by developing countries—each of them is an extremely hard nut to crack. Whether China can successfully bypass the "middle income tap" depends on whether it can jump these hurdles. The country's experience since its foundation has taught us that as long as there is no "rocking the boat" or getting sidetracked, any problem can be eventually solved. What is implied by this is avoiding the setbacks inflicted when information asymmetry leads to the state (government) and society (public) blindly following others and losing the sense of "self" on a national and social level, thereby erroneously believing what they are doing is for the better, when in fact it is detrimental. Specifically, not rocking the boat economically means averting radical booms and busts in development; not rocking the boat politically means preventing vacillation in the political direction; not rocking the boat socially means deterring illegal public demonstrations of "democracy"; and not rocking the boat ecologically means refraining from damaging the ecological environment. So, how can these be achieved? Fundamentally, we must not take futile actions, but opt for a proactive and steady approach to state building. Secondly, should another party attempt to intervene and rock the boat, we must keep a solid footing, and instead of following suit, we must confidently adhere to our own path, system and retain independence in our democratic political development.

China's development path of socialist modernization is neither ordinary nor simple. We have learned the hard way from history. From the founding of the PRC to the reform and opening-up, there have been two tumultuous times as a result of getting sidetracked. The first was on the economic front with the Great Leap Forward. During the First Five-Year Plan period, China's GDP grew at an annual average of 9.2%, with industrial and agricultural output growth at an average of 18% and 4.5% respectively. But this was not fast enough for Mao Zedong. He first criticized Zhou Enlai and others for their opposition to his ambitions, then suggested China could "surpass the U.K. and catch up with the U.S." and set off the Great Leap Forward movement with its sky-high targets which ultimately ended in failure. The second time was turmoil on the political front with the "Cultural Revolution". In 1963–1965, China's GDP grew at an average of 17.6%; even though the speed was partly owing to the economy being in recovery mode, it still signaled potential for fast development in the future. However, once again, a decision by Mao Zedong to launch the Cultural Revolution resulted in a polarized and damaged nation. In September 1981, Politburo Standing Committee member and Vice Premier of the State Council, Li Xiannian, urged the country to never again rock the boat.[22] In the three decades after, we have encountered threats and stumbling blocks, but even when there was unforeseen political turbulence, we have handled trouble in time and survived the test, avoiding significant turmoil. This is the fundamental reason for the three decades of high-speed economic growth and social progress in China. Based on this, we can safely say that not "rocking the boat" is the basic safety net for China when crossing the "middle income trap".

The world has been told the same cautionary tale. In the 1980s and 1990s, the Soviet Union and eastern European soviet states all underwent

[22] Li Xiannian pointed out that past setbacks in politics and the economy were caused by "class wars" and the Cultural Revolution, and unrealistically high targets such as those imposed during the 1958 Great Leap Forward. He also said he is certain that today's central government will never rock the boat like this again. Li Xiannian's speech, "Economic Growth Targets Must Be Realistic", September 2, 1981.

dramatic economic and political transformations, which caused a serious blow to their economies. According to Angus Maddison's calculations of per capita GDP by purchasing power parity (PPP, 1990 Geary-Khamis/international dollars), per capita GDP in seven eastern European country did not grow past their 1990 levels (5427 US dollars) until 1998. In Yugoslavia (five countries), it took until 2005 for per capita GDP to exceed what it was in 1990 (5646 US dollars). In the Soviet Union, it was not until 2006 that per capita GDP caught up to what it was in 1990 (8513 US dollars).[23] Aside from long-term economic slowdown or stagnation, these countries also saw high unemployment and soaring inflation among other phenomena, and declining standards of living in the 1990s. In 1996, the World Bank analyzed 28 countries undergoing economic transformation in its World Development Report: From Plan to Market. It found only China and Vietnam were able to circumvent negative economic growth and sustain high-speed growth. Whereas the other 26 countries experienced different degrees of V or L shaped economic growth, in particular Ukraine and Russia.

In retrospect, China's development successes of today are largely because the country did not sway from its path in the 1980s and 1990s, and resisted the changes spreading across the former Soviet Union and eastern European socialist states. If we posit that in the 1990s, China's prevailing purpose was to avoid the national fragmentation, economic stagnation and political meltdown experienced by the Soviet Union and Yugoslavia as they underwent economic transformation, then we can say the prevailing purpose today is to fend off the destabilizing factors to politics and society as China prepares to emerge from the middle-income development phase.

The forces that could destabilize Chinese politics come from both the outside and inside. The external factor is that the country must not blindly import Western democracy, but rather insist on developing its own socialist democratic political system. We can see from other developing countries that have imported Western values and the Western political system, that doing so does not necessarily guarantee economic development; instead, it can cause political fracturing, turbulence and social fissures. This often results in pertinent livelihood issues being pushed aside amid

[23]The 1990 rate of Geary-Khamis/international dollars used in calculations. Angus Maddison, Historical Statistics of the World Economy: 1–2008 AD.

political rivalries and thus sinking the country into the "democracy trap".[24] To cite a few examples, Thailand's "Red Shirts" movement, Georgia's "Revolution of the Roses", Ukraine's "Orange Revolution", Kyrgyzstan's "Tulip Revolution", and Tunisia's "Jasmine Revolution"—these eventually all boiled down into a show of "street democracy" and chaos. These "color-coded revolutions" brought only political and social unrest and government changes, and meant the public could not even meet their most basic material needs. In other words, for developing countries, the "middle income trap" is essentially a "Western democracy trap".

Internally, stable and progressive politics hinge on the CPC making relentless endeavors to improve and strengthen its leadership, as well as modernize its governance system and governance capability, in order to optimize the advantages of the socialist system and provide more for the people. In practice, since the reform and opening-up, the CPC has continued to self-improve, move with the times, meet the development aspirations of the people and the evolving national circumstances, actively deepen reform and optimize the advantages of a socialist system with Chinese characteristics. We could say that the leadership of the Party is the foundation of an optimal socialist system.

China's biggest difference from other middle-income country is also its biggest advantage—that is, its socialist system. This will prove to be the security that will help it cross the middle-income trap. The advantages of the socialist system are not rigid; it manifests itself in different manners at different historical times, and will become more elaborate as the system becomes more refined. Whether this advantage can be utilized depends on the CPC's leadership. Even with the setbacks of the Great Leap Forward and the Cultural Revolution before the reform and opening-up, we were still able to see the system's superiority, for example in the progress made in raising average incomes, life expectancy and education standards. With the reform and opening-up, China abandoned the "class struggle" doctrine and established the "one central task and two basic points" political line, which was to make economic development the central task, uphold the four cardinal principles and adhere to the reform and opening-up. This political mantra ensured stability after the reform and opening-up and enabled China's political development. It helped to shape the ensuing political consensus of the Deng Xiaoping theory, the important thought

[24] Xu Juezai, "The Four Types of Democratic 'Chaos' in the West", *HongQi WenGao*, Issue 14, 2014.

of the "Three Represents" as well as a scientific outlook on development to guide governance.

Since the reform and opening-up, we have seen in practice how China could apply foresight and flexible strategies to counter the conflicts arising from development. In regard to the political system, there are several favorable conditions that could help China bypass the "middle income trap": one, the ability to make independent national decisions; two, the sense of crisis and urgency in leaders of the CPC Central Committee and the State Council, which leads them to take very seriously conflicts and dilemmas encountered during the middle-income development phase; and lastly, the persistence toward the socialist goal of just and equitable shared development.

The first point: China has the ability to make independent national decisions. From the late 1980s to the early 1990s, China faced the big question of what development path to take, while beholden by the international backdrop and domestic reforms. The CPC Central Committee was able to steady itself in time to firmly champion national stability, and thus prevented the country from becoming the guinea pig of "western democracy" as well as averted political upheaval, securing the nation's autonomy. The Soviet Union and Yugoslavia are classic examples of the contrary. This also explains why so many middle-income countries struggle to join the ranks of developed countries—they lack the will to make independent decisions in regard to development and national democracy building.

If we compare China with the Soviet Union and eastern European socialist states, China's advantages are, to a large extent, due to the country insisting on its own development path. After the dissolution of the Soviet Union and the socialist camp, instead of closing itself off, China resolved to adhere to the aspirations of its socialist market economy, joined the WTO, elected to institute currency exchange reform and determined its own macroeconomic policies and development path. It is a rare example of a developing country that did not fall prey to the "Western democracy myth", or indiscriminately adopt the Washington Consensus economic reform package.

The leadership of the CPC ensured that Western interference in sovereign matters would be impossible, as would fostering of an "agent" or political force. Again, this is not something commonly observed in a developing country. The Chinese government has never capitulated to external pressure that came primarily from Western powers, but rather always made autonomous decisions in the interest of the nation. Even when compromise was necessary, it was only partial and for an "exchange". This explains why China was able to buffer both the Asian and global financial crises, as well as why destabilizing forces in society are unlikely to be converted into expressions of "street democracy". Provided there is "universal order", it is possible to attain economic prosperity and social harmony. Otherwise, there is simply no guarantee of stable development and improvements in the quality of life.

The second point is the sense of crisis and urgency in leaders of the CPC Central Committee and the State Council leads them to take very seriously the conflicts and dilemmas encountered during the middle-income development phase. In September 1995, Comrade Jiang Zemin said reform, development and stability are deeply intertwined, and this is the most important of "twelve major relationships" in building a modernized socialist society. He stressed that nothing can be accomplished without a stable political and social environment, and emphasized that the relationship among reform, development and stability must be balanced and mutually enhancing: advance reform and development in a stable political-social environment, and bring about political-social stability with reform and development.[25] This is both experience distilled from China's own successful economic development, and a lesson borrowed from the countries that had fallen into the democracy trap. This stands in sharp contrast with Soviet Union and the economic transformation of eastern European countries.

Upon entering the twenty-first century, China shifted from a low-income to a medium-low-income country. The concept of the "middle income trap" had not quite existed at the time, nonetheless, the CPC Central Committee had the foresight to predict the development challenges that could arise. In April 2003, General Secretary Hu Jintao, when visiting Guangdong province, talked about firmly adhering to a "holistic view of development". In October of the same year, at the Third Plenary Session of the 16th CPC Central Committee, major development problems were raised, such as irrational economic structure, inadequate distribution, slow climb in farmers' income, employment conflicts, increasing

[25] *The Selected Works of Jiang Zemin, Volume One*, pages 460–463, People's Publishing House, 2006.

pressure on resources and the environment and insufficient competitiveness of the economy overall. It was said that these problems exist because China is still in the fledgling stage of a socialist society, with an economic system that is not yet fully formed, and many systematic obstacles in the way of productivity. The plenary session proposed putting people first, establish a comprehensive, coordinated and sustainable view of development, in order to promote social and human development.

In reference to the direction that development should take in the middle-income stage, Comrade Wen Jiabao said at a forum of ministerial and provincial officials in February 2004, that Chinese per capita GDP had reached 1000 US dollars, and could reach 3000 US dollars by 2020, based on the existing roadmap currency exchange rate at the time. This was a critical phase in development, and marked the beginning of the deep shift in socio-economic structure. The development experiences of other countries have shown that there are two possible scenarios: one is that the economy will march forward and successfully attain industrialization and modernization; the other is huge income disparity, high unemployment, widened gap between urban and rural areas and among regions, exacerbated social conflict, deteriorated ecological environment, which would cause socio-economic growth to languish, and even social upheaval and regression.[26] Facing the challenge of this development stage, the CPC Central Committee raised the idea of a people-oriented, "scientific outlook on development",[27] abiding by a comprehensive, coordinated, sustainable development, taking all factors into consideration in handling conflict and problems, in order to avoid the latter scenario while aspiring for the former. This is both the Party's foresight and part of its grand plan to brace for the development difficulties of the middle-income stage, in anticipation of the "middle income trap".

The CPC Central Committee has prioritized the "middle income trap" since the 18th CPC National Congress. It has acknowledged the complexity and arduousness of crossing this trap, while expressing its confidence in succeeding. On November 10, 2014, General Secretary Xi Jinping spoke

[26] *Wen Jiabao: Raising Awareness, Aligning Thoughts, Firmly Establish and Implement a Scientific Outlook on Development – Speech at the Forum of Ministerial and Provincial Officials on "Establishing and Implementing a Scientific Concept of Development"* (February 21, 2004), Xinhuanet.com, February 29, 2004.

[27] The 17th CPC National Congress held in October 2007 incorporated the "scientific outlook on development" into the Party Constitution as an important element of socialism with Chinese characteristics.

at the APEC Business Advisory Council (ABAC) Dialogue with Leaders in Beijing. He said,

> For China, the 'middle-income gap' is bound to be crossed, and the key is when it will happen and how to better move forward after that. We have confidence in balancing reform, development and stability as well as steady growth, structural adjustment, improvement of people's livelihood and promotion of reform, advancing China's economy in a steady and long-term manner.[28]

Premier Li Keqiang has also elaborated on the understanding of "middle income trap" on several occasions. For example, at the 13 session of the 12 Standing Committee of the CPPCC National Committee in November 2015, he pointed out

> the 13th Five-Year Plan is the decisive stage for attaining a comprehensive moderately prosperous society. To win this victory means that by 2020, China's per capita GDP will close in on the levels of high-income countries, taking us across the 'middle income trap'; it will be another milestone in China's modernization. But the comprehensive moderately prosperous society will not materialize by itself, as there is no such thing as a free lunch. We face many risks and challenges, and we cannot underestimate the difficulty.

As soon as China saw the complex challenges ahead in the middle-income stage, it took active counter measures. This has become a development consensus reached by the entire Party and society: tenaciously enhance the country's governance capability in order to successfully bridge the middle-income trap and stride toward a high-income level. Considering that this is the critical period for building a moderately prosperous society and crossing the middle-income trap, General Secretary Xi Jinping said at the Fifth Plenary Session of the 18th CPC Central Committee:

> We must clearly recognize that to build a comprehensive moderately prosperous society, we are both fully equipped with the conditions and also faced with difficult tasks. The road ahead is not smooth; it is laden with conflicts, risks and complicated predicaments. If these are not properly addressed, or if we become susceptible to systematic risks, make subversive errors, the process of building a moderately prosperous society will be delayed or even halted.[29]

[28] *Xi Jinping: Speech at the APEC Business Advisory Council Dialogue with Leaders in Beijing* (November 10, 2014), People's Daily, November 11, 2014.

[29] *Xi Jinping: Extracts from Speech at the Second Conference of the Fifth Plenary of the 18th CPC Central Committee* (October 29, 2015), reprint on *Qiushi*, January 2016.

With this in mind, General Secretary Xi Jinping formally proposed adhering to the five major development concepts of innovation, coordination, greening, opening-up and sharing. This is to make strategic arrangements for the "targeted remedy" at the predicaments arising out of the economic new normal and middle-income phase. The five major development concepts have become the strategic thinking enabling China to stride to a high-income stage during the 13th and 14th Five-Year Plans.

Additionally, China has persistently endeavored to improve people's livelihoods in order to realize the goal of a shared development—this is the essential requirement of socialism and an important reflection of its superiority. Up to now, China has steadily built a public services system that is suitable to national conditions, fairly complete, with coverage of both urban and rural areas, and sustainable. It includes the six key areas of employment services, mandatory education, public health and basic medical care, cultural services, basic social security and social housing. These go to the root of the wellbeing of citizens, and embody the superiority of a socialist system.

Take the prevalence of the New Rural Co-operative Medical Care System as an example. China began pilot schemes in 2002; by 2005, it had 75.7% coverage and reached 98.9% by 2014, which is practically full coverage.[30] The Urban Resident Basic Medical Insurance scheme was launched in 2007. The number of urban residents enrolled started out at 42.91 million people in 2007, and shot up to 377 million people in 2015. At the end of 2015, 660 million urban residents and workers had basic medical insurance coverage, accounting for 85.7% of the urban population.

Turning to basic pension insurance: China launched the New Rural Social Endowment Insurance System in 2009, and the Social Endowment Insurance System for Urban Residents in 2012. Together with the Basic Endowment Insurance System for Urban Workers, these provide coverage for all groups. The number of urban residents enrolled under the insurance scheme increased from 103 million in 2010 to 505 million in 2015; combined with urban workers enrolled under the insurance scheme, the total number increased from 360 million people in 2010 to 858 million in 2015. The number of people with pension insurance account for 85.5% of the population over 15 years of age. We project that by 2020, China will have realized universal medical care and pension insurance.

Altogether, Chinese government has taken active measures to reduce poverty, build a public services system accessible to all and drive inclusive

[30] Source: *China's Health and Family Planning Statistical Yearbook 2015.*

development that embodies shared development with Chinese characteristics. The five major development concepts raised at the Fifth Plenary Session of the 18th CPC Central Committee make specific mention of shared development, which makes advancing social justice and equality its premise, with eradicating poverty, reducing the income gap, providing equal basic public services in both urban and rural areas as a means to shared prosperity as its objective. The shared development model is an important reflection of China's improvements in governance capability, and will remain a core tenet to China's long-term development. This will also be the foundation for a stable social and political environment, and provide a systematic guarantee for China's successful leap from an upper-middle income to high-income country.

3.2.8 Summary

To conclude, even though China is currently in the upper-middle income stage, and its economy is facing challenges of economic transformation, ecological and environmental burdens, an aging population, income disparity, social and political stability concerns, among others—it is also taking active measures to address these issues. For example, China is actively facilitating the transformation of its economic growth model, curbing ecological and environmental deterioration, narrowing income disparity and addressing factors causing social instability. The challenges presented by an aging population can be mitigated by the accumulation of "education dividend". Though threats to political stability could bear a long-term presence (particularly from externally), China's continued progress in political development and governance capability can still safeguard stability. Therefore, these impediments are unlikely to trip China into the "middle income trap". Besides, the country is armed with several favorable conditions to lift it over the "middle income trap". These include ever-improving strategic planning capability, steady economic structural transition and ever-maturing macroeconomic management. China is equipped with the fundamentals for sustainable growth; moreover, it has the benefits of the socialist system as the political safety net against the trap.

China will not retrace the steps of the Latin American, former Soviet and eastern European countries in stumbling into the "middle income trap", nor will it spiral into long-term stagnation. The key to guaranteeing this is to discover in time the primary factors that could push the country into the "middle income trap", accurately identify and adeptly avoid the "trap" and, all the while, readily take advantage of the favorable development conditions to propel the country right over it.

CHAPTER 4

How Can China Overcome the "Middle Income Trap"?

Whether a country can overcome the "middle income trap" is a test of its governance capability. The above comparative analysis of the practices in various countries shows that tackling the "middle income trap" is only possible when certain conditions are met, which may be summarized as follows.

First, an effective market. Effective market is the prerequisite for effective resource allocation, which ensures that the potential productivity of all productive factors is tapped to the full extent and that labor and capital factors are effectively utilized, while creating a sound market environment for innovation, fostering highly motivated innovative players and continuous improvement in total factor productivity, thus enabling a country to achieve economic growth by unleashing the potential of human capital. An effective market is reflected not only in building a unified domestic market but also in active participation in globalization, fully leveraging on the external economic opportunities while effectively addressing negative economic impact from the outside. From the 14th CPC National Congress announcing the establishment of socialist market economic system to the 3rd Plenary Session of the 18th CPC National Congress with the statement of "enabling market to play a decisive role in resource allocation", China has never ceased its efforts in institutional building for an effective market, which has laid a solid institutional foundation for its rapid economic growth in the long run.

S. Zhou, A. Hu, *China: Surpassing the "Middle Income Trap"*,
Contemporary China Studies,
https://doi.org/10.1007/978-981-15-6540-3_4

Second, a harmonious society. The concordance of economic growth and social development is the guarantee for sustainable economic development. A common cause for social discordance is the severity disparity and opposition between social classes resulting from the marginalization of certain members of the society in the growing economy, of which achievements fail to be shared among all members of the society. The accumulation of malaise in society tends to result in social upheavals and political instability, eventually leading to disruptions in economic prosperity. In 2004, a clear statement was made to "continuously enhance the capacity of building a harmonious socialist society" during the 4th Plenary Session of the 16th CPC National Congress; in October 2006, *Resolutions of the CPC Central Committee on Several Critical Issues in Building a Harmonious Socialist Society* was approved during the 6th Plenary Session of the 16th CPC National Congress, proposing the goal to build a harmonious socialist society by 2020. Since 2000, major achievements have been made toward this goal as China is gradually improving its social security system with socialist characteristics.

Third, a positive government. A positive government plays a key role in effective market operations and harmonious social development. First, a positive government builds up a market economy system by perfecting the legal and regulatory framework, hence safeguarding a fair and competitive market environment, inspiring the creativity of market players and facilitating domestic and overseas market growth, industrial restructuring and upgrading as well as technological innovation and so on; second, a positive government guarantees the stability of the macro economy through effective administration and provides public products (such as infrastructure) for market entities and public services for its people (such as minimum social security, pension scheme, healthcare and education); third, a positive government ensures the dynamic adaptability and prospectiveness of development strategies by formulating and implementing strategic plans such as five-year plan and mid- to long-term plan aiming at achieving long-term national development goals.

Obviously, in light of China's track of growth, the development path is a typical case of synergy of effective market, harmonious society and positive government. The goal of "modernization of the national governance system and governance capacity" proposed during the 3rd Plenary Session of the 18th CPC National Congress is also seen as the "top-level design" of further coordinated progress of the three factors. With the three prerequisites—effective market, harmonious society and active government—ensured, China ranking among high-income countries is just a matter of time.

Yet as a country with a population of 1.38 billion and significant disparity in regional development between urban and rural areas, China must undergo a process before ranking amongst high-income countries, and by no means will this goal be attained automatically without lifting a finger. The key question is: will China effectively address the current challenges as a middle-income country and achieve economic growth of higher quality and social development featuring more equality, justice and harmony? Besides, even if China becomes a high-income country, there is still a big gap in per capita income between China and developed countries, and supassing the "middle income trap" only represents a new starting point for China to narrow the development gap between China and developed countries. Therefore, in supassing the "middle income trap", China should consolidate the foundation for its development to continuously reduce the development gap with the developed countries, thereby achieving stable and sustainable growth of its gigantic economy. This, to a large extent, will depend on how China plans to address the various challenges in its current stage of development.

This chapter aims at answering the following question: how will China effectively respond to the various challenges as a middle-income country in the current stage and stride over the high-income threshold by fully leveraging on the favorable conditions. Distinct from the analysis framework rooted in traditional Western economics, this chapter provides an analysis framework based on political economics and, through an in-depth elaboration of characteristics of the middle-income stage, proposes that only by properly removing the constraints that impede the development of social productivity and circumventing from various possible traps, all guided by the Five Development Concepts, will China be able to effectively eliminate the systematic risk factors in economic development. Besides, it is argued that the strongest cornerstone for China's transition as a middle-income country requires continuous efforts in deepening reform and modernization of the country's governance system and governance capacity, so to ensure a steady long-term economic growth in China.

4.1 Breaking Out of the Middle-Income Trap Through the "Five Development Concepts"

Since the implementation of the reform and opening-up policy, China has maintained nearly four decades of rapid economic growth, rising from the world's 10th economy to the 2nd,[1] from the 29th biggest trader of goods to the biggest trading country in the world[2] and from an extremely low-income country to an upper-middle-income country. China's success in avoiding drastic slowdown in economic growth during the middle-income stage and its subsequent entering into the development phase of high income are critical for China's goal of building a moderately prosperous society in all respects by 2020 as well as for the world's economic landscape. A blueprint for China's development goals by 2020 was sketched during the 5th Plenary Session of the 18th CPC National Congress with the proposition of five new development concepts by the CPC Central Committee, namely "innovation, coordination, greening, opening-up and sharing", aiming at addressing the "middle income trap" with clearly defined target as these concepts are the basic approaches to overcome such trap as well as a foundation for China to continue on the healthy track of development afterward.

Why are the "five development concepts" clearly targeting the "middle income trap"? In drafting the 13th Five-Year Plan, the CPC Central Committee made a clear statement of "overcoming the middle income trap"; it is hence exactly on this basis that the CPC Central Committee innovatively proposed these five development concepts, which are clearly target-driven as well as problem-driven featuring pragmatism: innovation focuses on the momentum for development, aiming at maintaining mid-to-high-speed economic growth toward a mid-to-high level; coordination aims at addressing the disparity in development and focuses on strengthening the integrality of development; greening highlights the harmony between mankind and nature and building a beautiful China with blue sky, green grass and clear water; opening-up focuses on the interaction between

[1] According to World Bank Database, China was the world's tenth biggest economy in the world in 1978; in 2010, China overtook Japan to become the world's second biggest economy.

[2] National Bureau of Statistics: China Statistical Abstract 2015, p. 178, China Statistics Press, 2015.

internal and external factors in development and greater openness in economy; sharing underlines social equality and justice for continuous improvement in people's wellbeing and upgrading China's economic and social development. In light of China's current phase of development, we have identified at least five types of traps, namely the total factor productivity (TFP) trap, urbanization trap, environment trap, dependence trap and inequality trap.

And what are the possible solutions? Obviously, no readily executable answers are provided in the textbooks of Western economics from a theoretical perspective; while in practice, no country could offer China off-the-shelf experience as a reference. China's development since the reform and opening-up shows that instead of sticking to one development theory, China's efforts in development proceed from the objective circumstances in different stages, adhering to the key principle of people and development for the people; with integration of respect and encouragement for local practices for development with macro-coordination by the central government, China is gradually exploring into and constantly enriching the theory of socialism with Chinese characteristics, which is reflected in the plenary sessions and development plans of the CPC Central Committee. The five development concepts proposed by the CPC Central Committee during the 5th Plenary Session of the 18th CPC National Congress aim to address the above five traps that confront China in mid- to high-income stage, providing important ideas and fundamental approaches to break through the five traps. Therefore, with the five development concepts as the basic theoretical framework, we suggest the following solutions to tackle the five traps.

4.1.1 Avoiding the Total Factor Productivity Trap Through Innovation-Driven Development

Overcoming the "middle income trap" is essentially a matter of economic growth—a matter of economic growth in the middle-income stage. Generally speaking, economic growth for countries in this stage is mainly driven by economic restructuring and transition in the engine of economic growth, both of which have an impact on the growth of total factor productivity (TFP). From a longer-term perspective, increase in TFP is the key to sustainable growth. As is emphasized by Eichengreen et al. (2011, 2013), the core of transformation in the economic development pattern fostered by economic restructuring and innovation is enhancing the trap.

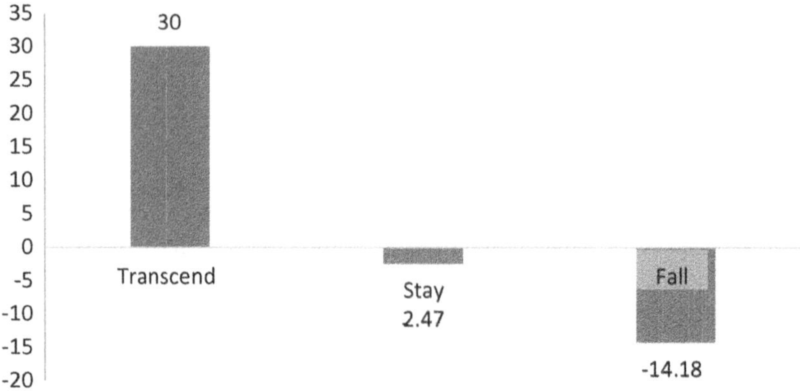

Fig. 4.1 Average changes in total factor productivity (TFP) in middle-income countries (1960–2010). (Note: 11 countries have overcome the "middle income trap"; 35 countries remain in the "middle income trap" while 11 countries are reduced to low-income level. Data Source: UNIDO Database)

contribution of TFP to economic growth, which is a prerequisite for successfully overcoming the "middle income trap".[3]

We have studied the experiences of middle-income countries in 1960 and grouped these countries into three types determined by whether they have passed through the middle-income stage by 2010: countries that have successfully crossed the threshold, countries remaining in the middle-income stage and countries reduced to low-income stage. Calculations of their performance in narrowing down the TFP gap with the U.S. (see Fig. 4.1) show that only countries that have passed through the middle-income stage show a narrowed gap in TFP, that is, a relative improvement in TFP level, while countries failing to cross the threshold have suffered a relatively reduced TFP level in various degrees. Therefore, failure in middle-income transition boils down to falling into the TFP trap. Furthermore, based on a relative standard, if China fails to improve its

[3] Eichengreen, B., Park, D., & Shin, K. When fast growing economies slow down: international evidence and implications for the People's Republic of China. *Asian Development Bank Economics Working Paper Series*, 2011 (262). Eichengreen, B., Park, D., & Shin, K. (2013). Growth slowdowns redux: New evidence on the middle-income trap (No. w18673). *National Bureau of Economic Research*.

TFP against the level of the U.S. in the future, or experiences TFP decrease, China will find itself in the TFP trap.

Long-term growth of TFP is the key to economic growth rate; in particular, catching up with the relative TFP level of leading developed countries (such as the U.S.) is the key in the transition from a catching-up country to an innovative country as well as the main driving force in the ascent from a middle-income country to a high-income country. It can therefore be safely stated that the sustained growth in TFP is a necessary condition for China to overcome the "middle income trap"; while the key to avoiding the TFP trap is to replace an economic growth model dominated by factor input with an innovation-driven growth model, and to increase the contribution of TFP to economic growth.

Placing China's economic development in the current context of the "new normal", the growth rate has switched gears from high to mid-to-high speed while the driving force of economic growth has undergone a transformation. Such transformation is the most critical factor in determining the progress and quality of speed adjustment and structural optimization[4]; it requires fostering new driving forces, expanding space for growth, earnestly implementing the innovation-driven development strategy, pressing ahead with agricultural modernization, and innovating and improving modes of macro-regulation and control to maintain high efficiency in China's economic growth.

Innovation as an important driving force of transformation of economic growth model is stated in the 13th Five-Year Plan where core indicators of innovation-driven development are explicitly listed. First, in terms of innovation input, the investment intensity of research and experiment shall increase from 2.1% of GDP in 2015 to 2.5% in 2020, higher than the average (2.37%) of OECD countries; total social expenditures on R&D shall increase from 1.42 trillion RMB to 2.32 trillion RMB, with an aggregate investment of 11.22 trillion RMB over five years, which translates into 1.93 times of total R&D expenditures of the 12th Five-Year Plan period (5.80 trillion RMB), closer or higher than the U.S.

Second, with respect to innovation output, a series of key indicators are listed in the 13th Five-Year Plan, including the one that patent ownership per 10,000 people shall be doubled, from 6.3 in 2015 to 12 in 2020 and the one that China's total patent ownership shall increase from 1.19

[4] Liu Yandong, On Earnest Implementation of Innovation-Driven Innovation Strategy, *People's Daily*, November 11, 2015.

million to 1.68 million, of which the actual result is highly likely to exceed expectation, reflecting both the accelerated accumulation of technical innovation capital stock in China and the continuous enhancement of its domestic independent innovation capacity. Besides, the contribution of innovation to economic growth is also clearly mentioned in the 13th Five-Year Plan, where the contribution by science and technological advancement shall increase from 55% in 2015 to 60% in 2020.

Third, the significant role of digital economy in innovation as a driving force is highlighted in the 13th Five-Year Plan, which, in terms of boosting the growth of digital economy, states that the household penetration of fixed broadband shall grow from 40% in 2015 to 70% in 2020, with users increasing from 688 million to 980 million, while the penetration of mobile broadband shall grow from 57% to 85%, with users increasing from 780 million to 1.19 billion. It is expected that the universal penetration of internet will by and large become a reality in China by 2020, making it the world's biggest internet economy with first-move advantage in new economies, new business models and new industries, while triggering restructuring and upgrading of traditional industries (such as labor-intensive and resource-intensive industries), expanding the geographical space for economy and penetrating the broader global market. A most typical example is the cross-border e-commerce of Alibaba, which, covering all provinces, municipalities and autonomous regions in China, has begun to establish a global footprint.

4.1.2 *Avoiding the Urbanization Trap Through Coordinated Development*

A key driver in a country's transition from the middle-income stage to the high-income stage is urbanization, which simultaneously represents the in-depth transformation of the economic and employment structures. Urbanization in benign interaction with economic growth will contribute to the liberation of agricultural labor, hence optimizing the labor structure and boosting economic growth; meanwhile, such economic growth will create more jobs in non-agricultural sectors, and thus driving the urbanization momentum. Nevertheless, excessive urbanization may weaken the bearing capacity of urban regions for economic growth, causing "urban maladies" such as mounting employment pressure, insufficient urban infrastructure, environmental pollution and poor efficiency of urban governance, eventually resulting in a situation with "growing urbanization

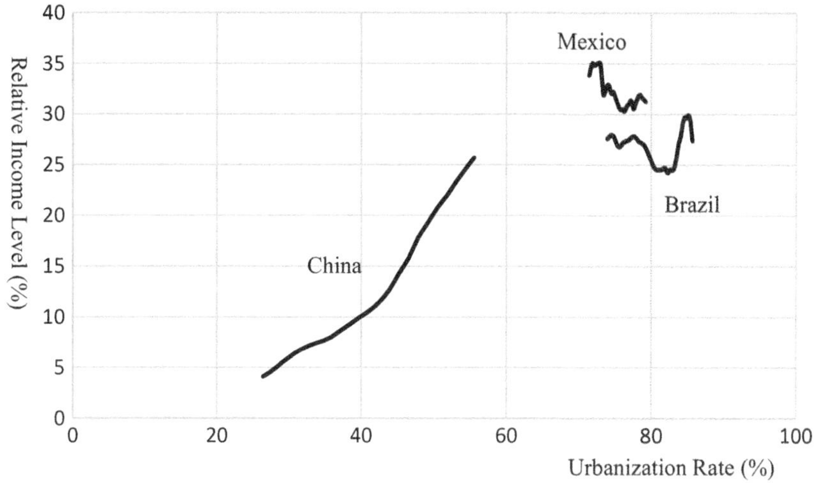

Fig. 4.2 Urbanization rate and relative income level. (Note: The vertical axis is the percentage of per capita GDP (in international US dollars in constant prices) in relation to that of the U.S. Data Source: World Bank, World Development Index, data from 1990 to 2015)

accompanied by zero economic growth", or, worse still, stagnated social development and aggravated social conflict—a fall into the urbanization trap.

Such commonplace situations in Latin America are what we are trying to avoid. For instance, some Latin American countries (such as Brazil and Mexico) are falling farther behind, rather than narrowing the gap with the U.S., despite their high urbanization rate (see Fig. 4.2). Although the urbanization level in many Latin American countries is on par with the average in high income countries,[5] the urbanization development and economic growth in these countries fail to stay in a relationship of benign interaction; on the contrary, a malicious cycle of urban development and economic development is formed. Polarization of wealth has aggravated as cities fail to create enough jobs to sustain its residents, leaving many impoverished urban residents living in slums, where urban utilities and

[5] According to World Bank statistics, in 2015, the average urbanization rate in Latin America and Caribbean Countries reached 80%, close to the average in high-income countries (81%).

public services tend to be insufficient, resulting in disadvantages in income, accessibility to education and healthcare, social security and so on for the slum residents as manifested in multi-dimensional poverty and even intergenerational transmission of poverty.[6] Besides, economic stagnation has put government in a position where it cannot afford to allocate sufficient budget to the planning and rejuvenation of slums, nor is it capable of effective social management of such areas; slums, as a result, have become the "tumors" for urban development.

The rapid development process of urbanization generates both economic gains and social challenges. Experiences of urbanization development in Latin American countries indicate that during the transition to the high-income stage, it is necessary to enable urbanization development in a steady manner and bring urbanization development into healthy interaction with economic growth, resolving conflicts and challenges incurred in the process of urbanization development by fully leveraging on the achievements of economic growth, and thereby fostering an efficient, inclusive and sustainable model of urbanization development. Otherwise, the risk of falling into the urbanization trap would be high.

China's urbanization rate in 2015 stood at 57.35%,[7] which is on par with the world's average yet is visibly lower than the average of high income countries (81% in 2015). In general, China has made great achievements in urbanization but improvement is expected in terms of quality. In 2016, urbanization rate for population with household registration was 41.2%, significantly lower than the percentage calculated from permanent population as statistical caliber, with a difference of 220 million people. In this regard, China still runs the risk of falling into the urbanization trap if this problem is not resolved properly.

Aiming to address this issue, China has developed a scientific plan to promote a new model of urbanization, that is, National Plan for New Urbanization Model (2014–2020) formulated in 2014, which is the strategic and fundamental plan on the macro-level for guiding the healthy development of urbanization in China. This plan is no less than a top design for China's new urbanization model aiming at efficient, inclusive and sustainable urbanization. The strategy of coordinated development proposed in the 13th Five-Year Plan is also a major move to circumvent

[6] Wu Sun Pei-jing, Zhao Xuemei (2016), Poverty and Poverty Alleviation Policies in Latin America from Multiple Perspectives, *Journal of Latin American Studies*, Vol. 3.

[7] Data source: National Bureau of Statistics, January 20, 2017.

the urbanization trap, including an emphasis on the new urbanization model with "urbanization of the people" at the core, deepened reform of the household registration system, full coverage of the residential permit system for permanent population without household registration in urban areas, increased coverage of employment services, and affordable housing and public services for migrants.

From a holistic perspective, the institutional mechanism for the new model of urbanization is gradually improving in China, and China's construction for new urbanization is generally on a healthy track, which represents not only a driving force for economic restructuring but also opportunities for the social transformation and progress in China. The key to attaining these goals is the conscientious implementation of the new urbanization plan, which in turn requires highly motivated and creative local government on various levels to plan for the space of urban development on a scientific basis, focus on the integrated development of urbanization, urban infrastructure and industries and constantly enhance its social governance capabilities. Besides, agricultural modernization and new countryside construction must be incorporated into the context of facilitating the construction of the new urbanization model, with higher quality of rural planning, strengthened development of infrastructure as well as coverage rate and quality of public services in rural areas, improvement in investment mechanism for the development of rural areas, agriculture and farmers, a revolutionary transformation in the urban-rural dualistic development pattern and narrowed gap between urban and rural regions.

The coordinated development strategy proposed in the 13th Five-Year Plan also includes coordinated regional development, which requires improved overall strategy for regional development, down-to-earth implementation of the main functional zone strategy as well as population and economic growth that are compatible with the resource bearing capacity. Moreover, inter-regional coordinated development mechanism shall be built to boost development with unique competitiveness, coordinated and win-win development through the Belt and Road Initiative, Beijing-Tianjin-Hebei Economic Zone and the Yangtze River Delta Economic Belt, and hence creating new space for regional development.

4.1.3 *Avoiding the Ecological Environment Trap Through Green Development*

Developing countries tend to use natural resources in an exhaustive way, resulting in ecological damage. On one hand, development pressures compel developing countries to import industrial projects, causing severe pollution and mounting environmental burdens. The growth model featuring intensive resource consumption and high environmental cost is unsustainable and may lead to grave consequences. On the other hand, some of these consequences of pollution are very expensive to remediate or even irreversible. Therefore, economic development at the cost of ecological environment will likely result in a malicious cycle of economic development and eco-environment, which is known as the "eco-environment trap".

China is a heavily populated country with limited resources, where ecologically vulnerable areas account for a considerable portion of the national territory.[8] With urbanization and industrialization in progress, the environment has become an important indicator of urbanization quality but with people's health and wellbeing at stake. In this sense, green development is the guarantee for the safety of ecological environment. The development trajectory of developed countries shows that although the development path characterized by "pollute first and clean up later" has eventually broken free from the malicious cycle between economic development and eco-environmental protection, the costs of this "old track" are by no means negligible.[9] Therefore, from a long-term perspective, the development model of "pollute first and clean up later" is not only economically unviable but also incurs heavy burden on sustainable economic development. Related studies also show that the mechanism where environmental improvement automatically comes alongside national income growth simply does not exist; therefore, the model of development at the cost of environment may highly likely result in a fall into the "environmental trap".

[8] White Paper: Ecological Protection in China publicly released by the General Administration for Environmental Protection for the first time in 2006 shows that ecologically vulnerable areas account for over 60% of China's territory.

[9] Such as Meuse River Valley episode in Belgium in 1930, Los Angeles photochemical smog episode in U.S. in 1943, Donora smog disaster in U.S. in 1943, Great Smog in London in 1952, water pollution incident in Kyushu, Japan, in 1953 and itai-itai disease in Toyama, Japan, that lasted 40 years (1931–1972).

Since the reform and opening-up, China has suffered continuous environmental degradation alongside its high-speed economic development, and environmental pressure has become a significant constraint for China's economic growth. Although ecological environment was listed as a binding indicator in the 11th Five-Year Plan, the eco-environmental degradation has not yet seen a reverse. In 2010, cost of eco-environmental degradation throughout the country registered at 1.53895 trillion RMB, accounting for approximately 3.5% of GDP and an increase of 200.7% as compared to 2004,[10] and the environmental loss has amounted to 5%–6% of China's GDP,[11] a further increase of the probabilities of falling into the environmental trap. It must be noted that the CPC Central Committee is conscientiously addressing the eco-environmental challenge for China's sustainable development, and such an attitude is not only reflected in its development practices but has also become a principle upheld by China in its participation in international governance.

A strengthened prospective of green development is exactly a response to this trap, aiming at the harmony between man and nature and a beautiful China with blue sky, green land and clear water through pursuing green development. Generally speaking, China's eco-environmental remediation is in the "braking" stage featuring significant slowdown in eco-environmental degradation and visible improvement in certain areas before it may "take a U-turn" on this basis, that is, overall improvement in eco-environmental, lowered ecological vulnerability and distinctive amelioration of ecological environment, hence circumventing from the environmental trap. In the long run, green development is not only a key topic on the agenda of the 13th Five-Year Plan period but also a mandatory path for long-term development for China's socialist modernization undertakings. Arguably, without green development, China is likely to lose the momentum for further steps in catching up with developed countries due to eco-environmental degradation.

4.1.4 Avoiding the Dependency Trap Through Open Development

International experience shows that all countries that have successfully overcome the "middle income trap" are open economies. For middle-income countries, catching up with developed countries in economic

[10] *2010 Green National Economic Accounting*, CAEP 2013.

[11] Xinhua News Agency, December 11, 2013

development level should, from an objective viewpoint, be based on full participation in economic globalization, with continuous adjustment of self-positioning in this globalization process, hence fostering new edge in global competition. Either refusal of economic globalization to protect national industrial development or participating in the global economy merely by exporting resources or excessive dependence on international capital will possibly result in the "dependence trap". The failure of import replacement strategy which used to be universally practiced in Latin American countries proves that breaking away from international division of labor regardless of the reality of national economic development would unavoidably result in falling into the "middle income trap" with factor allocation deviating from the basic principles of comparative advantage, which in turn increases production cost and leads to worsened international balance of payments.

Southeast Asian countries provide another example from which much can be learned. Prior to the Asian financial crisis in 1997, these countries prematurely opened up their capital markets before their own industrial competitive edge was fully established, eventually resulting in massive international capital flight and grave devaluation of their domestic currencies, triggering a financial crisis that eventually evolved into an economic crisis. A typical country was Malaysia, which joined the ranks of high-income countries as early as in 1996 and yet never staged its comeback until now after being swirled into the Asian financial crisis in 1997.

Since its reform and opening-up, China has been gradually moving from the edge to the center of limelight on the international stage as it became the world's second largest economy and the No. 1 trading country, with the share of China's merchandise export increasing from 2.24% in the world in 1992 to 12.37% in 2014. Overall, China's opening-up strategy has achieved significant success as it has become the external driving force for China's economic growth. However, it should be equally noted that China is facing new challenges in its engagement in economic globalization. First, China urgently needs to generate a new competitive edge in innovation as the competitiveness of its labor-intensive exported goods is facing challenges with rising labor cost. Second, China must strengthen its resilience to external shocks as the impact of the international financial crisis is transmitted through external demand to China's domestic economy. Third, the pressing need is felt for China to enhance the capacity of its participation in global governance if it is to remain active in future economic globalization. This requires China to assess its own capabilities and act accordingly while making fruitful efforts and playing an active role in building new international development mechanisms (such as the Belt and Road Initiative and AIIB) in global climate change governance, coordination of international macroeconomic policies and participation in regional economic development organizations of various types. These challenges for China's opening-up, indicating potential opportunities on one hand, may place China in a passive position, or even lead to a fall into the "dependence trap" if engagement in economic globalization is inappropriately handled.

Open development has clarified China's strategy in participating in economic globalization and global governance in all dimensions in the future: on one hand, China must circumvent the "dependence trap" and create new opportunities for its economic growth; on the other hand, it will set an example and generate opportunities for "Southern countries" which shall have far-reaching and long-term implications on the world economy. Moreover, China's open development contributes to building a future-oriented new international political and economic order by avoiding the Thucydides trap where conflicts would inevitably occur between rising powers and established powers—which is exactly the win-win concept emphasized by Xi Jinping.

In general, China possesses the capabilities to resist external shocks and risks and to avoid the dependence trap. First, China's foreign exchange reserve of 3 trillion US dollars makes a sovereign debt crisis seen in some European countries impossible in China. Second, the numerous world-class enterprises in China have become another source of the country's resilience to external crises. Moreover, China's massive outbound FDI, of which resource projects constitute a considerable share, has secured the resources necessary for China's future economic development. Finally, China has accumulated abundant experience in external shock response after surviving the Asian financial crisis in 1998 and the global financial crisis in 2008.

The world today is characterized by the ongoing complicated and profound changes in the external environment, with development issues and challenges in globalization remaining grave for all countries, which must therefore make concerted efforts for joint response. China finds it necessary to participate in global governance through better communication and dialogues while improving its domestic institutional foundation accordingly through deepened reform in order to avoid falling into a passive situation in future economic globalization and global governance.

4.1.5 *Avoiding the Inequity Trap Through Shared Development*

International experience shows that grave income disparity constitutes an essential threat to economic development during the middle-income stage, as it is highly likely to cause accumulated social malaise and economic stagnation, resulting in the "inequality trap". As a typical Latin American country, Argentina saw its Gini coefficient hike from 0.428 in 1986 to 0.507 in 1998,[12] causing the country to fall into both the "inequality trap" and the "middle income trap". As for China, despite the aggravation tendency brought under control, the country is not to be blindly optimistic about its income distribution. According to statistics released by the National Bureau of Statistics, from 2003 to 2008, China's Gini coefficient was on a continuous rise from 0.479 to 0.491, with the relative gap between average disposable income per capita for urban residents and average net income for rural residents escalating from 3.23 times in 2003 to a peak of 3.33 times in 2009. In recent years, the income disparity in China has been mitigated to some extent as the Gini coefficient of national average disposable income per capita decreased from 0.473 in 2013 to 0.462 in 2015, and the relative gap between average disposable income per capita for urban and rural residents narrowed down from 2.81 times in 2013 to 2.73 times in 2015.[13] However, on an international scale, income disparity remains a prominent problem for China due to multiple reasons: urban and rural gaps, regional disparity, internal gaps within urban regions as well as within rural regions, and coexistence of the salary income gap and the capital income gap. Therefore, resolving China's income disparity will remain a standing issue on its development agenda.

It must be pointed out, though, that Kuznets curve graphs the hypothesis that economic inequality is first increased and then decreased with economic development, yet international development studies show that income inequality will not automatically narrow down as the economy grows to a higher level. Therefore, income distribution policies are necessary in mitigating inequality in distribution. Shared development is an exact response to the "inequality trap" as sharing the accomplishments of development among people is the only way toward common prosperity, and crossing the threshold of a moderately prosperous society with

[12] Data source: The World Bank.

[13] Data source: China Statistical Abstract 2015, pp. 57, 59, China Statistics Press, Beijing; statistics of 2015 are published by National Bureau of Statistics.

common prosperity represents the true essence of overcoming the "inequality trap" and the "middle income trap". Sticking to shared development and highlighting social equality and justice, China shall make continued progress in people's wellbeing and open up new horizons for its economic and social development.

In general, the key to circumventing the "middle income trap" is accelerating the transformation of the economic development model through economic dimensions, shifting from low-level development to high-level development, from low-quality development to high-quality development, from inequal development to equal development, from poorly coordinated development to well-coordinated development and from unsustainable development to sustainable development, which, for China, means the full implementation of the Five Development Concepts to overcome the multiple traps during the middle-income stage.

4.2 Supply-Side Structural Reform Is the Key to Overcoming the "Middle Income Trap"

China experienced prominent structural contradiction in 2011 with the implementation of the 12th Five-Year Plan and the phasing downturn of its economic growth. In this context, the Central Economic Work Conference in 2015 explicitly proposed supply-side structural reform, which was identified as the mainline of the 13th Five-Year Plan. Supply-side structural reform is an inevitable choice as China's economic development enters into the new normal, and appropriate understanding and effective implementation of such reform would bear profound strategic significance for China to comprehensively build a moderately prosperous society in by 2020 and to overcome the "middle income gap". Progressing with the supply-side structural reform requires not only a deep understanding of the in-depth structural problems prevailing in China's current economic development but also a clear view of the structural characteristics of China's long-term economic development. This in turn is built on clearly understanding the basic rationale of supply-side structural reform from a theoretical perspective as well as properly handling the critical relationships between supply-side structural reform and other reform measures in practice.

For supply-side structural reform, first of all, an understanding of the historical rationale, theoretical rationale and realistic rationale is indispensable; second, the relationship between supply-side structural reform and macroeconomic regulation and control should be clarified in light of China's current economic situation; last but not least, a practical approach for China to proceed with supply-side structural reform should be outlined based on the outstanding problems facing China's current economic development and the mandate for economic development during the 13th Five-Year Plan period.

4.2.1 The Three Rationale Behind Supply-Side Structural Reform

First, we have to understand the historical rationale of the supply-side structural reform in the context of the overall process of China's economic reforms since the reform and opening-up.

China's economic reform is essentially an innovation of the practice and theory of Marxist political economy, which is oftentimes neglected. Communique of the 3rd Plenary Meeting of the 11th CPC Central Committee pointed out that

> achieving the four modernizations requires significant improvement of productivity, which inevitably requires a multi-dimensional change of production relations and superstructures that are unfit for the development of productivity, a change of all modes of management, activities and thinking that are unsuitable, hence is an extensive and profound revolution. Appropriate reforms must be conducted to change production relations and superstructures that are unfit for the rapid development of productivity.[14]

However, how to liberate and bring significant increase to productivity through reforms? How to bring production relations and superstructures in line with the rapid development of productivity? There were no ready answers to these questions in the beginning of the reform and opening-up, which, objectively, means that China's economic reforms need to "feel its way forward", allowing and encouraging local experiments, with continuous practice, continuous trial and error and hence continuous accumulation of experience, with continuous exploration into the top design for economic reform, continuous enhancement of conscientious awareness of the practice of economic reform, continuously enriching the theoretical construction of socialism with Chinese characteristics and continuously adding its value as

[14] Communique of the 3rd Plenary Meeting of the 11th CPC Central Committee (approved on December 22, 1978).

guidance for China's economic reform at the same time. From a holistic perspective, China's economic reform features a dual-way interaction between "top-down" and "bottom-up" efforts.

In retrospect of China's economic reform since 1978, nearly 40 years of reform practice has been a typical example of "supply-side structural reform" in itself. In a sense, supply-side structural reform is a summary of China's economic reform trajectory and quintessence of development that include three key words in organic linkage.

First, reform as the backbone. A fundamental view in Marxist political economy is that productivity determines production relations, and that the development of productivity inevitably requires adjustment in production relations, which, nevertheless, do not automatically initiate a self-adaptation process in consistence with the development of productivity. Instead, production relations that fail to adapt to the development of productivity may survive for a considerably long duration until the contradiction between the two accumulate sufficiently to trigger a passive and drastic adjustment of production relations. Reform, on the other hand, takes the initiative to adapt to the objective demand of development of productivity through active adjustment of production relations, which is essentially adjustment of production relations through continuous institutional improvement to liberate productivity.

Second, supply-side as the keypoint. The essential goal of reform is to facilitate the liberation of productivity, of which improving the efficiency of factors of production such as labor, capital, technology, knowledge and information is the pre-condition; these factors are on the supply side. Besides, the development of productivity has a positive impact on the supply of factors, for instance, by increasing savings and boosting human capital.

Third, structure as the distinctive feature. The history of economic development is a history of structural transformation, and economic development is inevitably accompanied by structural transformations of various kinds, including changes in industrial structure, employment structure, consumption structure, ownership structure, urban-rural structure, and so on. These structural factors, being the results of economic policy impact of the previous stage, may influence economic growth as structural factors. In a sense, various structural factors do not necessarily opt for the optimized track for evolution in economic development, since irrational economic policies in the previous stage may cause certain structural factors to deviate from the optimal track for evolution, or to trigger structural problems in factor allocation on the supply side, eventually hampering the growth of total factor productivity.

Since China's reform and opening-up, reforms in different phases of development with distinctive characteristics and differentiated key areas of each phase have been implemented, which facilitated structural changes while influencing the allocation of factor resources, though the term "supply-side structural reform" was not yet used at the time. Master plans of economic development targets of each phase as well as overall planning and corresponding measures for deepening the economic institutional reforms were proposed during the five "3rd plenary sessions" of the CPC since China's reform and opening-up which fully reflected the characteristics of the "supply-side structural reform" corresponding to each phase.

The decision of the 3rd Plenary Session of the 11th CPC Central Committee began the first round of reform and ignited the engine of China's economic structural reform. This period featured very low average income per capita and a pressing need to alleviate extreme poverty as the population was struggling below the subsistence level. During the 3rd and 4th Plenary Sessions of the 11th CPC Central Committee, *Decisions on Certain Questions of Accelerating Agricultural Development* was issued, promulgating 25 policies to launch reforms in rural areas and implement the household contract responsibility system on a full scale, which, as the key institutional system in rural economic reform, drastically boosted the economic growth during this period. First, the rural population saw an unprecedented high growth in average income per capita. Between 1978 and 1985, at constant prices, the average net income per capita increased by 2.7 times for rural residents, with an average annual growth of 15.2%. Second, a major decrease was seen in population living in extreme poverty. Based on the poverty threshold in rural area in 1978, the impoverished rural population registered at 250 million in 1978, which reduced to 125 million in 1985, and the occurrence of poverty decreased from 30.7% to 14.8%. According to the poverty threshold of 2010, impoverished rural population in China amounted to 770 million in 1978, which decreased to 661 million in 1985, and the occurrence of poverty reduced from 97.5% to 78.3%[15]; moreover, rural enterprises created many new jobs, with total employment increasing by 1.47 times from 28.27 million in 1978 to 69.67 in 1985.

[15] China Statistical Abstract 2016, p. 70, China Statistics Press, Beijing, 2016.

Decision of the second round of reform was made in 1984 at the 3rd Plenary Session of the 12th CPC Central Committee. China was struggling in extreme poverty and had to prioritize subsistence for its population as the country was at the starting point of full-scale reform. According to the task of "systematic economic structural reform" proposed during the 12th CPC National Congress, *Decision on Economic Structural Reform* was made by the CPC Central Committee, which drafted a blueprint for multi-faceted reform, proposing a planned commodity economy based on public ownership to build a dynamic socialist economic system. This Session opened a new chapter of overall economic restructuring focusing on urban area though the reform was still conducted in the framework of planned economy to address the issues of "insufficient incentives" or "absence of incentives" in the existing institutional system. From this point on, the central government gradually shifted its main approach to managing enterprises from direct control to indirect control, significantly reducing the scale of the planned economy. Mandatory plans, guiding plans and full market-based regulation were implemented based on actual situation and a "dual-track" system was put in place for pricing and other issues. Active measures were taken to diversify ownership models including ownership of the whole people, collective ownership and private ownership, leading to a boost in the private sector. China's opening-up pattern was preliminarily defined with strategic priority given to the coastal regions to take a pioneering start in development. It can be safely stated that China's economic reform in the mid-1980s was a transitional phase toward the socialist market economic system.

The third milestone was the 3rd Plenary Session of the 14th CPC Central Committee in 1993, which released the clear statement that the direction for China's economic reforms was "to build a socialist market economic system". At this time, China was in a development stage featuring low income and pursuit for a moderately prosperous society. Based on goals and fundamental principles defined in consistence with the 14th CPC National Congress, *Decisions on Certain Questions About Building Socialist Market Economic System* containing 50 articles were released, identifying key tasks including building a modern corporate system, building a universal and open national market system, shaping and improving macroeconomic regulation and control system, constructing an income distribution system and social security system and so on. These decisions became the fundamental framework and key pillars for the new system and have been inherited by the reforms in later periods. It has to be pointed out that an important international context for the 3rd Plenary Session of the 14th CPC Central Committee was the collapse of the former Soviet Union and drastic political and social changes in socialist Eastern European countries. China's brave proposal to build a socialist market economic system against such historical background demonstrated China's confidence in its path to reach a system of socialism with Chinese characteristics.

The fourth important session was the 3rd Plenary Session of the 16th CPC Central Committee in 2003, ushering China into the phase of "improving the socialist market economic system" as well as the development stage of building a moderately prosperous society as a lower-middle-income country. *Decisions on Certain Questions About Improving Socialist Market Economic System* was released. The document containing 42 articles became the guideline for China's reform in the first decade of the twenty-first century, greatly boosting the growth and dynamism of market players. In 2002, market players in China (including private enterprises and individual business owners) totaled 32.11 million, which jumped to 54.26 million in 2012, with the proportion of total population increasing from 2.42% to 4.00%. Among these, the number of private enterprises increased from 2.64 million to 10.86 million, an annual growth rate of 15.2% on average; the number of employees increased from 19.99 million to 75.57 million, an annual growth rate of 14.2% on average. This sufficiently demonstrates this period's significant growth of diversified market players who became the key actors in boosting the economy and trade volume as well as creating new jobs.

The fifth one was the 3rd Plenary Session of the 18th CPC Central Committee as China was entering the stage of "comprehensively deepening reform", development for building a moderately prosperous society and ranking among upper-middle-income countries. *Decisions of the CPC Central Committee on Some Key Questions About Comprehensively Deepening the Reform* contained 16 parts and 60 articles. It comprises 336 key moves, proposing the guiding philosophy and principles for comprehensively deepening the reform, mapping out the overall target for comprehensively deepening the reform and milestone targets up to 2020, planning for the "five-in-one" reform and institutional reform in national defense and military forces as well as reform in the Party's construction systems, laying out the strategic highlights, priorities, key directions, working mechanisms, implementation approaches, timetable and roadmap. An example of commercial affairs system reform shows that by 2015, the number of market players in China (including private enterprises and individual business owners) increased to 77 million, accounting for 5.62% of the total population, an increase of 23 million compared to 2012. Among these, private enterprises employed 111.8 million people and individual business owners employed 78 million people, that is 190 million in total. Up to 2015, according to rural poverty line, the number of impoverished rural residents decreased to 55.75 million, with the poverty occurrence rate falling to 5.7%.[16] It is expected that poverty would be fully eradicated by 2020.[17]

These five third plenary sessions show that China's reform and opening-up has highlighted three key themes from the very beginning: effectively improve the factor input and allocation on the supply side through reform to facilitate restructuring and optimization in various areas in China. In 2015, China's per capita GDP registered at 13,571 international US dollars (PPP, international US dollars in 2011), merely 25.7% of that of U.S. (52,704 international US dollars),[18] representing a major gap compared to the U.S. Narrowing down such gap would eventually depend on continuous improvement of productivity. Therefore, supply-side structural reform is the only way to facilitate China's moderately high growth over the long term, and more importantly, to enable constant structural optimization in various dimensions. This shall be manifested in the continuous decrease of the proportion of agriculture and continuous increase of the percentage of the service sector in GDP, and visible decrease (since 2006) following an increase in the proportion of industry and manufacturing. The population and urban-rural structures will see continuous decrease in rural population and rural workforce and continuous increase in urban population and urban workforce, constant increase in the average years of education for the working-age population as well as in productivity level. Additionally, comparative productivity across different industries shows a tendency of convergence. Despite the differences in TFP growth across stages, China still maintains a high growth from the global perspective despite being lower than some developed countries in relative contribution. Currently, a major constraint for China's TFP growth is the structural contradiction in its economic development that must be solved

[16] China Statistical Abstract 2016, p. 70, China Statistics Press, 2016.

[17] The 13th Five-Year Plan for Economic and Social Development of the People's Republic of China, March, 2016.

[18] Data source: World Bank Database: http://data.worldbank.org/indicator/.

by addressing the structural problems in factor allocation on the supply side, which further requires eliminating the low efficiency in factor allocation due to structural contradictions through deepening reforms in all areas, so as to achieve sustainable economic growth and maintain relatively high growth.

Furthermore, the theoretical origins and development trajectory of supply-side reform must be fully understood and the theoretical logic of supply-side structural reform be clarified if such reform is to be correctly interpreted. A typical interpretation of supply-side structural reform is to relate it with the so-called supply-side economics, and to place China's supply-side structural reform on par with the policies of Reaganomics based on supply-side economics. Therefore, it is necessary to introduce the main arguments of the school of supply-side economics as well as the background and consequences of Reaganomic policies if China's supply-side structural reform is to be understood in depth.

Supply-side economics has its origins in classical liberalism advocated by French economist Say (1767–1832), who proposed Say's Law, that is, demand is automatically created by supply, which is the most important statement on demand-supply relationship in classical economics.[19] Economic policies based on Say's Law basically feature laissez-faire and non-intervention, emphasizing the absolute dominating position of the market, which is exactly the economic policy pursued by major capitalist countries in the beginning of the twentieth century. However, the Great Depression looming over the capitalist world from 1929 to 1933 posed a daunting challenge to economic policies based on classical liberalism. Unlike the idea of automatic market clearing emphasized by Say, Keynesianism with "insufficient effective demand" at the foundation gradually gained popularity in principal macroeconomic policies in capitalist countries.

Keynesianism emphasizes government intervention and control of the economy with demand management at the core. In practice, the New Deal implemented by Roosevelt since 1933 effectively addressed the economic crisis in U.S. through a series of economic policies characterized by

[19] Say's Law is of great significance in classical economic and neo-classical economic theories; it laid an important theoretical foundation for general equilibrium theory in later years. Neo-classical economics emphasizes the absolute effectiveness of the market, believing that automatic market clearing and Pareto optimality are possible.

demand management.[20] In the wake of World War II, Keynesian economic policies gradually became the universally adopted means of macroeconomic management in capitalist countries.

After capitalist economies soared in the wake of World War II, up to the 1970s, "stagflation", that is high unemployment rate accompanied by high inflation rate stirred up doubts about Keynesian economic policies, which, centered upon "demand management", proved ineffective in addressing stagflation. The liberalism school even blamed the stagflation on government intervention of the economy, which inhibited the dynamism of market economy. As a result, supply-side economics represented by the viewpoints of Robert A. Mundell and Arthur B. Laffer was back in the limelight and became the theoretical foundation for the economic policies of the Thatcher administration in the U.K. and the Reagan administration in the U.S. Economic policies implemented by the Reagan administration, nicknamed "Reaganomics", included supporting free market competition, deregulation for enterprises, reducing tax and public expenditures, advocating balanced budget, emphasizing combating inflation by controlling money supply. In general, the "stagflation" problem was resolved during Reagan's presidency[21] even though it remains disputable whether the alleviation of stagflation in the U.S. was a result of Reaganomic policies. However, the sequela of Reaganomics was quite visible. The U.S. fiscal deficit continued to aggravate during the Reagan administration and even became "normal" for the U.S. economy during Reagan's presidency until the mid-1990s. Meanwhile, the income disparity was also worsening.

In essence, Reaganomics is neoliberal economics with "omnipotence of the market" at its core, which tends to label necessary and helpful governmental regulation as "distorting the market and creating inequality"; its

[20] The contents of the New Deal include: reorganizing the financial system, rebuilding the banking and credit system, abolishing the gold standard, stabilizing agricultural product prices by government subsidy, launching public works as a relief for the unemployed, creating jobs and stimulating consumption, improving the social insurance system, formulating the Social Security Act and other acts concerning labor protection, reforming administrative institutions, emphasizing the budgeting function of the federal government.

[21] The inflation rate in U.S. decreased from 10.35% when Reagan took office (in 1981) to 3.55% at the end of his first term of presidency (in 1985), and remained on a moderate level during his second term. The economic growth generally remained above 3.5% from 1983 to 1989 with the negative growth in 1982 as the only exception, indicating that the overall growth was better than the 1974–1980 period.

policies, opposing to government intervention, aim to boost the proportion and role of the private sector through free trade, open market, privatization, deregulation, tax cuts and public expenditure reduction. Nevertheless, in light of the transformation of Latin America, the former Soviet Union and East European socialist countries from the late 1980s to the early 1990s and the Asian Financial Crisis in the late 1990s, many failures of the "Washington Consensus" prescribed based on neoliberal economics have been witnessed in the developing world and the countries in transition. The eventual results of pursuing neoliberal economics are weakened macroeconomic regulation capacity of the government, market disorder, aggregation of systematic risks in economy, all of which will eventually result in economic crises and social turbulence. Even developed countries, such as the U.S., have failed to free themselves from the consequences of neoliberal economic policies as a matter of fact, with their economic development still troubled by aggravating income gap and soaring deficits. In a sense, the global financial crisis triggered by the sub-prime mortgage crisis in the U.S. indicates another typical failure of the adoption of neoliberal economic theory in the financial sector.

It has to be noted in particular that although supply-side economic theory as the basis of Reaganomics and the "supply-side structural reform" currently highlighted in China pursue a similar goal of revitalizing the economy and boosting economic growth, distinct differences do exist in policy goals and development stages between China's supply-side structural reform and Reaganomics.

The first and foremost goal of Reaganomics is to curb inflation.[22] The stagflation looming over the U.S. economy in the late 1970s was related to the energy price hike due to the blow on oil supply and the rising military expenses to a large extent, resulting in the stagnation of economic growth and inflation at the same time. Yet despite the minor inflation pressure,[23] China is now burdened by severe structural overcapacity that is causing distortion in resource allocation. Besides, despite the slowdown in economic growth, China is still maintaining a moderately high-speed growth of approximately 7%, which is distinct from what the

[22] From 1973 to 1981, the U.S. economy entered into a period of continuous high inflation, with average inflation rate reaching 9%, marking a period of high inflation over a relatively long term after the Great Depression.

[23] For example, CPI has been staying under 3% since 2012; while deflation is seen in PPI for a succession of 45 months since March 2012.

U.S. experienced in 1980 when the country was trapped in negative growth. This has created conditions for China's supply-side restructuring from an objective perspective.

Concerning the development phase, the current economic structure in China shows clear difference from the U.S. economy during Reagan's administration. In 1980, the urbanization rate of the U.S. was 73.74% and added value of the service sector in GDP registered at 63.57%, employing 65.70% of the working population in the U.S. All these indicators are typical of developed economies. In contrast, China's urbanization rate in 2015 was 56.1%, with added value of the service sector accounting for 50.5% of GDP, employing 42.4% of the working population in China, and the income level of the Chinese population remains in the middle-income range.

The two differences illustrated above determine that China's policies of supply-side structural reform must avoid repeating the economic policies implemented by Reagan in the 1980s, with Reaganomic policies highlighting tax cuts (especially for capital income and the rich) and deregulation in an effort to tackle stagflation.[24] China, on the other hand, focuses on economic restructuring and transformation of the economic development model as the core of its supply-side structural reform, aiming to improve TFP by developing the adaptability and flexibility of the supply structure. Therefore, China's supply-side structural reform is essentially distinct from the U.S. policies in the early 1980s based on Reaganomics in terms of policy target and development stage. In this sense, directly applying Reaganomic policies to China's supply-side structural reform would be a mismatch and a misconception, hence China's supply-side structural reform should by no means be taken as the Chinese version of "Reaganomics".

Furthermore, a key contributor to China's successful economic reforms is the country's self-awareness and autonomy in implementing the economic reforms. From the perspective of self-awareness, during the implementation of economic reforms, China did not miss the right timing for reform and development due to overcaution in facing various possible

[24] In 1980, the marginal tax rate for individual income tax in the U.S. ran as high as 70% at the maximum; while the maximum corporate income tax registered at 46%. Despite the visible economic recovery in the U.S. during the Reagan administration as compared to the mid-1970s and 1980s, many analysts believe that such recovery was not completely attributable to Reagan's economic policies.

risks triggered by reform; while from the perspective of autonomy, China's economic reforms are based on the reality of the country's economic development with readiness to adapt to the objective trend of economic globalization rather than blindly copy the so-called international experience. For example, when making the decision to build the socialist market economic system, China refused to blindly adopt the approaches prescribed in the "Washington Consensus". Likewise, the current supply-side structural reform in China also reflects the self-awareness and autonomy in pressing ahead with economic reforms.

Thirdly, as China's economic growth enters into the "new normal", supply-side structural reform has its rationale in reality. The downturn of China's economic growth is not only a pressing issue of the current economic fundamentals but also has raised global concerns, as China is not only the second largest economy (in exchange rate) or the largest economy (in purchasing power parity) but also the biggest trading country in the world. Therefore, the future trend of China's economy will have a direct spillover effect on 240 countries and regions in the world, which is especially true to 130–140 countries and regions for which China is an important trading partner. This is the biggest difference from the economic reforms from the previous stages. A clear understanding of the realistic rationale of the supply-side structural reform is, in itself, a correct answer to why supply-side structural reform should be identified as the backbone in the 13th Five-Year Plan period. Sticking to the backbone is to focus on the principal factors determining economic development and main contradictions to be addressed for future economic growth. Once these factors are clear, the details will fall into place. This in turn requires a clear understanding of two major questions facing the current economic growth: first, how to correctly interpret the economic downturn during the 12th Five-Year Plan period? Second, how to secure growth by restructuring during the 13th Five-Year Plan period rather than boosting domestic demand in 1998 and 2008 in the context of financial crisis?

The economic slowdown during the 12th Five-Year Plan period highlights the necessity for supply-side structural reform. China's average economic growth stood at 9.6% between 1978 and 2015, on par with Japan's average economic growth of 9.35% between 1950 and 1972 and higher than that of South Korea (8.6%) between 1961 and 1996.[25] In terms of

[25] GDP calculated in US dollars of 1990, data source for calculation: Angus Maddison, 2011, *Historical Statistics of the World Economy: 1–2008 AD.*

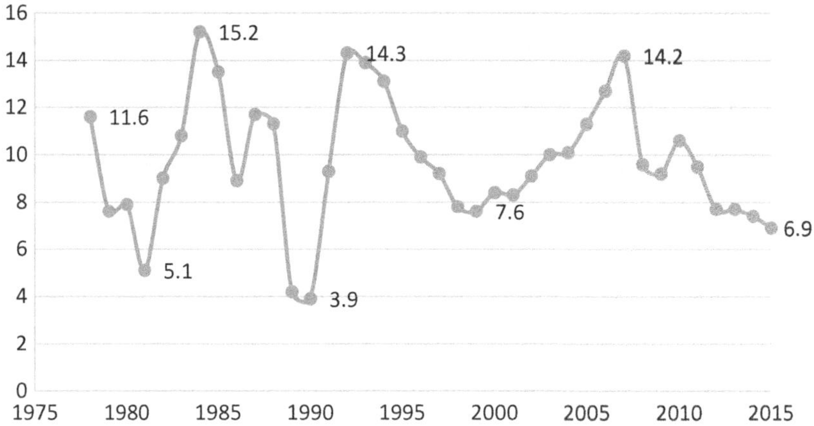

Fig. 4.3 China's economic growth rate (1978–2015). (Data Source: National Bureau of Statistics: *China Statistical Abstract 2016*, p. 24)

economic fluctuations, China's rapid economic growth was not exempted from several rounds of temporary decrease (see Fig. 4.3), including the forced adjustment from 1978 to 1981 resulting in a slowdown from 11.6% to 5.1%, a second round of forced adjustment between 1984 and 1990 resulting in a slowdown from 15.2% to 3.9%, a fallback from 14.3% to 7.6% during the 1992–1999 period and a further slowdown from 14.2% to 6.9% from 2007 to 2015. In general, China's economic growth shows more stability since the reform and opening-up, in particular, no major boom and bust characteristics of the planned economy occurred in China since 1992, indicating the country's maturing capability of macro regulation and control. Overall, changes in the economic growth rate are the result of combined effects of external demand factors (or cyclical factors), internal structural factors and macro regulation and control. However, each round of adjustment involves economic restructuring that in turn lays the foundation for growth in the next phase.

China's economic growth has entered into the "new normal" since 2011, with growth gradually slowing down from 9.5% in 2011 to 6.9% in 2015 (falling below 7% for the first time since 1991). An important viewpoint on such downturn is that China's economy is impacted by cyclical factors, that is, its growth hampered by the slowdown (or even negative growth) of external demand. With regard to external demand, the 2008 global financial crisis did deliver a heavy blow on China's economy, which is directly related to China's openness and deep involvement in the world economy. In light of the current world economic fundamentals and China's economic growth trend in recent years, the sluggish or even shrinking external demand does explain, to a large extent, China's economic growth downturn: during the 12th Five-Year Plan period, the proportion of China's import and export volume of goods in GDP shrank from 49.16% in 2011 to 35.74% in 2015, which was even lower than prior to China's entry into WTO (38.8% in 2001).

In the wake of the financial crisis, the world economy has been ushered into a period of fluctuation, transition, transformation and adjustment with clashes of old and new thinking modes, shift from obsolete to emerging driving forces, comparison of conventional and unconventional powers and alternation of traditional and newly established rules.[26] In general, the world economy in recent years has been facing a new reality characterized by "low growth in trade, sluggish economic growth and high public debt"[27] as it undergoes structural changes, generally turning for the better and yet facing tremendous uncertainties. On one hand, the role of emerging economies as an engine for world economic growth is weakening and disintegrating; on the other hand, the contribution of developed economies for boosting growth is too limited to enable a smooth recovery of the world economy. Moreover, uncertainties that may influence world economic growth should by no means be overlooked. For instance, the negative interest rate policy implemented respectively by the European Central Bank at the end of 2015 and by Bank of Japan in late January 2016 has confronted the stability of the global financial system with new uncertainties; economic growth in Europe is highly likely to suffer from the consequences of Brexit, which will in turn trigger a profound impact on the global capital market. Besides, Donald Trump's vowing into presidency and the interest rate hike in the U.S. will also prove to be pivotal factors influencing the world economy. Altogether, the negative impact of the "reverse-globalization trend" emerging in recent years on the growth of

[26] Chen Wenling, Yan Shaojun, New Trends and New Characteristics of World Economic Development of Today [J], *Nanjing Social Sciences*, 2016 (5): 1–9.

[27] In October 2014, Christine Lagarde, Managing Director of IMF, pointed out that the world economy entered the "new mediocre", that is, low growth over the long term. In April 2015, she warned again that we must prevent the "new mediocre" from evolving into the "new reality" of lower growth today.

global trade and world economic growth inevitably constitutes an adverse impact on China's economic growth.

Although the impact of external factors on China's economic growth should by no means be overlooked, it would be too much of a one-sided view to argue, on this basis, that the major problem currently confronting China's economy is a cyclical one, as the impact of structural problems on China's economic growth is not to be neglected. The cyclical factors arising from the global financial crisis caused China to launch a massive economic stimulation plan from late 2008 to 2010 to "stabilize the growth", which in turn aggravated the structural contradiction of China's economy and became increasingly visible during the 12th Five-Year Plan period. Therefore, the sluggish external demand is the external and secondary cause for the economic downturn in recent years while structural problems prevailing in the domestic economy is the internal and primary cause.

A significant factor exacerbating the structural problem of China's economy is the impact of real estate investment on economic growth (see Fig. 4.4). Prior to the global financial crisis, the nominal growth rate of real estate investment in urban China reached 27.4% between 2000 and 2007, close to twice the nominal GDP growth (15.1%). After the outbreak of the global financial crisis, the growth rate of urban real estate investment shrank to 14.1% in 2009 and bounced back to 32.8% in 2010. The beginning of the 12th Five-Year Plan period saw a significant decline

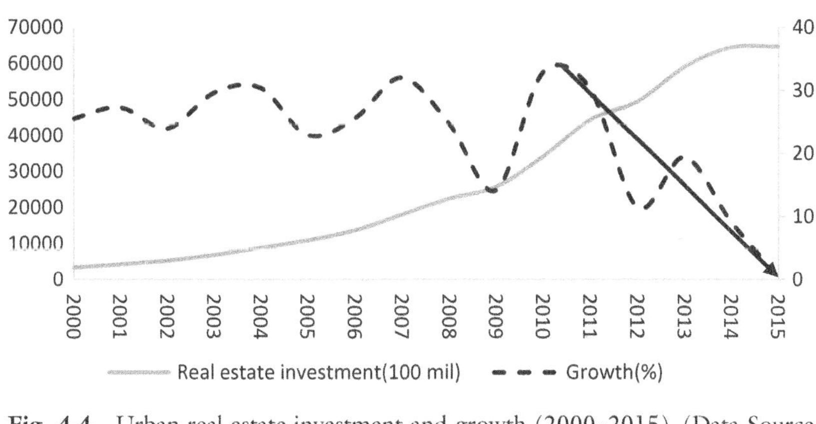

Fig. 4.4 Urban real estate investment and growth (2000–2015). (Data Source for Calculation: National Bureau of Statistics: China Statistical Abstract 2016, p. 91)

in urban real estate investment growth, hitting 0.38% in 2015, resulting in the economic downturn in recent years. More importantly, the sluggish growth in real estate investment directly led to declining demand growth in sectors closely related to real estate investment (such as coal, steel, cement, construction materials), hence constituting a key cause for overcapacity in coal and steel industries, and so on, resulting in the current pressure of de-inventory and de-capacity. Furthermore, in an effort to combat the international financial crisis, the economic stimulation plan launched in late 2008 encouraged banks to grant loans to real estate, steel, cement, and so on. With enthusiastic support from the local government, local financial platforms also received massive credit loans from the bank. The explosive expansion of trust loans between 2011 and 2013 resulted in mounting debts and continuously growing leverage of local governments, which has contributed to the de-leveraging pressure of today.

During the 13th Five-Year Plan period, supply-side structural reform has become the key item on the economic development agenda. Despite the economic downturn during the 12th Five-Year Plan period, visible achievements have been made in economic restructuring, which is in line with the direction of economic restructuring aiming at long-term economic growth. On a macro level, restructuring during the 12th Five-Year Plan period is mainly manifested in the following aspects: visible decrease of the proportion of the secondary industry and significant increase of the proportion of the tertiary industry.[28] The proportion of the tertiary industry rose from 44.2% in 2010 to 50.5% in 2015, that is, an increase of 6.3 percentage points; while the proportion of the secondary industry dropped from 46.2% to 40.5%, that is, a decrease of 5.7 percentage points, both rates of change are significantly higher than all previous five-year plan periods. Furthermore, restructuring will inevitably trigger changes in the growth momentum, yet there tends to be a time lapse between the obsolete momentum phasing out and the new momentum playing its leading role. In the case where the recession of the obsolete momentum is much faster than the growth of the new momentum, economic growth would stay sluggish for a short term. Therefore, the economic slowdown is but a natural result of restructuring. A comparative analysis of the average provincial GDP growth and the rate of change of the secondary and tertiary

[28]The proportion of the primary industry only dropped by 0.6 percentage point from 2010 to 2015, much lower than other Five-Year Plan periods. In 2010, the proportion of the primary industry in GDP was 9.6%, which has basically entered into a period of slow change.

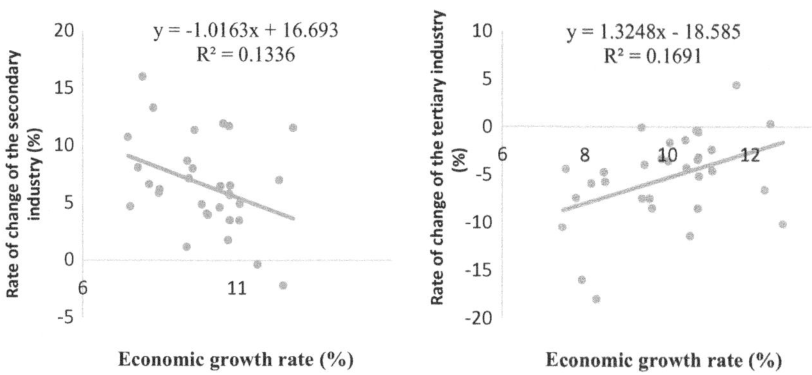

Fig. 4.5 Changes in economic growth rate and structure in various regions during the 12th Five-Year Plan. (Data Source for Calculation: National Bureau of Statistics: China Statistical Abstract 2011–2016)

industries during the 12th Five-Year Plan period (see Fig. 4.5) shows, to a certain extent, a negative correlation between GDP growth and the change of the proportion of the tertiary industry as well as a positive correlation between GDP growth and the change of the proportion of the secondary industry, that is, in regions with sharp increase of the tertiary industry and sharp decrease of the secondary industry would see comparatively sluggish GDP growth. Therefore, considering the structural factors, the economic slowdown during the 12th Five-Year Plan period was reasonable and should not have prompted excessive pessimism, not to mention that the average economic growth during this period registered at 7.8%, which, although lower than 9.9% growth between 1978 and 2010, still exceeded the expected target of 7%.

In terms of comprehensive development indicators, the quality of economic growth improved significantly during the 12th Five-Year Plan period, as indicators of industrial structure, urban-rural structure, science and technology (except for the proportion of R&D expenditures in GDP), education and environment have basically achieved the expected goals of the 12th Five-Year Plan period. An evaluation of all previous five-year plans based on the method of goal congruence shows that the fulfillment rate was 64% for the 10th Five-Year Plan, 86% for the 11th Five-Year Plan and 96% of the 12th Five-Year Plan. Therefore, it can be seen that the comprehensive fulfillment rate of the 12th Five-Year Plan was higher than that of the two previous five-year plans despite the economic downturn during this period, and this has created favorable conditions for moderately high economic growth and implementation of supply-side structural reform during the 13th Five-Year Plan period. Generally speaking, the structural changes emerging during the 12th Five-Year Plan period were fundamental; they were positive and benign long-term changes that were basically consistent with the long-term development trend of China's industrialization (in the later stage of decrease of the proportion of secondary industry) and urbanization (in the stage of rapid growth of the proportion of urban population), with continuous upgrading in the consumption structure of residents (in particular, Engel's coefficient for both urban and rural residents fell to 30% approximately, marking the attainment of a better-off level),[29] this is in line with the fundamental direction of China's economic restructuring and optimization over the long term.

Despite the remarkable achievements of China's economic restructuring during the 12th Five-Year Plan period, the structural problems remain prominent and the restructuring efforts are far from sufficient, with the pressure of "stabilizing growth" and the challenge of "restructuring" co-existing, which, if not properly handled, would tumble into aggravated contradiction. On one hand, economic growth during the 13th Five-Year Plan period remains an important indicator measuring development during this period, as whether China would achieve its goal to double the country's economic size by 2020 on the basis of 2010 is at stake. A well-grounded understanding of the economic growth during the 13th Five-Year Plan period must be based on a thorough evaluation of the potential growth of China's economy, which refers to the achievable growth on the condition of effective allocation of economic factors that can be sustained over a considerably long term. Multiple evaluations exist for China's potential economic growth in the future. For example, Cai Fang believes that the country's potential economic growth during the 13th Five-Year Plan period is 6.2%,[30] his main argument being the workforce shortage resulting from the aging population and the subsequent decline in returns on capital investment; Zhang Jun, on the contrary, argues that China's

[29] In 2015, Engel's coefficient was 30.6% for all residents in China, 29.7% for urban residents and 33.0% for rural residents.

[30] Cai Fang: Growth Potential + Reform Dividend—How to View China's 7% Economic Growth in the First Half of the Year, *People's Daily*, 2015-8-5(2).

potential growth rate for the next decade is approximately 7%–8%, mainly for the reason of the major per capita income gap between China and developed countries[31]; Justin Yifu Lin, on the other hand, believes that China could achieve an 8% potential economic growth for at least another ten years, with similar argument that the per capita income for Chinese residents is on a relatively low level, hence will still benefit considerably from the late-mover advantage.[32]

Based on a multi-dimensional consideration of the late-development advantage, the momentum of industrial restructuring, the driving force of urbanization, the aggregate effect and economies of scale of human capital and the innovation-driven potential, it can be reasonably and safely stated that China's potential economic growth rate is likely to stay close to 7% in the next decade. The economic growth target established in the 13th Five-Year Plan is above 6.5%, which is the bottom line for economic growth but not without some margin of adjustment; it does not exceed China's potential economic growth rate while leaving adequate room for restructuring. In the long run, structural factors remain the key determining factors for China's potential economic growth rate in the future, which, if properly handled, would be crucial for aligning the actual growth rate with the potential growth rate for China's economy in the future.

In terms of external demand, if the "new reality" becomes the "new normal" for the world economy, China would reduce itself to a passive position in "stabilizing growth" if we identify our hopes to overcome the current economic dilemma in improved external demand. Therefore, restructuring must aim at securing the initiative for stabilizing growth. China's economic growth rate in the future will both depend on the external demand factor (or cyclical factor) and, more importantly, restructuring at a deeper level. Considering structural factors, a key driving force for China's rapid economic growth since the reform and opening-up is the continuous optimization of the economic structure. Currently, the structural problem is particularly visible in the high inventory of real estate and over-capacity of certain industrial sectors with hiking leverage and soaring costs of business operation.[33] From 2012 to 2016, China's PPI (producer

[31] Zhang Jun: Potential Growth Rate of China's Economy, *The Financial Times* (Chinese), 2013-10-28.

[32] Justin Yifu Lin: China's Economy Possesses Potential to Maintain 8% Growth for At Least Another 10 Years, *The Economic Daily*, 2015-3-22 (4).

[33] On February 23, 2016, *New Year gambling hints at Chinese entrepreneurial vigour* published on The Financial Times cited BIS estimation that by the end of the second quarter of

price index) underwent deflation for a succession of four years, demonstrating that the major problem prevailing in China's economy is on the structural level, with visible overcapacity in traditional industrial manufactured goods and capacity utilization rate of certain industries apparently lower than the international level. This shows that China's traditional industrialization is running into a dead end and that the poor efficiency of factor allocation is highly likely to cause mounting financial risks. To solve these problems is the short-term goal of supply-side structural reform, which, nevertheless, is unlikely to be achieved within a matter of one, two or a few years' time.

China is at a critical moment with its economic growth shifting gears, labor pains in restructuring and a process to digest the stimulation policies in the previous stage "overlapping" with one another. With profound transformation of the strategic window of opportunities, China is still facing daunting challenges in seizing and leveraging on this strategic window, especially considering that TFP improvement and steady economic growth are constrained by the outstanding structural problems accumulated over the long term. In this sense, pressing ahead with supply-side structural reform on a deeper level is not only a palliative to address the current structural contradictions, but also a far-sighted move to create strategic opportunities for sustainable economic development in the future. During the 13th Five-Year Plan and even a longer period, China will carry on with its restructuring efforts and its economic growth rate will be subject both to the impact of internal and external demand and to the actual allocation of supply-side factors, that is, structural factors to a large extent. Changes in China's future economic structure will still be seen in the changing proportions of the secondary and tertiary industries. Therefore, identifying supply-side structural reform as the cardinal line of economic development during the 13th Five-Year Plan period is consistent with the realistic need of China's sustainable economic development over the long term. Stabilizing growth through restructuring at a deeper level is on the top of the current economic development agenda.

The 13th Five-Year Plan has explicitly identified supply-side structural reform as the priority for development, indicating that it does not only

2015, the proportion of debt of non-financial enterprises in China has exceeded 160% of GDP, remarkably higher than that of Europe and Japan at close to 110%, visibly higher than that of the U.S. and U.K. at around 70% and significantly higher than that of India (50.1%), Brazil (75%) and Russia (57%) approximately.

focus on addressing the highlighted structural contradiction currently facing China's economy, but also aim at mid- and long-term economic development of the country. In terms of the short-term goal, the main tasks such as de-capacity and de-inventory identified during Central Economic Work Conference must be accomplished, not to ignore stabilizing growth and reducing risks. From a mid- to long-term perspective, the fundamental goal of supply-side structural reform is to accelerate the transformation of the economic development model and to improve labor productivity and TFP so as to stabilize potential economic growth. In particular, the 13th Five-Year Plan highlights green development while emphasizing restructuring. The Chinese government has pledged to achieve the peaking of CO_2 emissions around 2030 and to make best efforts to peak early.[34] This shows that emission reduction and environmental quality improvement would be binding conditions for China's long-term economic growth as well as important structural factors influencing such growth in the future. In this sense, structural issues are the long-term factors at play for China's economic development.

4.2.2 *Supply-Side Structural Reform Ushers in China's New Normal*

Theoretically speaking, implementing supply-side structural reform has three implications. First, on a micro level, it requires improvement of allocation efficiency of production factors on the supply side as well as higher TFP for the transformation of growth drivers. Second, on a meso level, it implies optimization of economic structure, reducing ineffective demand through de-inventory and de-capacity while expanding effective demand and innovating demand models through development of new industries and creation of new business models to rectify the mismatch between supply and demand, and hence enabling economic development to build upon the dynamic equilibrium between supply and demand. It must be pointed out, however, that supply-side structural reform is not a synonym of "shock therapy" of economic restructuring, which is the normal for

[34] On November 12, 2014, U.S.-China Joint Announcement on Climate Change was officially published by the heads of state of China and the U.S. On September 3, 2016, at G20 Summit in Hangzhou, Chinese President Xi Jinping and U.S. President Obama successively submitted documents of approval of the Paris Climate Change Agreement to UN Secretary-General Ban Ki-Moon.

China's economic development and a long-term mission; instead, such structural reform must remain aligned with the objective demand of economic restructuring. Third, on an institutional level, synergy of reform should be built by in-depth execution of various institutional arrangements (such as decentralizing and organizational streamlining, facilitating new urban construction, deepening SOE reform, deepening capital market reform, accelerating the implementation of innovation-driven development strategy), with the market playing a decisive role in resource allocation. Meanwhile, the government shall play an active role where the market fails to function (e.g. environmental protection, poverty alleviation, provision of public services, anti-monopoly, basic research, etc.).

In general, supply-side structural reform was proposed in the context of China's practice of economic development and reform and represents a new exploration of the CPC Central Committee into China's economic development theory since the 18th CPC National Congress; it is gradually shaped based on the principal issues and milestone targets of China's economic development both currently and in the future.[35] The idea of supply-side structural reform is proposed in light of some prominent difficulties facing China's economy in the current stage (such as excessive inventory of real estate, overcapacity, soaring debts, high costs burdening enterprises), the solution of which constitutes short-term goals for supply-side structural reform yet it would be unrealistic to expect such goals to be achieved within one or two years. Therefore, no once-for-all or instant

[35] First, "enabling the market to play a decisive role in resource allocation" was first proposed during the 3rd Plenary Session of the 18th CPC Central Committee in 2013, followed by President Xi Jinping's statement in 2014 that China's economy has entered into the "new normal", whose main features are summarized from the aspects of growth speed, economic structure and growth momentum, that is, from high speed growth to moderately high speed growth, continuous optimization and upgrading in economic structure, switching from investment-driven to innovation-driven growth. Third, in 2015, the five development concepts described as "innovation, coordination, greening, opening-up and shared" development were first proposed at the 5th Plenary Session of the 18th CPC Central Committee, focusing not only on the transformation of the economic growth model but also on that the achievements of economic development should be shared by the people. Fourth, in 2015, President Xi Jinping stated that "efforts should be made to strengthen Supply-side structural reform" for the first time during the 11th Session of the Leading Group for Financial and Economic Affairs, which was further clarified at the Central Economic Work Conference. Furthermore, in the group study organized by the Politburo at the end of January 2016, "pressing ahead with structural reform, especially on the supply side" was identified as a strategic highlight in the 13th Five-Year Plan.

solution possibly exists for supply-side structural reform due to the long process of China's urbanization and transformation of the demand structure, which corresponds to the stage of China's development from a moderately high-income country to a high-income country. This, from an objective point of view, determines the importance, necessity and long duration of the supply-side structural reform.

From 2010, China has ranked among the upper-middle-income countries in terms of economic development level. The "new normal" during the 12th Five-Year Plan period featured a slowdown in economic growth, a change of gears, and in-depth economic restructuring, which have built a solid foundation for supply-side structural reform. In light of the current development state, China's economy is at a critical moment of transitioning to the next phase: new urbanization construction has entered into the key stage, with urbanization rate in China reaching 56.1% in 2015, which is expected to exceed 60% in 2020 and approximately 70% in 2030. China's economic restructuring in a post-industrialized society is also in a pivotal phase. With industrial structure upgraded from an industry-dominated one to a service-dominated one, it is expected to attain relative stability by 2030, with industrial output accounting for around 23% of GDP while the percentage of service sector in GDP exceeding 60%, making it a key period in overcoming the "middle income trap". It is estimated that China's national income per capita shall rank among high-income countries by 2025. A holistic overview shows that the period from now up to 2030 represents a critical stage for China's industrial restructuring and transformation in the economic growth model driven by industrial and consumption upgrading, during which pressing ahead with supply-side structural reform on a deeper level bears strategic significance for China's economy to evolve into a more advanced stage featuring more efficient models, more sophisticated division of labor and a more rationalized structure.

4.2.3 How to Promote Supply-Side Structural Reform: The Formula

As the country's economy evolves to a more advanced phase, it has to confront a more sophisticated economic growth as well as more daunting challenges of industrial restructuring and upgrading at the core of this growth. Economic restructuring indicates varying growth rates among industries, some of which are in a fast-growing cycle while others are in decline. Therefore, both "addition" and "subtraction" are seen in the industrial development trend. Besides, upgrading of industrial structure includes both continuous improvement in technical competence and capacity building for green development in various industrial sectors with effective containment of risks in different links of economic growth; thus, industrial structure upgrade requires "multiplication" and "division" as well. Based on the above analysis, deepening supply-side structural reform is a wise combination of "addition, subtraction, multiplication and division" in the industrial structure adjustment and upgrading by comprehensively leveraging on the policy portfolio for optimized economic structure and higher level of sustainable development in economic growth. The following formula shows how the arithmetic fundamentals—addition, subtraction, multiplication and division—are used to facilitate supply-side structural reform.

$$\text{Policy portfolio} = \left[\text{Increase effective supply} + \text{eliminate ineffective supply}\right] \times \frac{\text{Innovation} - \text{driven}}{\text{Green development}}$$

"Addition" refers to the expansion of new space for economic development, building room for basic sectors (such as agriculture) in the national economic system, and meeting the demand for people's wellbeing and expectations for higher quality of life as well as building up the effective supply capacity. This includes higher levels of professional, scaled-up and modernized agricultural production and advancement in agricultural industrialization and market-oriented development to satisfy people's demand for high quality agricultural products; facilitation of emerging industries of strategic significance and acceleration in industrial restructuring in the manufacturing sector to boost the development of new products, new industries and new business models; adaptation to the trend of higher proportion of the service sector in national economy and acceleration of its overall development through institutional innovation, lowering the bar for private capital to invest in high-end services to release the potential of private capital in boosting the development of the service sector, especially in areas related to people's wellbeing and quality of life such as elderly care, health services, tourism, culture and entertainment and so on. Efforts should be made to promote coordinated regional development and to build a solid foundation for "new space" of regional development, pressing ahead with the three regional strategies, that is, coordinated development of Beijing, Tianjin and Hebei, the Yangtze River Economic Belt and the Belt and Road Initiative, conscientiously implementing the new urbanization strategy, quickening up the pace to enhance the urbanization rate for the registered population and exploring for various public-private partnership (PPP) models in infrastructure and public utilities.

"Subtraction" refers to the elimination of ineffective supply, obsolete productivity as well as institutional barriers restraining economic agents from active engagement and unnecessary government intervention of corporate activities, thereby stimulating the dynamism of enterprises as micro-agents. At present, efforts in de-capacity and de-inventory should continue, building on the basis of preliminary success in these areas. Discriminatory institutional environment placing private capital at a disadvantaged position should be reversed while regulations and practices impeding single market and fair play should be abolished, so as to eliminate institutional discrimination against private capital in its access to industries. Investment scope should be broadened for private capital by implementing measures to relieve tax burdens for enterprises and raise the taxation threshold for small, medium-sized and micro enterprises. Optimizing the development pattern of state-owned enterprises also depends on "subtraction" with the following key tasks identified: stripping non-core businesses with poor market competitiveness and low profitability which are not serving public benefit; eliminating "zombie enterprises" among SOEs and building up the scale, quality and competitiveness of SOEs by lean management and core capacity building.

"Multiplication" refers to shaping an innovation-driven development model in all aspects, with innovative development ranking first among the five development concepts proposed in the 13th Five-Year Plan and "innovation-driven" as a major indicator of economic and social development during the 13th Five-Year Plan period. In general, innovation as a driving force will impact all dimensions of transforming the economic growth model and produce a multiplier effect in industrial upgrading and economic growth quality improvement. The success of "multiplication" will depend on three pillars: first, building an innovation input mechanism in society with institutional innovation playing a steering role, while improving the national innovation system; second, reviewing the income distribution system with more incentives for those possessing science and technology expertise, thus inspiring various stakeholders to innovate; third, allowing capital markets to function as a catalyst in translating innovation findings into application, deepening the reform of capital markets and shaping a capital market environment that encourages innovation and entrepreneurship, quickening the pace of transformation of scientific and technological achievements, thereby achieving a healthy development of innovation with application of science and technology. In general, as China strides toward the bar of high-income countries, the "multiplication effect" of innovation as a driving force would play a decisive role.

"Division" refers to the reduction of resource consumption, pollution and emissions per unit of GDP. For example, saving energy and water while cutting emissions of waste water, exhaust gas, solid waste and CO_2, essentially aiming to achieve green development and building capacity for sustainable development. An overview of the implementation of the 11th and 12th Five-Year Plans shows that targets related to natural resources and the environment have been by and large achieved; while 10 among 25 targets during the 13th Five-Year Plan period are under the category of natural resources and environment, all of them being obligatory, indicating that green development is promoted to a new height of overall national development. Success in "division" depends on both stronger social awareness of green development, the facilitation of which being integrated in every link of production and daily life, and the establishment of a set of strict "division" standards of energy saving, consumption reduction and emission cut as the baseline in production, which is to be conscientiously implemented without compromise. Additionally, guiding policies such as green finance (the strict implementation of green standard in government procurement) encourage green production by enterprises and green consumption by citizens. In general, the success of "division" is to facilitate green development, which influences every dimension in improving the quality of China's economic growth and helps to consolidate the foundation of sustainable development, ensuring the steady and sustainable development of China's economy.

It has to be pointed out that the application of these four "arithmetic fundamentals" in various fields are not isolated from one another; on the contrary, policy portfolios incorporating "addition, subtraction, multiplication and division" should be developed based on actual needs, leveraging on the synergy of different policy measures, adapting to and actively leading the new normal of economy. These policy portfolios include: (1) fully leveraging on "multiplication" for "addition", for example, boosting the development of new industries and business models with technological innovation, of which the currently thriving "platform economy" is a typical example. (2) "Subtraction" based on the standards of "division". For example, "division" standards may be set for energy use, resource consumption, pollution and emissions of industrial sectors undergoing de-capacity, eliminating enterprises that fail to comply with the standards. (3) "Multiplication"-enabled "division", that is, promoting energy saving, consumption reduction and emission cut among enterprises through technological innovation.

In addition, continuing with supply-side structural reform is not a risk-free move, especially considering the release of internal risks such as social risk triggered by unemployment due to restructuring in certain industrial sectors and financial risk due to various structural factors. In the meantime, changes in external economic environment (for instance, the impact of de-globalization on world trade growth) may also put pressure on China's efforts to stabilize its economic growth and to optimize its structure, which may be regarded as external risks. Apart from active prevention and early identification of these internal and external risks, proactive countermeasures are also needed through macro regulation and control; that is to say, in pressing ahead with supply-side structural reform, various measures of massive regulation and control need to be taken, enabling fiscal policies, monetary policies, foreign trade policies and investment and funding policies to play their roles in stabilizing growth and alleviating risks.

In order to create a favorable social environment for the deepening of various reform schemes, internal risks such as social risks can be effectively circumvented and controlled by targeting the weaknesses. De-leveraging should be continued as a proactive measure to mitigate and prevent financial risks, which, to some extent, may create conditions for reducing costs. To tackle external risks, we should provide guidance for Chinese enterprises to go global, actively engage in various regional economic organizations and forums and firmly oppose the trend "de-globalization" in any disguise. External risk assessment and stress test should be strengthened in all areas such as international trade, outbound investment, regional economic cooperation, foreign exchange reserves and stabilization of exchange rate to avoid passivity. In a word, with deepening supply-side structural reform and increasingly sophisticated relationships between stabilizing growth, restructuring and controlling risks, it is necessary to stabilize growth by means of macro regulation and control in order to prevent risks deriving from releasing too quickly, which may result in a more challenging situation of restructuring.

On the whole, the key to deepening supply-side structural reform is to adapt to the objective trend of China's economic development, taking the initiative to adapt to the "new normal" and actively guiding it with policy portfolios of "addition, subtraction, multiplication and division" as well as effective containment of various internal and external risks. This will help facilitate China's economic restructuring and transformation in economic growth model, enable its economic transformation and upgrading, with its growth momentum shifting from investment to consumption and its leading sector from industry to services, eventually making China's economy better in steadiness, quality and sustainability as it moves toward a more advanced stage of development, enabling it to better fuel the world economic growth in a sustainable manner.

4.3 Supply-Side Structural Reform: China's Practical and Theoretical Innovation

For the first time in history, "supply-side structural reform" was stated in *The 13th Five-Year Plan for Economic and Social Development of the People's Republic of China* as the theme of the Five-Year Plan, epitomizing the three key words—"reform", "supply-side" and "structural" since the reform and opening-up while functioning as the backbone for China's economy to enter and lead the way of the "new normal". A statement of President Xi Jinping explains this reform fully: "the key to supply-side reform is to liberate and develop productivity, promoting restructuring through reform, reducing ineffective and low-end supply while expanding effective and mid-to high-end supply, strengthening the adaptability and flexibility of the supply structure to changing demands and improving total factor productivity". "In terms of political economy, the essence of supply-side structural reform is to enable China's supply capacity to satisfy the people's constantly rising, upgrading and personalized material, cultural and eco-environmental demands, so that the aim of production in a socialist economy can be achieved".[36] Supply-side structural reform is essentially the constant adjustment of production relations. It adapts to

[36] Xi Jinping, Speech on the Workshop of Studying and Implementing the Principles of the 5th Plenary Session of the 19th CPC Central Committee for Key Officials on Provincial and Ministerial Levels, January 18, 2016, *People's Daily*, May 10, 2016.

productivity while liberating and developing productivity, reflecting both the fundamental principles of Marxist political economy and China's practices and theories in the context of China's reform and opening-up today.

Primarily an interaction between China's innovation in practice and in theory, supply-side structural reform is the guiding theme of the country's future economic development and transformation of the development model, providing a theoretical foundation and a political consensus for the next step in practical innovation. As it is well said by Mao Zedong: correct ideas come from nowhere but social practice. Once correct ideas representing the advanced class are mastered by the mass, they shall transform into material forces to rebuild the society and revolutionize the world.[37]

[37] Mao Zedong, *Where Do Correct Ideas Come From?* Selected Writings of Mao Zedong, Volume VIII, pp. 320–321, The People's Publishing House, 1999.

CHAPTER 5

Looking Ahead: China Becoming a High-Income Economy

Nearly four decades of reform and opening-up shows that China is one of the few successful cases of development. First, sustained high growth became a reality in China. China's GNP grew by 32.19 times from 1978 to 2016 at constant prices, that is, an annual increase of 9.6%, of which the annual GDP growth hit 9.9% and 7.8% from 1978 to 2010 (high-speed growth) and from 2011 to 2016 (moderately high-speed growth) respectively on average.

Second, China has achieved leapfrog development from an extremely low-income level to upper-high-income. In 1978, China's GNI per capita was less than half of the average of low-income countries and ranked close to the bottom of the world. According to statistics provided by the World Bank, China ranked 175th among 188 economies with available statistics, 13th from the bottom and amongst the last 6.9%, indicating a typical least developed country; by 1990, China ranked 178th among 200 economies with available statistics, 22nd from the bottom and amongst the last 11.0%, by which China basically resolved the subsistence challenge for its population[1]; in 2000, China ranked 141st among 207 economies with

[1] Report of the 14th CPC National Congress pointed out that the subsistence problem has been basically resolved for 1.1 billion people, as China is striding toward a moderately prosperous society. Jiang Zemin: *Quickening the Pace of Reform, Opening-up and Modernization Construction, Aiming for Greater Victories of the Cause of Socialism with Chinese Characteristics—Report at the 14th CPC National Congress* (October 12, 1992).

S. Zhou, A. Hu, *China: Surpassing the "Middle Income Trap"*,
Contemporary China Studies,
https://doi.org/10.1007/978-981-15-6540-3_5

available statistics, 66th from the bottom and amongst the last 31.9%, marking the country's entrance into the lower-middle-income bracket with a moderately prosperous society shaped in general[2]; by 2015, China ranked 96th among 214 economies with available statistics, 44.6% from the top as the country stepped into the upper-middle-income phase and is at a critically strategic stage to build a moderately prosperous society in all aspects. The basic plan for the next step is to enter the high-income phase and successfully become a high-income country within the next decade through overcoming the "middle income trap".

5.1 Income Group Classification of China's Provincial Regions

Based on the World Bank statistics, we have conducted an analysis of countries and regions with population over 1 million from 1995 to 2015 using absolute income method (GNI per capita in US dollars, statistics based on *Atlas* method) and relative income method (PPP, international dollar in 2011), aiming to understand China's development track from a low-income to a moderately high-income level from the perspective of international development. Statistics of 1995, 2005 and 2015 have been chosen with data samples spanning 20 years.

5.1.1 Absolute Income Method

According to the absolute income method, in 1995, the aggregate population of low-income countries (GNI per capita below 765 US dollars) accounted for 57.0% of the world population; that of lower-middle-income countries (GNI per capita between 765 and 3035 US dollars) accounted for 18.2% of the world population; that of upper-middle-income countries (GNI per capita between 3035 and 8955 US dollars) accounted for 8.6% of the world population while that of high-income countries (GNI above 8955 US dollars) accounted for 16.2% of world

[2] Report of the 16th CPC National Congress pointed out that the people's livelihood has basically achieved the historical leap forward from basic subsistence to a moderately prosperous society. Yet the moderate prosperity currently achieved is at a low level, incomplete and imbalanced. Jiang Zemin: *Building a Moderately Prosperous Society in All Aspects and Opening a New Chapter in the Cause of Socialism with Chinese Characteristics—Report at the 16th CPC National Congress* (November 8, 2002).

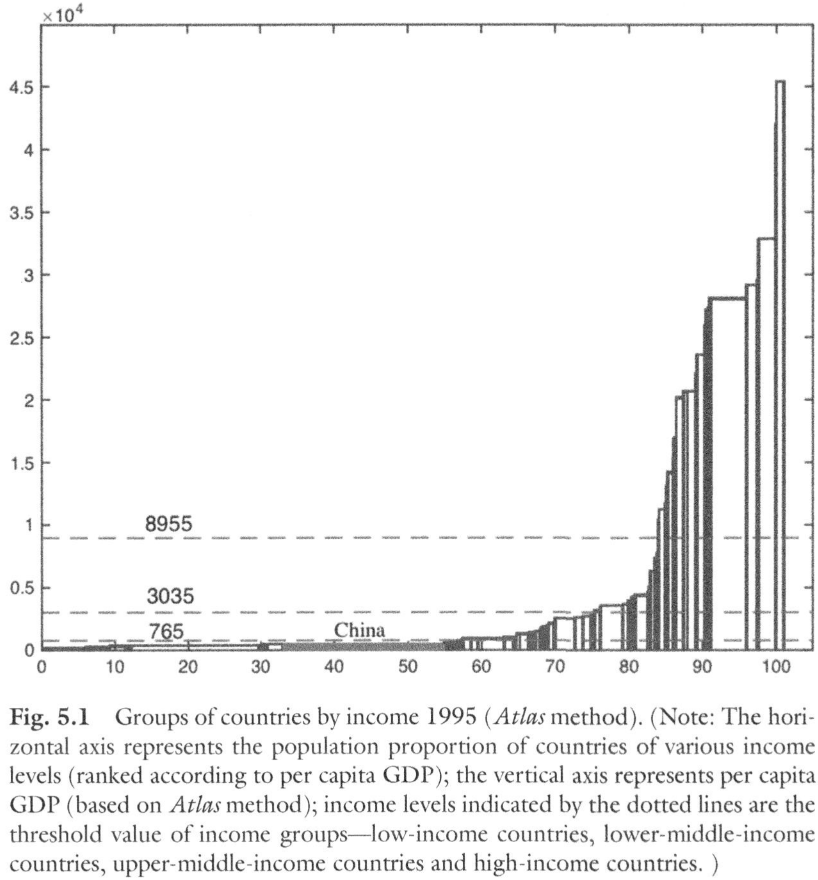

Fig. 5.1 Groups of countries by income 1995 (*Atlas* method). (Note: The horizontal axis represents the population proportion of countries of various income levels (ranked according to per capita GDP); the vertical axis represents per capita GDP (based on *Atlas* method); income levels indicated by the dotted lines are the threshold value of income groups—low-income countries, lower-middle-income countries, upper-middle-income countries and high-income countries.)

population. In 1995, China was categorized as a low-income country with GNI per capita of 540 US dollars, accounting for 38.4% of the total population of low-income countries (see Fig. 5.1).

According to the absolute income method, in 2005, the aggregate population of low-income countries (GNI per capita below 825 US dollars) accounted for 36.6% of the world population; that of lower-middle-income countries (GNI per capita between 825 and 3465 US dollars) accounted for 35.2% of the world population; that of upper-middle-income countries (GNI per capita between 3465 and 10,725 US dollars)

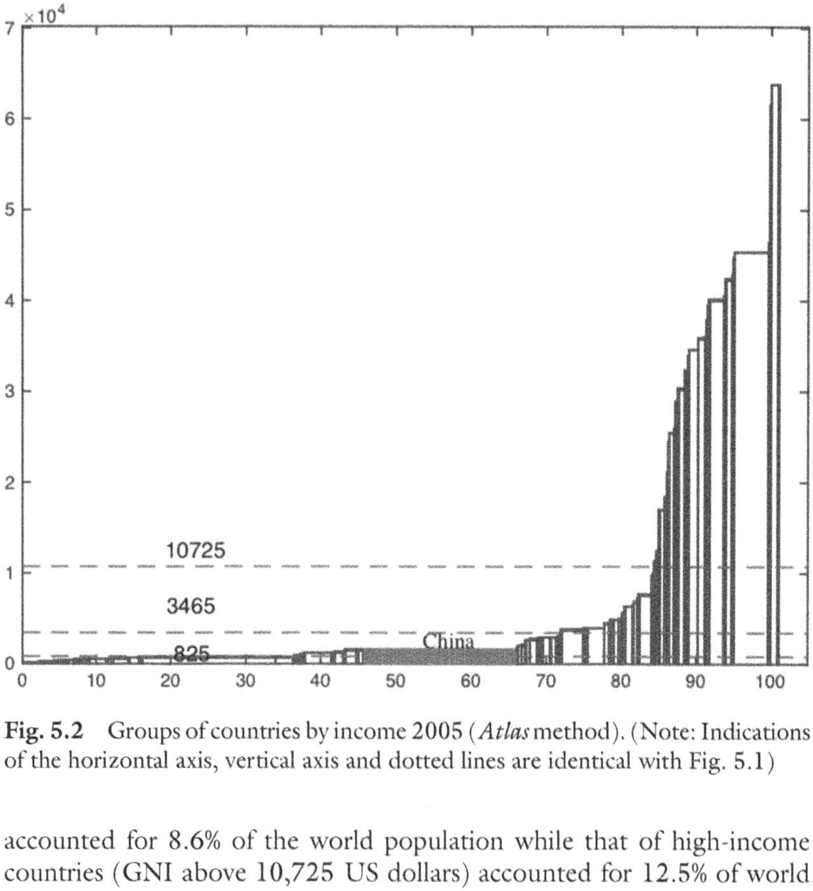

Fig. 5.2 Groups of countries by income 2005 (*Atlas* method). (Note: Indications of the horizontal axis, vertical axis and dotted lines are identical with Fig. 5.1)

accounted for 8.6% of the world population while that of high-income countries (GNI above 10,725 US dollars) accounted for 12.5% of world population (see Fig. 5.2). In 2005, China was categorized as a lower-middle-income country with GNI per capita of 1760 US dollars, accounting for 57.9% of the total population of lower-middle-income countries.

According to the absolute income method, in 2015, the aggregate population of low-income countries (GNI per capita below 1045 US dollars) accounted for 8.4% of the world population; that of lower-middle-income countries (GNI per capita between 1045 and 4125 US dollars) accounted for 40.7% of the world population; that of upper-middle-income countries (GNI per capita between 4125 and 12,735 US dollars) accounted for 37.7% of the world population while that of high-income countries (GNI above 12,735 US dollars) accounted for 16.2% of world

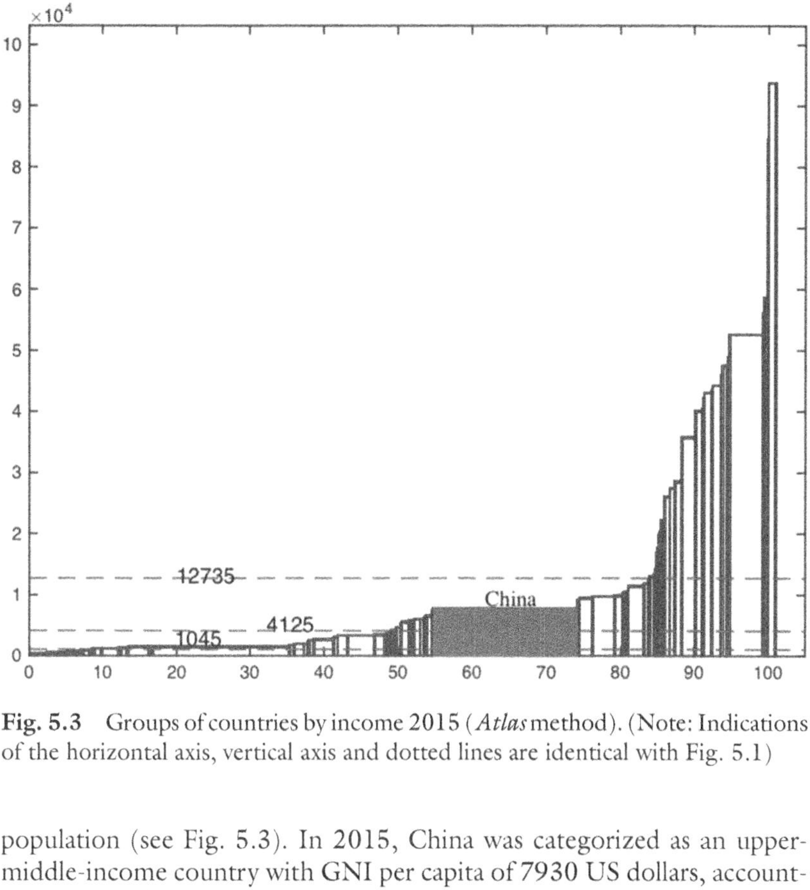

Fig. 5.3 Groups of countries by income 2015 (*Atlas* method). (Note: Indications of the horizontal axis, vertical axis and dotted lines are identical with Fig. 5.1)

population (see Fig. 5.3). In 2015, China was categorized as an upper-middle-income country with GNI per capita of 7930 US dollars, accounting for 51.3% of the total population of upper-middle-income countries.

5.1.2 *Relative Income Method*

Based on the relative income method, in 1995, the aggregate population of low-income countries (per capita GDP at constant prices of 2011 below 5% of the U.S.) accounted for 9.2% of the world population; that of middle-income countries (per capita GDP at constant prices of 2011 between 5% and 40% of the U.S.) accounted for 74.2% of the world population while that of high-income countries (per capita GDP at constant prices of 2011 above 40% of the U.S.) accounted for 16.6% of the world

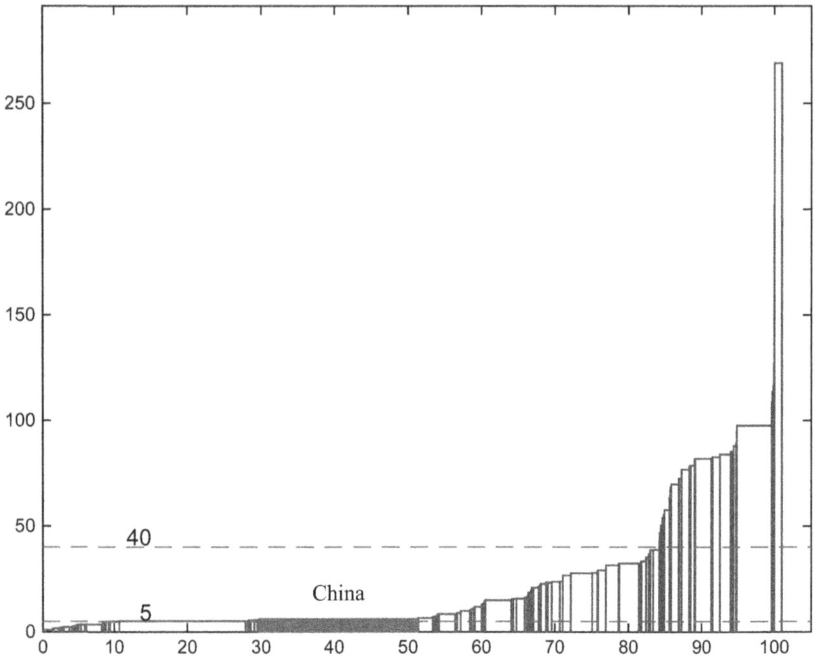

Fig. 5.4 Per capita GDP of countries in 1995 relative to that of the U.S. (Note: The horizontal axis represents the population proportion of countries of various income levels (ranked in the order of per capita GDP); the vertical axis represents the percentage of per capita GDP (PPP, in international dollar in 2011) in relation to the U.S.; the dotted lines correspond to 5% and 40% respectively, representing the threshold value of low-income countries, middle-income countries and high-income countries according to the relative income method)

population (see Fig. 5.4). Based on the relative income method, China's per capita GDP in 1995 was 6.5% of the U.S., slightly above the 5% threshold of low-income countries.

Based on the relative income method, in 2005, the aggregate population of low-income countries accounted for 11.1% of the world population; that of middle-income countries accounted for 72.9% of the world population while that of high-income countries accounted for 16.0% of the world population. According to the relative income method, China's per capita GDP in 2005 was 11.5% of the U.S., an increase of 5 percentage points compared to 1995, during which China ranked among

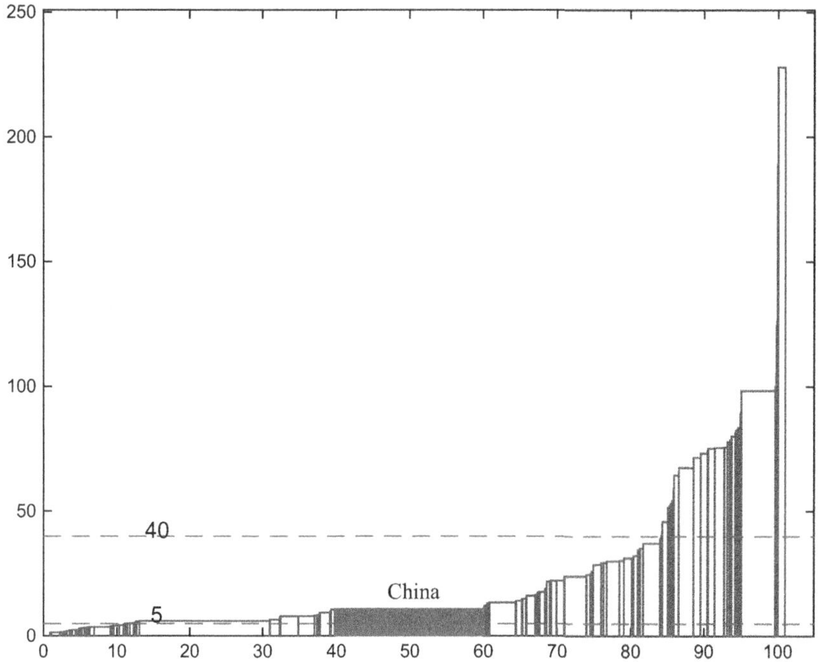

Fig. 5.5 Per capita GDP of countries in 2005 relative to that of the U.S.

middle-income countries. Between 1995 and 2005, the convergence coefficient of per capita GDP between China and the U.S. was 5.9% annually (see Fig. 5.5).

Based on the relative income method, in 2015, the aggregate population of low-income countries accounted for 8.9% of the world population; that of middle-income countries accounted for 72.2% of the world population while that of high-income countries accounted for 18.9% of the world population (see Fig. 5.6). Based on the relative income method, China's per capita GDP in 2015 was 25.4% of the U.S., an increase of 13.9 percentage points compared to 2005, indicating that the gap of per capita GDP significantly narrowed down between China and the U.S. despite China remaining a middle-income country. Between 2005 and 2015, the convergence coefficient of per capita GDP between China and the U.S. was 8.2% annually, which was higher than that between 1995 and 2005,

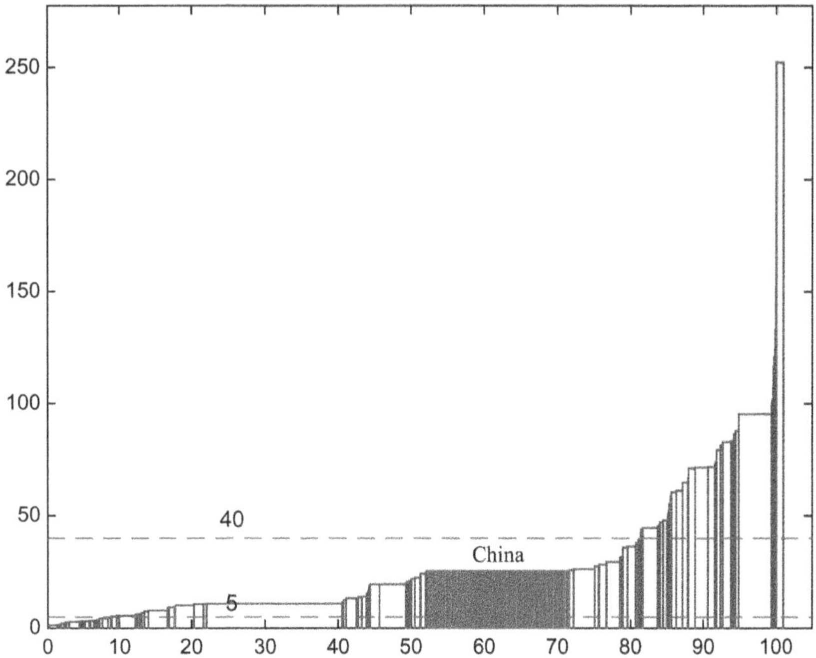

Fig. 5.6 Per capita GDP of countries in 2015 relative to that of the U.S.

indicating that despite the slowdown in growth of per capita GDP during this period, China had quickened its pace in catching up with the U.S. in per capita income.

5.2 A Region-by-Region Statistical Analysis of Overcoming the "Middle Income Trap" in China

Showing the most significant regional disparity in the world, China is referred to as "one China, four worlds (i.e. four income groups)", which is part of the basic reality of China. Nevertheless, rather than remaining static, such a pattern is changing dynamically, constantly leaping toward a higher level. Therefore, understanding China's gradual transition from a low-income country to a high-income one would also require putting this process in various regional contexts. Based on the amount of US dollars of

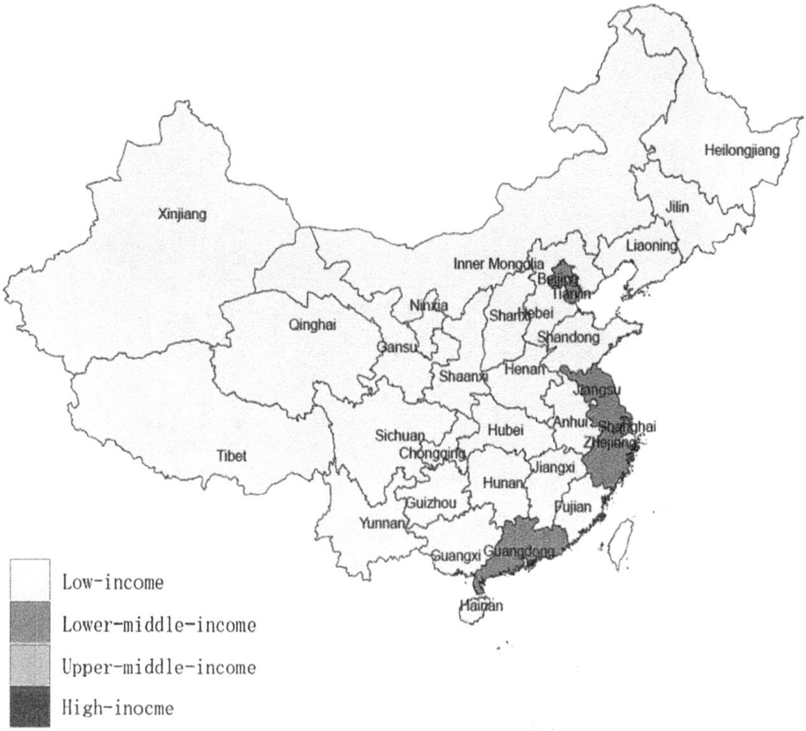

Fig. 5.7 Income groups by region (1995)

per capita GDP (*Atlas* method) and the threshold of income groups announced by the World Bank every year, we have illustrated the income groups that various regions in China belonged to between 1995 and 2015.

In 1995, Shanghai was the only Chinese city in the upper-middle-income group, while coastal regions in Eastern China, the three provinces of Northeast, Inner Mongolia, Xinjiang, Hubei and Chongqing reached lower-middle-income level, and other parts of Central and West China all belonged to low-income regions (see Fig. 5.7). Therefore, from a holistic view, China was an economically backward country in 1995 in relative terms.

In 2005, Shanghai, Beijing and Tianjin all crossed over the upper-middle-income threshold while all other regions except for Guizhou, which remained in the low-income group, were amongst the lower-middle-income ranks (see Fig. 5.8). Therefore, in 2005, China worked its

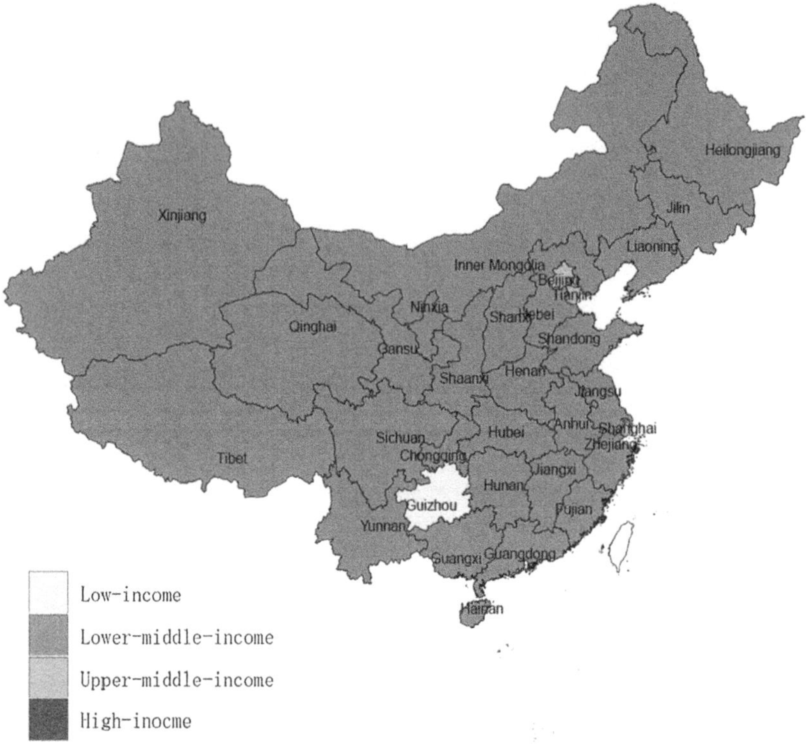

Fig. 5.8 Income groups by region (2005)

way into the lower-middle-income group on the whole, showing remarkable improvement as compared to 1995.

In 2015, five regions in China secured their positions in the high-income group, namely Beijing, Tianjin, Shanghai, Jiangsu and Zhejiang, while all other regions in China crossed over the upper-middle-income threshold (see Fig. 5.9). Additionally, per capita GDP of Inner Mongolia, Liaoning, Fujian, Guangdong and Shandong exceeded 10,000 US dollars, adding up to 507.8 million permanent residents which accounted for 36.9% of the Chinese population (1.3746 billion), equal to the total population of the EU (509.9 million) and 1.58 times of the total population of the U.S. (321.4 million). The population in the rest of the 21 provinces, municipalities and autonomous regions also entered the upper-middle-income stage, accounting for less than two-thirds of the population. This means that over one-third of China, mostly the coastal regions, has successfully overcome the "middle income trap" and entered high-income

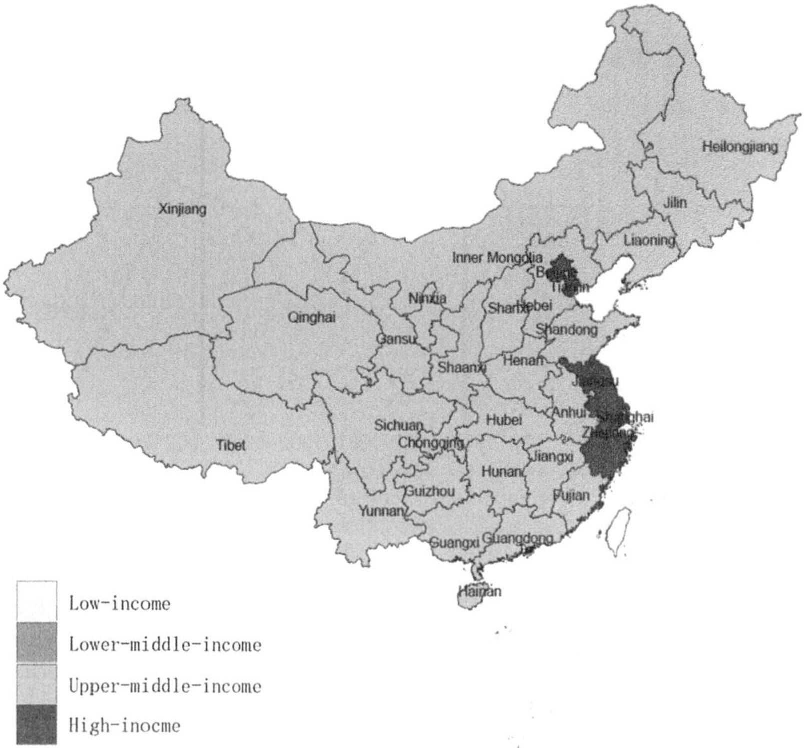

Fig. 5.9 Income groups by region (2015)

stage, which is expected to ignite the momentum for the entire country to sail through the middle-income stage and cross the high-income threshold.

Seen from the changes in income groups based on per capita GDP from 1995 to 2015, all regions maintained the momentum of progressing toward the higher-income group, while no province remained in the low-income or lower-middle-income stage, which was consistent with the trend of changing regional disparity in economic development. From the perspective of regional disparity in economic development, the relative difference coefficient of per capita GDP saw an increase from 64.0% in 1995 to the peak value of 75.1% in 2004 before a continuous decrease of up to 43.5% in 2014, reflecting a tendency of continuous convergence (see Fig. 5.10). This also indicates that overall, relatively backward regions in China are catching up with relatively developed regions, with economic development gaps narrowing down and a more balanced development among regions. If such trend is to continue, economic development across

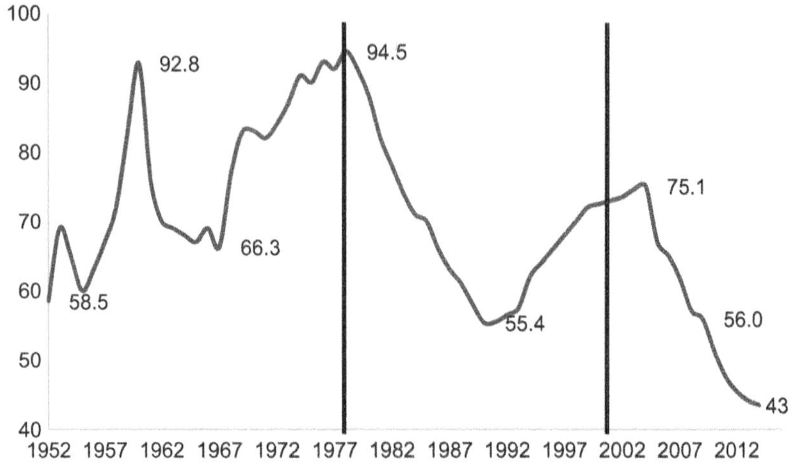

Fig. 5.10 Relative difference coefficient of per capita GDP across regions (1952–2014)

regions in China shall make their way toward the high-income level together with the overall development of China's economy, and regions currently struggling in underdeveloped economy shall gradually earn their positions in the high-income group.

Such trend is also attributable to the strategy of balanced regional economic development implemented in the new millennium. For over a decade, the masterplan of development of Western China, rejuvenation of the Northeast, rising of Central China and pioneering role of Eastern China has taken shape, which, in the context of an increasingly open economy and more efforts in infrastructure improvement of landlocked regions, has enabled the development of coastal regions to boost the development of other regions, with Beijing, Tianjin, Shanghai, Jiangsu and Zhejiang entering the high-income group while other coastal regions and Inner Mongolia are ready for the crossover as well. This will drive other regions currently in the middle- and upper-middle-income groups to leap into the higher-income bracket, which is comparable to the opening and economic take-off of the eastern region in boosting the opening-up and soaring economy of the entire country.

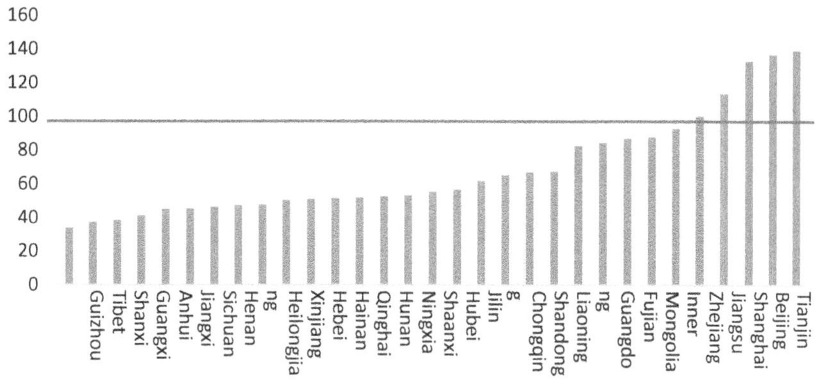

Fig. 5.11 Per capita GDP of various regions as a percentage of high-income threshold (%) in 2015. (Note: Based on China's per capita GDP (international dollar value) in 2015, the international dollar value of per capita GDP of various provinces is calculated based on the relative value of per capita GDP against national per capita GDP; these values of provincial per capita GDP are divided by the high-income threshold value to calculate the percentage of per capita GDP of various regions in comparison with the high-income threshold)

Fourthly, a new pattern of "four zones and three strategies" has been shaped in recent years with China's design and implementation of three key strategies, namely the Belt and Road Initiative, the coordinated development of Beijing, Tianjin and Hebei and the Yangtze River Economic Belt. They have invigorated the dynamism of the four zones while building channels for their connectivity, releasing tremendous momentum for the integration of zones, regions and countries. These trends will also help regions in China to overcome the "middle income trap" and step into the high-income group sooner or later.

Of course, the journey toward the high-income bracket is not a synchronized process for all regions in China. Seen from the percentage of per capita GDP (PPP, in international dollar, 2011) of various regions in 2015 in comparison with the high-income threshold value (Fig. 5.11), there exists remarkable regional disparity in the gap between such threshold values, indicating the overall regional characteristics of China in its efforts to advance toward a high-income country.

5.3 Forecast and Outlook for China's Overcoming of the "Middle Income Trap"

The essential precondition to overcome the "middle income trap" is economic growth. Since the 12th Five-Year Plan period, China has been experiencing economic slowdown due to the external impact of the international financial crisis, especially the subsequent global economic downturn. As China's economy steps into the "new normal",[3] its growth rate shows a decrease compared to approximately 10% at the turn of the century yet still maintained a 7.8% growth during the 12th Five-Year Plan period.

The goal of overcoming the "middle income trap" has been clearly stated in the 13th Five-Year Plan for Economic and Social Development. To this end, the anticipatory economic growth target is set at above 6.5% in light of the goal defined at the 18th CPC National Congress (GDP shall double by 2020 on the basis of 2010), changing growth speed, structural optimization and changing growth drivers in the context of the "new normal" of economic development, which is expected to contribute to the growth of better quality and higher efficiency.

Considering the natural population growth of approximately 0.5%, the anticipated growth rate of per capita GDP would exceed 6% during the 13th Five-Year Plan period, so an analysis of China's per capita GDP can be conducted at different growth scenarios according to the World Bank's criteria of income groups (*Atlas* method). China's estimated GNI per capita in 2015 was 7930 US dollars according to the World Bank, and the following provides three forecasts of the growth rate of China's GNI per capita, where the conservative forecast is 5%, the neutral forecast is 6% and the optimistic forecast is 7%. In all three scenarios, China's GNI per capita would range between 10,121 and 11,122 US dollars by 2020, close to the high-income threshold and between 12,917 and 15,600 US dollars by 2025, crossing the threshold of high-income countries (see Fig. 5.12).[4]

Based on the *Atlas* method, we may back-calculate the economic growth rate required for China's GNI per capita to reach the high-income threshold as in 2015 (12,745 US dollars). Figure 5.13 shows the average growth rates required for China to cross over the high-income threshold in any year between 2020 and 2025. It is expected that China will enter

[3] Refer to Angang Hu (2015) for the description of the "New Normal" of economy.

[4] According to the criteria defined by the World Bank in 2015, income per capita of 12,735 US dollars (based on *Atlas* method) is the threshold of high-income countries.

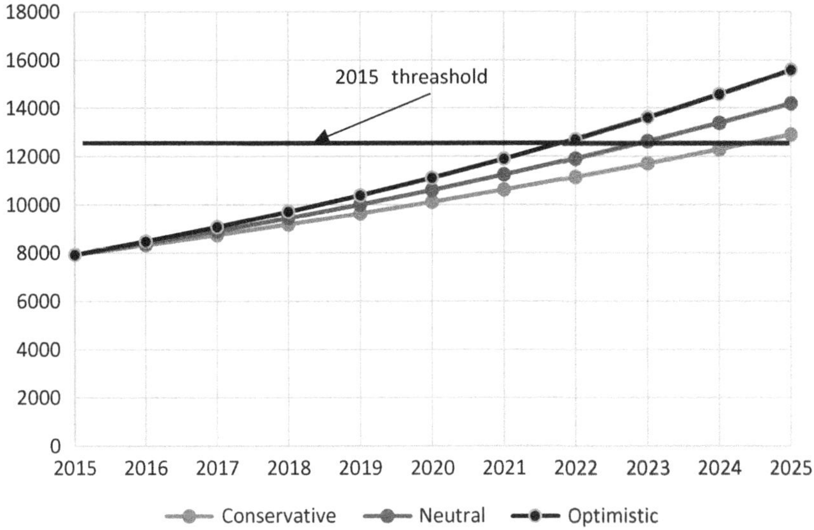

Fig. 5.12 China's GNI per capita (2010–2025)

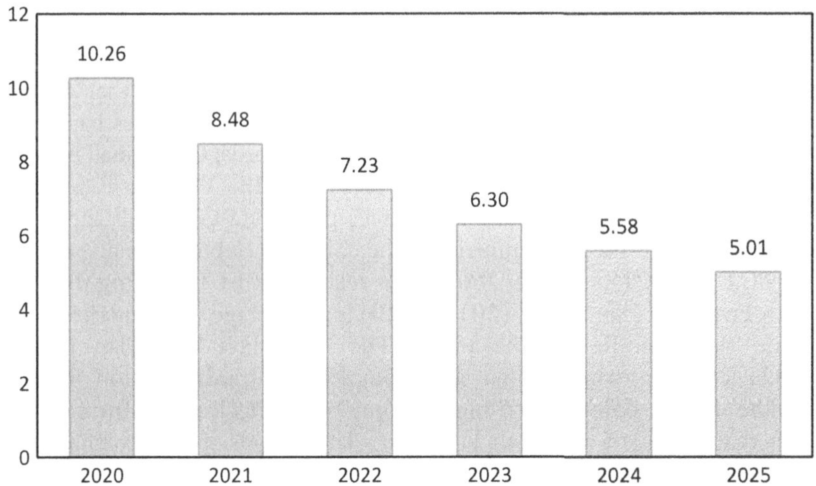

Fig. 5.13 Average growth required of China to cross the high-income threshold in various years (2020–2025)

the high-income group by 2025 provided that the growth rate of per capita GDP remains above 5% during the 14th Five-Year Plan period. In addition, as China strides toward the ranks of high-income countries, its GDP will also overtake that of the U.S. based on the exchange rate method. It will be another milestone after China's GDP exceeded that of the U.S. based on the PPP method in 2014.

Based on the calculation method of relative income, the World Bank has provided the relative criteria of per capita GDP (PPP, international dollar in 2011) as compared to the U.S. in purchasing power parity, where countries whose per capita GDP is below 5% of that of the U.S. are categorized as low-income countries while those with per capita GDP above 40% of that of the U.S. are recognized as high-income countries. According to the World Bank database, in 1990, China's per capita GDP accounted for 4.11% of that of the U.S., and increased to 8.05% in 2000, 19.29% in 2010 and 25.75% in 2015. In terms of the difference in growth rate of per capita GDP, China was ahead of the U.S. by an average of 8.45 percentage points from 2005 to 2015, of which the difference was 6.02 percentage points from 2010 to 2015. Likewise, three assumptions have been made for China's efforts to catch up with the U.S. in per capita GDP, that is higher by 5%, 6% and 7% compared to the U.S. between 2016 and 2025, corresponding to the conservative estimation, neutral estimation and optimistic estimation, respectively. Based on the assumption of the three scenarios, China's per capita GDP (PPP) will exceed 40% of that of the U.S. by 2022 to 2024, ranking among high-income countries based on the relative income criteria (Fig. 5.14). In other words, China shall be able to overcome the "middle income trap" before 2025.

The above forecasts show that China's per capita GDP will approach the level of high-income countries as the country celebrates its first centenary (i.e. in 2021), in either absolute or relative terms, indicating that the 13th Five-Year Plan period (2016–2020) is a key stage for China to overcome the "middle income trap". The 14th Five-Year Plan period (2021–2025) is when China shall complete its transformation from a middle-income country to a high-income one. This leads to the conclusion that the 13th and 14th Five-Year Plan periods are a key phase for China to overcome the "middle income trap", which also represents the core targets and development measures in understanding and implementing both Five-Year Plans.

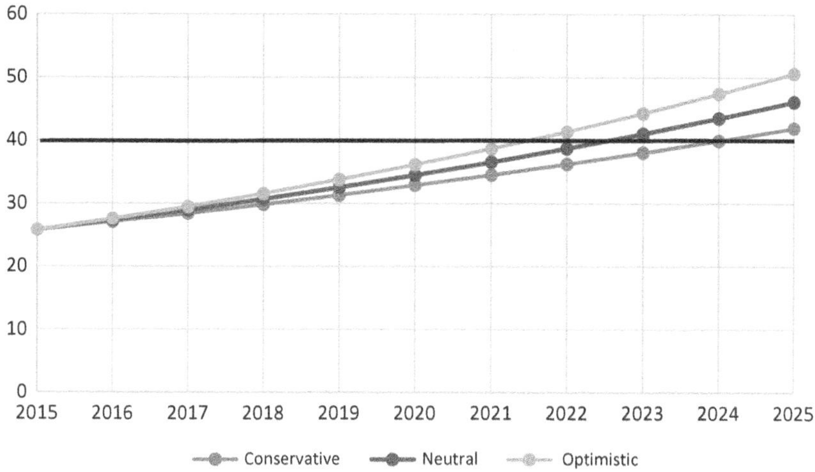

Fig. 5.14 China's per capita GDP relative to the U.S. (2015–2025)

5.4 Formation of the Chinese Path

In retrospect of China's modern history, since the Opium War, the country has undergone over 100 years of humiliation by big powers, internal unrests and endless sufferings of the people, with neither basic conditions nor capabilities to explore the Chinese path of development based on the needs and will of its people. From 1949 to 1978, after three decades of arduous efforts exploring the Chinese path as an independent nation, from 1978 to around 2022, dedication and perseverance of two generations are transforming a country amidst poverty and backwardness into a country overcoming the "middle income trap" and securing its position among high-income countries, making the great rejuvenation of the Chinese nation a reality for the first time.

A review of the world economic development since the 1960s shows that overcoming the "middle income trap" is indeed a major challenge for developing countries. As the above analysis indicates, based on nearly four decades of socialist development since the reform and opening-up, China sees its socialist institutional system maturing, accommodating China's reality while taking the initiative to address challenges posed by changing external conditions. China's development since the founding of the country in 1949 testifies to its evolution from an underdeveloped country struggling in the dire fate of poverty and weakness to a socialist power achieving its goal of building a moderately prosperous society through hardships in pursuit of socialist modernization. This is a remarkable achievement not only in the history of the Chinese nation but also in the development of mankind. Such a brilliant feat is attributable fundamentally to the fact that China has persevered in choosing its development path on its own initiative based on the country's reality and people's desire for development.

Since the early years after the founding of new China in 1949, the Communist Party of China has never ceased its exploration for the country's unique development path. The first generation of central collective leadership represented by Mao Zedong were the designers, pioneers and practitioners of the Chinese path. For example, the people's congress system was established rather than the parliamentary system of the West or the soviet system of the former Soviet Union; the system of multi-party cooperation and political consultation under the leadership of the CPC was created rather than two or multiple parties ruling in turn as seen in the West or the single-party system in the former Soviet Union; a multi-ethnic unified country with regional ethnic autonomy in place rather than federalism in the U.S. or the former Soviet Union. The facts since the founding of new China in 1949 proves that these fundamental political systems are suitable for China's reality as a heavily populated country with vast territory, significant regional differences and rural-urban disparity; they are in line with the historical path and future trend of development as a unified and powerful nation featuring both diversity and solidarity.

The trials and practices of the Chinese path are not without frustrations and setbacks, which have been more attributable to internal determinants than to external factors. For example, in the late 1950s and early 1960s, the radical ups and downs in economic development due to the Great Leap Forward and the three years of natural disasters almost nullified the good start of the First Five-Year Plan. Subsequently, a decade of havoc of the Cultural Revolution from 1966 to 1976 inflicted major damages to the fundamental systems of the country and heavy loss on the Party and the nation, causing China to miss the golden opportunity to catch up with developed countries. An overview of the development of the world economy in the wake of World War II leads to the observation that the period between 1950 and 1973 was a golden era of world economic development with rapid growth recorded in all major developed countries. Although the growth of China's per capita GDP during this period was not far from the world's average, such growth indicated a major economic underperformance considering China's growth potentials. From a longer historical perspective, had it not been for these major setbacks, China would have highly likely already crossed the high-income threshold. The root cause of such frustrations includes two dimensions: first, an unrealistic path of development, such as the Great Leap Forward that taught China a hard lesson; second, failure in grasping the basic contradiction in the country's development by emphasizing on "politics as priority" and "class struggle" while ignoring the basic contradiction between the growing material and cultural demand of the people and underdeveloped productivity.

As the saying goes, "a fall into the pit, a gain in your wit", the failure in Mao Zedong's late years provided experience and lessons for his successor, Deng Xiaoping, who was both a participant and practitioner of the Chinese path initiated by the first generation of leaders and an heir to this path dedicated to its rectification, exploration and re-innovation. As the chief designer of China's reform and opening-up, he was driven by a sense of urgency as he witnessed the backwardness of China after the Cultural Revolution; meanwhile, as a victim of this political and social havoc, he truly understood the dire consequences of damages done to the nation's fundamental system and the importance of rebuilding the institutional system. Refusing to pour new wine into the old wineskins, Deng Xiaoping objectively commented on Mao Zedong's historical contribution, safeguarding the authority of the Party. Rejecting the doctrine of "two whatevers", he re-established the ideological direction to seek truth from facts, opening up the path of socialist modernization with Chinese characteristics constituting three major factors: modernization, socialism and Chinese characteristics. Modernization is to initiate change in the underdeveloped country which, of course, places economic development at the core; socialism refers to the goal of common prosperity and development for the wellbeing of all; Chinese characteristics indicate that socialist development must proceed from China's reality and that the Chinese path of development shall be shaped with an innovative mind.

Since the reform and opening-up, "economic development at the core" has been at the central position in the basic line of the primary stage of socialism, which essentially secured China's stability in development and enabled the country to survive the trials of international political storm. In the late 1980s and early 1990s, a wave of abandoning the socialist path for the capitalist path engulfed the former Soviet Union and former socialist countries in Eastern Europe, all of which suffered from economic recession, significant deterioration of people's wellbeing to various extents and even division of the nation. Undoubtedly, such transition was an erroneous move and the internal and external political vicissitudes during this period posed a daunting challenge at China's stability and development at the time. However, rather than taking the wrong turn by changing its nature and abandoning its system, China unswervingly adhered to the leadership of the Party, and did not retrace its steps to the rigidity and isolation of the past. Rather, China renewed its efforts in firmly pressing ahead with the cause of the reform and opening-up, clarifying the direction for its economic transition and opening a new chapter of building a socialist market economy.

More than 20 years have passed since the beginning of the 1990s, almost equivalent to one generation's time. In retrospect, the significant indication of China's firm position at this critical historical moment is self-explanatory for the country's development in over two decades that followed. It can be safely stated that China would have possibly missed some major opportunities for development had it not been for the country's pursuit of both socialism and market economy with Chinese characteristics. Such conclusion can be easily drawn with reference to what Russia experienced in the 1990s. With its entry into WTO at the turn of the century, China took an unprecedented active role in economic globalization. By 2013, China had become the world's biggest trading country in goods. Moreover, China overtook Japan in becoming the world's second largest economy in 2010 (based on exchange rate). If calculated by PPP, China ranked the biggest economy in 2014, replacing the U.S. The vision of the first generation of leadership in the early years of new China finally came true.

The fundamental reason for China's enormous achievements in building socialism with Chinese characteristics is that the Party has firmly stood with the people, incorporating the historical mission of the Party with its affinity to the people, proactively explored the Chinese path in line with China's reality, fundamental interests of the people and the general trends of global development. China's practice in development since the reform and opening-up is the Chinese path.[5] In a sense, the secret for China's feat since the reform and opening-up is no other but China's perseverance in its own course of development, dedicated to an unceasing exploration into building socialism with Chinese characteristics. From the 13th to the 18th CPC National Congress, "socialism with Chinese characteristics" has remained the key phrase in the theme of every report. The targets, tasks and safeguard mechanisms identified for building socialism in each development stage represent not only unrelenting efforts in pursuing the socialist path but also stage-specific innovations in the form of socialism in practice. As President Xi Jinping stated, "this is the correct path found by the Chinese people after long and arduous efforts in exploration".[6]

Not only securing China's development, the Chinese path also constitutes an important pillar in the development of the world, which is reflected in China's contributions to the world economy in the wake of the Southeast Asian financial crisis in 1998 and the global financial crisis triggered by the U.S. sub-prime mortgage crisis in 2008. The Southeast Asian financial crisis sweeping across Southeast Asia in 1998 reduced numerous Southeast Asian countries as well as neighboring countries including South Korea and Russia into economic recession to various degrees. Likewise, China's firm position and pledge that RMB will not devalue played a key role in stabilizing the economy in East and Southeast Asia.

Amidst the global financial crisis in 2008, China again became the cornerstone of the stability of the world economy. The global impact of this economic crisis might be second to none in the post-war world, its scope and severity comparable to the Great Depression between 1929 and 1933, with the world economy still not yet fully recovered from this havoc up to now. Objectively speaking, despite the fact that China was also victimized by this global financial crisis with symptoms of economic downturn, it still played a pivotal role in stabilizing the global economic growth. According to the World Bank statistics, at constant prices in US dollars in 2010, the annual contribution of China's economic growth to the world economy reached 30.5% during the 12th Five-Year Plan period, overtaking the U.S.; China ascended to the first place in the world with the contribution of

[5] Deng Xiaoping made the statement of pursuing our own course and building socialism with Chinese characteristics in the opening address of the 12th CPC National Congress.

[6] Xi Jinping's speech at the meeting with foreign delegates attending the Twenty-First Century Council Beijing Conference on November 2, 2013.

17.8% for the U.S. and 4.4% for the euro zone during the same period.[7] Also, China's contribution increased by 16.3 percentage points compared to 14.2% annually during the 10th and 11th Five-Year Plan periods.

President Xi Jinping pointed out at the G20 Saint Petersburg Summit (the eighth meeting of the G20 heads of state) the impact of China's economy on the world economy:

> China, with close integration of its economy and the world, more stability in economic operation, higher quality of growth and more sustainable growth, is in the interest of the world economy in the long run; China has the conditions and abilities to achieve a sustainable and sound economic development and create for other countries an even broader market and more development space.

In fact, China's contribution to the world economic growth overtaking that of the U.S. has already become "normal". At constant prices in US dollars in 2010, the GDP of the U.S. in 2015 was 16.6 trillion US dollars while that of China registered at 8.91 trillion US dollars, that is, the GDP of U.S. was 1.86 times of China's GDP which indicates that as long as China's economic growth is above 1.86 times of the U.S., China's contribution to the world economic growth would overtake the U.S. The long-term trend of economic growth of the U.S. shows that over 2.5% growth would be deemed impressive. Despite the forecast of further slowdown in China's future economic growth, in the next 15 years, that is by 2030, there is still a high probability that China's average economic growth would exceed 5%, meaning that it would be normal for China's contribution to the world economic growth to overtake that of the U.S., which would be of significant impact on world economic landscape. In this sense, the Chinese path is of global significance.

It goes without saying that China will continue confronting various challenges in pursuing the Chinese path ahead, as the path is exactly shaped and improved by taking on such challenges. Nevertheless, it would be unwise to hold the Chinese path in suspicion or even allege that China is about to collapse. For over two decades, the scaremongering forecast of the collapse of China has never ceased in the international community, yet such cry-wolf assertions would not change their nature of pseudo-preposition. Likewise, the theory that China has fallen into the "middle

[7] During the 12th Five-Year Plan period, in terms of annual contribution rate, the contribution rates of China's economic growth respectively reached 28.6%, 31.7%, 32.5%, 29.7% and 30.0% from 2011 to 2015; while that of the U.S. economic growth were respectively 11.8%, 20.4%, 15.2%, 19.6% and 21.9% during the same period.

income trap" has been looming over the international arena, which is as much of a pseudo-preposition as the previous assertation. Be it the "poverty trap" when China was struggling as a low-income country, or the "middle income trap" encountered in the middle-income stage or even the "high income trap" in the future when China ranks among high-income countries, development is always accompanied by challenges while progress is never without traps, yet China has successfully overcome each trap in its journey from extremely-low-income to low-income level, then to lower-middle-income and upper-middle-income level, eventually crossing the high-income threshold. With three decades of reform and opening-up, both the CPC central committee and the general public are growing in rationality, maturity and wisdom, therefore China will by no means stray into the "middle income trap".

The next step in China's development is to achieve high-income level and gradually attain the goal of common prosperity.[8] Despite the considerable gap between China and developed countries in the Western hemisphere as well as Japan in terms of economic development level when China leaps over the "middle income trap", China is on track to maintain the high speed in catching up with developed countries provided that its economic transformation proves successful and that an innovation-driven development model is in place. Take South Korea as an example, the country's per capita GDP exceeded 40% of that of the U.S. in 1994 for the first time (PPP, international dollar in 2011), followed by its membership in OECD in 1996 when its per capita GDP was around 44% of that of the U.S., which may be regarded as a milestone of South Korea to preliminarily make it as a moderately developed country. In 2015, South Korea's per capita GDP increased to 65.2% of that of the U.S., by which the country fully deserved its position as a moderately developed country. This also shows that South Korea maintained a considerably high speed in catching up with the U.S. after crossing the threshold of high-income countries. Therefore, if China's per capita GDP reaches 5% of annual growth between 2016 and 2030, by the year 2030, it will be on par with South Korea in per capita GDP in 2007 and 2008 (approximately 28,200 US dollars). In this sense, it is highly possible that China will, on the whole, rank among moderately developed countries between 2030 and 2040, fulfilling the third step of Deng Xiaoping's "three-step strategy" ahead of time.

[8] Hu Angang, Yan Yilong, Wei Xing: *China in 2030: Towards Common Prosperity*, Beijing, China Renmin University Press, 2011.

5.5 The Global Significance of China's Overcoming of the "Middle Income Trap"

In September 2000, the Millennium Development Goals (MDG) were announced by the United Nations, covering global development goals in eight areas. Jiang Zemin, Chinese president at the time, pointed out at the United Nations Millennium Summit that "the economic globalization that we need is one that features win-win, equality, fairness and co-existence among all countries, and the key to promoting common development of mankind is to establish a new international economic and social order characterized by justice and rationality". From 2000 to 2015, China actively responded to the initiative of MDGs and successively mapped out and implemented the 10th, 11th and 12th Five-Year Plans, achieving not only key economic and social development goals in China but also MDGs, and becoming the top performer in MDG fulfillment in the developing world with excellent achievements. Meanwhile, China has also actively engaged in South-South cooperation, assisting over 120 developing countries in MDG implementation, which has been unanimously recognized by the international community. During this period, China also completed its journey from a low-income country to an upper-middle-income one, driving the total population of upper-middle-income countries up to 2.594 billion.

In September 2015, 193 member countries of the United Nations officially approved the Sustainable Development Goals (SDG) on the UN Sustainable Development Summit held at the UN headquarters in New York. Sustainable Development Goals aim at thoroughly addressing development issues in social, economic and ecological dimensions by taking comprehensive measures from 2015 to 2030, gearing toward sustainable development. President Xi Jinping gave a speech titled *Towards a Mutually Beneficial Partnership for Sustainable Development* at the Summit, encouraging the international community to step up cooperation in the joint implementation of the Post-2015 Development Agenda, with an aim to achieve a win-win outcome. To this end, President Xi Jinping made the following four proposals: to build up capacity for development, improve the international environment for development, optimize the partnership for development and to strengthen the coordination mechanisms for development. Meanwhile, he announced to the international community that China will continue to strike a balance between justice and its own interests by putting justice before such interests, contributing

China's strength to realize the sustainable development goals.[9] China has incorporated the 17 sustainable development goals into the 13th Five-Year Plan in order to drive the implementation of these goals. It is anticipated that with China ranking among high-income countries by 2025, China will make greater contributions to sustainable development proposed by the UN. We believe that China's striding toward a high-income country shall produce the following positive impact on world development.

First, China as a high-income country will dramatically enhance the current global economic landscape, thus producing positive impact on shaping a more reasonable and equitable international political and economic order. From a global perspective, the population in low-income, middle-income and high-income countries respectively totaled at 8.9%, 72.2% and 19.9% (relative income method) in 2015, representing an olive-shaped pattern of demographical distribution. Apart from those in the Western hemisphere, countries that genuinely ascended from middle-income to high-income level or joining the "developed world club" were very few in number, while most countries stumbled into the "middle income trap" to varying degrees and were unable to overcome it, which is exactly why Robert Zoellick, former president of the World Bank, pointed out that China's experience in the transition from a lower-middle-income society to a high-income one is of reference value for other middle-income economies.[10] China's entrance into a high-income society from the middle-income group will bring significant changes to the pattern of demographical distribution of low-income, middle-income and high-income countries in the world. By that time, the total population of high-income countries will exceed approximately 40% of the world population, which will be a major contribution to world development as such

[9] Including the following: China will establish an assistance fund for South-South cooperation, with an initial pledge of 2 billion US dollars to support developing countries in their implementation of the Post-2015 Development Agenda; China will continue to increase investment in the least-developed countries, aiming to attain a level of 12 billion US dollars by 2030; China will write off the debt on outstanding intergovernmental interest-free loans due by the end of 2015 owed by designated least-developed countries, landlocked developing countries, and small island developing countries; China will establish an international development knowledge center for studying and exchanging between countries on the theories and practice of development best-suited to their respective national conditions; China will propose a discussion on establishing a global energy internet to facilitate efforts to meet global power demand with clean and green alternatives.

[10] Xinhuanet, September 13, 2010, Beijing.

transformation is conducive to building an international governance system better suited for the appeals and demands of the vast developing world.

Besides, a high-income China will not only benefit the wellbeing of the Chinese people but also bring positive impact on the economic development of other countries through China's foreign trade and outbound direct investment. Evolving into a high-income country on the whole, China will gradually become the world's largest importer, generating trade and employment opportunities for developing countries and emerging economies. Calculated on the current dollar, China's import value of goods and services accounted for merely 0.88% of the world's import, followed by increases to 2.83% in 2000, 7.49% in 2010 and 9.87% in 2015, making China the second largest importer of goods and services after the U.S. (whose import value of goods and services accounted for 13.44% of the world's total). In particular, China has become the engine for world trade growth in the aftermath of the global financial crisis in 2008.

Between 2010 and 2015, the nominal growth of China's import of goods and services calculated on current dollar registered at 10.9%, higher than that of the U.S. (8.7%) and the world average (8.3%). It has to be pointed out that China harbors enormous potential for import. In 2015, the average percentage of import in goods and services in GDP was 25.8% globally, yet only 18.6% in China. With China's economic transition from an investment-driven growth to a consumption-driven growth, it is expected that China will become the world's No.1 importer of goods and services with total import exceeding 4 trillion US dollars.[11]

Furthermore, China is a major player in direct outward investment, with outward FDI reaching 145.7 billion US dollars in 2015 and the accumulated outward investment amounting to 1.0979 trillion US dollars in total, its share in accumulated global outward FDI increasing from 0.4% to 4.4%.[12] It is predicted that China's total outward FDI will range from 3 to 5 trillion US dollars between 2016 and 2025. Especially with the implementation of the Belt and Road Initiative, China will become the most important source of FDI for the developing world. Both the trend of international trade and the momentum of FDI show that China will be a

[11] China's GDP growth in US dollars is assumed to be 6% between 2016 and 2025, and import is estimated to account for 20% of GDP by 2025.

[12] Data source: Ministry of Commerce, PRC, National Bureau of Statistics, State Administration of Foreign Exchange, 2016, *2015 Statistical Bulletin of China's Outward Foreign Direct Investment*, China Statistics Press.

powerhouse for world economic and trade growth as it becomes a high-income country, creating enormous job opportunities for its trading partners and investment destinations.

Thirdly, China will contribute Chinese strength and Chinese wisdom to the world's green development as it evolves into a high-income country. As the biggest developing country and the most influential emerging economy in the world, China should not neglect its national conditions as well as the global trend and follow the path of "black development" traditionally pursued by Western countries in their industrialization; instead, China must seek its own path of green development in line with the global trend of green industrialization. Since the 11th Five-Year Plan, China's green development strategy has evolved in clarity, with the green development concept and path with Chinese characteristics explicitly stated in the 13th Five-Year Plan. In June 2007, the Chinese government formulated *China's National Climate Change Programme*, which was the first national plan specializing in combatting climate change in the developing world. Since then, China's top leadership over two terms (Hu Jintao and Xi Jinping) successively expanded China's position and commitment in tackling climate change.[13]

Regarding China's participation in the global governance of climate change, from Copenhagen Climate Change Conference to the Paris Conference, China is a key driver in the global governance of climate change, perhaps even playing an indispensable and pivotal role. In particular, China's active efforts represented a major contribution to reaching the Paris Climate Agreement at Paris Climate Change Conference in December 2015. In June 2016, China published *Enhanced Actions on Climate Change: China's Intended Nationally Determined Contributions*,

[13] In September 2009, President Hu Jintao stated China's position concerning climate change for the first time at the UN Climate Change Summit, pledging that China will step up efforts to conserve energy and improve energy efficiency and strive to reduce carbon dioxide emissions per unit of gross domestic product (GDP) by a considerable margin by 2020 from the 2005 level. In November of the same year at the executive meeting of the State Council, the proposal was made to reduce carbon dioxide emissions per unit of GDP by 40% to 45% from the 2005 level, which is incorporated in the mid- to long-term plan of national economic and social development. On November 12, 2014, President Xi Jinping and Barack Obama, then President of U.S., signed *U.S.-China Joint Announcement on Climate Change*, stating the two countries' respective post-2020 actions on climate change, in which China intends to achieve the peaking of CO_2 emissions around 2030 and to make best efforts to peak early and intends to increase the share of non-fossil fuels in primary energy consumption to around 20% by 2030.

establishing the goals of nationally determined actions up to 2030: to achieve the peak of carbon dioxide emissions around 2030 and make best efforts to peak early; to lower carbon dioxide emissions per unit of GDP by 60% to 65% from the 2005 level; to increase the share of non-fossil fuels in primary energy consumption to around 20%; and to increase the forest stock by around 4.5 billion cubic meters from the 2005 level, thus making another remarkable contribution to the global governance of climate change after mapping out the intended action plan by 2020 at the 2009 Copenhagen Climate Change Conference.

Moreover, China announced its contribution of 20 billion RMB to initiate the "China Climate Change Fund for South-South Cooperation" in order to assist other developing countries with capacity building in climate change finance. Currently, taking proactive steps to address climate change is identified as a key strategy for China's national development, with pressing ahead with the low-carbon development strategy being prioritized on China's development agenda and pinpointed as a major binding target in the Five-Year Plan. Therefore, it can be concluded that as the world's biggest emerging economy, China has become an initiator, innovator and forerunner of global governance of climate change and global green development. China's implementation of the green development strategy has not only carved out a new path of leap-frog development for China but also demonstrates worldwide significance by providing reference and inspirations for the development of other developing countries. In contrast, the future trend of climate change policies of the U.S. may constitute the biggest uncertainty in the global governance of climate change. For instance, Donald Trump signed an executive order of "energy independence" at the onset of his presidency which contained multiple articles on the restriction of clean energy, even to the extent of repealing the climate policies inaugurated by the Obama administration.

Fourthly, China will become a major innovator as it strides toward the high-income group and produce significant spillover effect on world development. Currently, the strategy of innovation-driven development has been placed at the top of China's development agenda, and China has developed multiple action plans for innovation-driven development to boost the transition from "Made in China" to "Created in China". By the time China ranks among high-income countries, it will have become the global center of technological innovation and a pioneering innovator in a multitude of high-tech areas. While shaping itself into an innovative country, China will play a proactive role in promoting international cooperation in technological innovation for global progress in science and technology. It must be pointed out that all major innovation projects planned by China pursue the wellbeing of mankind and sustainable development of the world as their goals, an embodiment of the mission of advancement in science and technology—serve all.[14]

Fifthly, while pursuing its target of becoming a high-income country, China will continue to promote common prosperity and the development of mankind on top of eradicating poverty by 2020, which is not only an embodiment of China's efforts in facilitating shared development but also an important example for developing countries to achieve development for the benefit of all. UNDP statistics show that China's Human Development Index (HDI) in 1980 was at a lower-medium level of 0.423. But China has become a high HDI country with the figure rising to 0.719 in 2014. This indicates that China, though not yet a high-income country, ranks high in human development. It is expected that by 2025, China's HDI will exceed 0.80, of which over two thirds will be contributed by education and health indicators. Undoubtedly, the Chinese experience in advancing human development is of referential value for the vast developing world. During the last two decades (1995–2015), China has made two leaps: from a low-income country to a lower-middle-income one and from a lower-middle-income country to an upper-middle-income one. Moreover, China also crossed the threshold for high human development level. By 2020, China will have built a moderately prosperous society in all respects and thoroughly eradicated poverty. China shall rank among high-income countries and attain a higher level of human development by 2025, contributing Chinese strength and Chinese wisdom to world economic growth, global green and innovation-driven development as well as win-win development of the world for the wellbeing of all.

[14] In *National plan on Scientific and Technological Innovation During the 13th Five-Year Plan*, key core technologies including core electronic devices, high-end generic chips, fundamental software, integrated circuit equipment, broadband mobile communication, CNC machine tools, oil and gas development, nuclear power, water pollution abatement, GMO, research and development of new pharmaceutical products, prevention and control of contagious diseases are listed as National Science and Technology Major Projects; aero-engines and gas turbines, deep sea space stations, quantum communication and quantum computing, brain science and brain-like intelligence technology, national cyberspace security, deep space probing and in-orbit services and maintenance systems for spacecraft are listed as Major Science and Technology Projects; independent innovation in seeds, clean and efficient use of coal, smart grid, integrated space and terrestrial information network (ISTIN), big data, intelligent manufacturing and robots, R&D and application of key new materials, comprehensive environmental management of Beijing, Tianjin and Hebei, healthcare, and so on are listed as major projects.

The achievements made and to be made by China show that on the basis of safeguarding the country's independence, ensuring political stability, proceeding from basic national conditions and adhering to independent development, China has not only achieved four decades of high economic growth but has also continuously enhanced people's livelihood through improving the socialist market economic system with Chinese characteristics and strategic guidance of national development planning, releasing the innovation potentials of market players while actively engaging in economic globalization. Through continuous fine-tuning of the social policy system featuring inclusive development, the achievements of economic development are intended to benefit all members of society, reflecting shared development. Through improving the institutions and mechanisms of sustainable development, the country's development is by and large steered on the track of green development. Through implementing the rule of law in all respects, comprehensively strengthening Party discipline and improving the democratic system with Chinese characteristics, constant progress is made in the country's governance capacity and governance system, thereby realizing the target of political development, which in turn will become the cornerstone for economic development and social stability.

China's success in overcoming the "middle income trap" and in becoming the world's biggest high-income country would not only make a pivotal and positive difference in the wellbeing of nearly 1.4 billion Chinese population but also have a far-reaching impact and profound significance for world development, since it will more than double the population in high-income countries from the current 1.187 billion (16.6% of the world population) to 2.637 billion, with an increase of 1.45 billion by 2030. More importantly, China will never seek hegemony even when it becomes a high-income country and the largest economy in the world; instead, it shall facilitate "win-win development" and "shared development" of China and the rest of the world through expansions in foreign trade, outward FDI, development assistance and aid and so on.

As the biggest developing country in the world, China has explored a path of development with Chinese characteristics since the reform and opening-up,[15] completing the process of transformation from a country

[15] The State Council Information Office of the People's Republic of China issued the white paper *The Right to Development: China's Philosophy, Practice and Contribution*, December 1, 2016, Xinhua News Agency, December 1, 2016, Beijing.

with the largest population living in absolute poverty to the world's biggest upper-middle-income country, that is the largest moderately prosperous society on track to rank among high-income countries by successfully overcoming the "middle income trap". China's development shows that the development path with Chinese characteristics is visibly different from the development model in the West. Its path of development has not only broken free from blind faith in the "Western model" but is also a transcendence from such model characterized by democracy and neo-liberalist economy paraded in the West. What China has undergone in the past has set an example for the rest of the world, and it is well expected that China will make even more profound and positive changes to world development in its ongoing efforts toward a high-income country, becoming a powerhouse for global sustainable development.

Epilogue

The proposal, debate, development and theorization of any academic concept requires time, experience, research, and all the more, tests through long-term social practice. From 2007 when the concept of the "middle income trap" was officially brought up by the World Bank to 2016 when "redoubling the efforts to overcome the middle income trap" was identified as a strategic goal of national development during the 13th Five-Year Plan period, China has undergone the process from intensified practice to deepened awareness in the transition from a planned economy to a market economy.

Personally, I also have gone through a journey of rethinking, repeated discussion and meticulous and deliberate research over a period of almost eight years, and this book is exactly the on-site record and genuine portrayal of this process. The following is a brief introduction of how this concept was proposed, how analysis has been carried out through investigation and study and how a solution is found to tackle this worldwide challenge, enabling China to overcome the "middle income trap" and smoothly march toward a high-income level characterized by common prosperity.

"Preparedness ensures success while unpreparedness spells failure". In March 2002, Wang Shaoguang, Hu Angang and Ding Yuanzhu published *Social Instability Behind a Prospering Economy* on *Strategy and Management*. We believe that China was again ushered into a period of

S. Zhou, A. Hu, *China: Surpassing the "Middle Income Trap"*,
Contemporary China Studies,
https://doi.org/10.1007/978-981-15-6540-3

instability at the turn of the century, which was prominently evident in the world's largest economic restructuring and the unprecedented overwhelming tides of unemployment, the world's most glaring urban-rural and regional divide, one of the fastest growing Gini coefficient and the most extensive eco-environmental damage in the world. We also argue that a prospering economy does not necessarily or automatically produce social stability. In retrospect of China's history, it is observed that severe social crises tend to occur during periods of economic prosperity; while experience of many developing countries indicate that unfair and inequitable growth usually triggers economic stagnation, recession or even collapse due to social crisis. Our analysis shows that inequitable distribution of social wealth is one of the major roots of instability; therefore, curbing such inequitable distribution and rectifying social injustice have transcended the scope of social ethics to become political issues involving social stability and legitimacy of the government. In fact, this is the biggest development challenge and dilemma confronting China as it moved into the twenty-first century and crossed the lower-middle-income threshold, though not named the "middle income trap" at the time. Aiming at addressing this challenge, in 2003, in *The Second Transformation: On China's Institutional Building* (Tsinghua University Press, 2003) written by Hu Angang, Wang Shaoguang and Zhou Jianming, it is argued that the essential purpose of institutional building for a country is to achieve "good governance" and to ensure the realization of fundamental interests and development goals of the country, which includes national security and territorial integrity, economic development and economic stability, social justice and human security, clean politics and social stability, ecological balance and environmental protection. This article has garnered massive attention in Chinese academia.[1]

In 2004, the important proposition of avoiding the "middle income trap" was made by the CPC Central Committee for the first time, with the creative notion of a scientific outlook on development proposed as a countermeasure. Wen Jiabao, then premier of the State Council, clearly stated at a workshop for key officials at provincial and ministerial levels that "China's per capita GDP has reached 1000 US dollars, which, according to the development plan and calculated on the current exchange rate, will reach 3000 US dollars by 2020. This marks a pivotal stage in the modernization process and a key phase heralding profound changes in economic

[1] This article has been cited nearly 500 times up to now (see CNKI).

and social structures. As is indicated by the courses of development in many other countries, two possible scenarios may occur during this phase: if the process is wisely managed, economic and social development will continue, eventually realizing industrialization and modernization; on the contrary, if it is poorly managed, wealth polarization, soaring unemployment, gaping rural-urban and regional disparity, aggravating social contradictions and worsening ecological environment will ensue, leading to painful and prolonged economic and social stagnation, or even social upheavals and retrogression.[2] Obviously, the latter scenario is a typical indication of the "middle income trap". Highly aware of the issues at stake, the CPC Central Committee innovatively proposed the notion of a "people-oriented" scientific outlook on development, firmly pursuing coordinated and sustainable development in all respects, making overall plans and preparations and addressing various contradictions and challenges. Only by doing this can China avoid the latter scenario and make the former one a reality.

In December 2008, when conducting research and survey in Guangdong Province, I was invited to organize the Guangdong Learning Forum[3] at the Provincial CPC Committee Center, where I gave a lecture titled *Transformation of Development Model of Guangdong and Addressing the Financial Crisis*. I made it clear from the very beginning that a specific economic development model tends to take shape as reform and development enter a new historical stage, possibly resulting in "path-dependent" and "path-locked" phenomena, which, if not addressed with timely and proactive initiatives, may constitute barriers for future reform and development and a fall into the "middle income trap" of economic development. For Guangdong Province that is right in the middle-income stage,[4] the key to overcoming the "middle income trap" is to shift from a traditional economic development model to a modernized one. I also shared my observation that the leapfrog development of Guangdong Province would spearhead the entire country to overcome the "middle income

[2] Wen Jiabao: *Enhance the Awareness, Reach a Common Understanding, Firmly Build and Implement the Scientific Outlook on Development—Speech on the Workshop on Building and Implementing the Scientific Outlook on Development for Key Officials on Provincial and Ministerial Levels* (February 21, 2004). Xinhuanet, February 29, 2004, Beijing.

[3] Wang Yang, then secretary of CPC Committee of Guangdong Province, and Huang Huahua, then provincial governor, were among the attendees.

[4] Per capita GDP of Guangdong was 5400 US dollars in 2008 (according to RMB/USD exchange rate in 2008), within the middle-income range.

trap". This lecture was greeted with tremendous enthusiasm among senior officials of Guangdong Province. I later submitted a proposal (of approximately 26,000 words) to the officials of the central government in the form of Report on National Conditions (December 19, 2008), which was not published.

In retrospect, my observation at the time was quite visionary. The economic model of Guangdong Province was thoroughly remolded after 2008, making it a forerunner in innovation-driven development in China. In 2015, Guangdong Province with a population of approximately 100 million was the first in China to join the three "ten-thousand clubs" at the same time: per capita GDP exceeding 10,000 US dollars (per capita GDP registered at 67,503 RMB, i.e. 10,838 US dollars), soon to cross the threshold of the high-income development stage; GDP exceeding 1 trillion US dollars (regional GDP reached 7.281255 trillion RMB, i.e. 1.1961 trillion US dollars), accounting for 10.8% of China's GDP and 1.67% of the world, equivalent to the world's 16th largest economy; total trade in goods exceeding 1 trillion US dollars (1.1658 trillion US dollars), accounting for 3.51% of the world's total (33.248 trillion US dollars), ahead of South Korea (ranking 8th), Netherland (ranking 7th), France (ranking 6th) and U.K. (ranking 5th).

This research and survey in Guangdong marks the start of our study on how China shall overcome the "middle income trap", yet the scope is not limited to Guangdong Province. In fact, our study targets the entire country from the very beginning and is blended with the research on formulating the five-year plans, adhering to the subject of "measures and approaches for China to address the "middle income trap".[5]

When the 12th Five-Year Plan was just beginning to be developed, China underwent its transition from the lower-middle-income stage to the upper-middle income stage. The 12th Five-Year Plan clearly indicated the need to "take scientific development as the theme and accelerating transformation of economic growth as the priority". This fundamental strategic adjustment holds the key for China to avoid falling into the "middle income trap".

China is currently in a critical stage striding toward the high-income group. In 2015, Tianjin, Beijing, Shanghai and Jiangsu all crossed the high-income threshold (12,700 US dollars or above in per capita GDP),

[5] Hu Angang: *How Does China Overcome the Middle Income Trap*, Contemporary Economics, Volume 15, 2010.

while Zhejiang (12,466 US dollars), Inner Mongolia (11,547 US dollars), Fujian (10,913 US dollars), Guangdong (10,838 US dollars), Liaoning (10,467 US dollars) and Shandong (10,305 US dollars) exceeded 10,000 US dollars in per capita GDP. The total GDP in the above ten provinces, municipalities and autonomous regions added up to 38.60 trillion yuan, accounting for 57.0% of China's GDP, their resident population adding up to 510.8 million, which constitutes 37.1% of the Chinese population, equivalent to the total EU population and 1.64 times of the US population. In fact, these provinces in the coastal regions have successively leaped over the "middle income trap", hence leading other regions across the country in avoiding the trap, just like beating a path out of poverty in the past. Therefore, we argue that the "middle income trap is a pseudo-proposition for China".

The year 2016 marked the beginning of the 13th Five-Year Plan, where "endeavoring to overcome the middle-income trap" was proposed for the first time in history. Our research shows that the five major development concepts established by the CPC Central Committee are both the core development concepts in overcoming the "middle income trap" and the five major development approaches for the successful accomplishment of this task. The 13th and 14th Five-Year Plan periods are the key phase in leaping over the "middle income trap", which will not be plain sailing. The research findings presented in this book suggest that China will successfully overcome the trap and become a high-income country featuring common prosperity between 2020 and 2025, achieving the first centennial goal as planned and laying a more solid foundation for the second centennial goal.

Traps may be encountered at any stage of development: poverty trap in the low-income stage, inevitable "middle income trap" in the middle-income stage and "high income trap" even in the high-income phase. From an international perspective, answers may vary to the question "why the probability of successful transition from middle-income to high-income is lower than that from low-income to middle-income?", and different viewpoints exist. My observation is that the "middle income trap" is more of a political trap than an economic one. As early as 25 years ago, the Soviet Union and Eastern European countries already earned their positions in the middle-income range; however, they never managed to avoid the political trap as middle-income countries and achieve high-income status in the wake of political upheavals. Some middle-income countries in the Middle East over a decade ago are now struggling in warfare after the Arab Spring, entailed by endless sufferings of their people who had to flee as refugees. For instance, as early as 2007, Libya's per capita GDP had exceeded 10,000 US dollars, which peaked in 2010 at 12,250 US dollars. Mired in the interventions from the West and the subsequent outbreak of civil wars, Libya's per capita GDP dived to 4660 US dollars in 2011 with the collapse of the Kaddafi regime, slowly regaining its momentum but only to 7820 US dollars in 2014.

These failures show that political stability is the prerequisite in creating a favorable environment for economic development and addressing the "middle income trap", that is to say, peace and order are the biggest national product for public welfare, which, similar to the invisible and intangible clean air, is indispensable yet cannot be self-provided by individuals, hence should be valued, treasured and protected by all. This is why peace and order are deemed the overarching product for public welfare. It lies with the fundamental interests of all people, so individual interest must give way to collective interest, and personal principles are subordinate to public principles of the country. China, with a population of over one billion, is a country with shared interests, destiny and development, rising or falling together.

Then, who is the provider of national product for public welfare in today's China? The answer is the CPC and the Chinese government, for whom this is the main responsibility and task. It is exactly on the basis of such overarching national product for public welfare that China managed to attain remarkable development, crossing over the "poverty trap" characteristic of an impoverished country and again successfully overcoming the "middle income trap", bringing wellbeing and prosperity to the 1.3 billion population and realizing the Chinese dream of great rejuvenation. Will China be able to leap over the trap? How to make it happen? What are the approaches and measures to be implemented? This is a practical as well as a theoretical question. Engaged in research projects at the Institute for Contemporary China Studies of Tsinghua University, my colleagues and I have internally published multiple *Reports on China Studies* with policy influence and many monographs in journals with academic influence since 2008. *Supply-side Structural Reform—Adapting to and Leading China's Economic New Normal* (Journal of Tsinghua University, Philosophy and Social Sciences, Vol. 2, 2016) published by Hu Angang, Zhou Shaojie and Ren Hao has been cited 210 times and downloaded over 30,000 times, producing prominent academic influence. In addition, the above-mentioned questions are studied on a deeper level and answered in a more systematic and comprehensive approach in *China: Successfully Overcoming the "Middle Income Trap"* authored by Zhou Shaojie and Hu Angang, providing background and policy recommendations as China prepares to embark on a journey toward the high-income range with common prosperity. Post-doctorate researcher Lu Yufeng and PhD candidate Ren Hao also participated in the research project on tackling the "middle income trap", and Ren Hao undertook data calculation in this research.

President Xi Jinping stated that "for China, the middle income trap is bound to be crossed, and the question is when it will happen and how to better move forward after that. We have confidence in balancing reform, development and stability as well as steady growth, structure adjustment, improvement of people's livelihood and promotion of reform, thereby advancing China's economy in a steady and sustainable manner".[6] This is a profound question presented by the era, and of the era.

Taking China's success in overcoming the "middle income trap" as the theme, this book consists of five chapters: Chap. 1 defines the "middle income trap" in terms of both the absolute and relative criteria; Chap. 2 introduces how China successfully addressed the "poverty trap", which lays an important foundation for China to leap over the "middle income trap"; Chap. 3 touched upon various development challenges during the middle-income stage and favorable conditions for China to overcome the trap; Chap. 4 provides an analysis of how China can cross over the "middle income trap", with five major development concepts addressing this multi-dimensional trap and Supply-side structural reform as the key to tackling the "middle income trap"; Chap. 5 looks into China's future development as the country navigates over the trap and moves toward a high-income country with common prosperity in all dimensions.

Practice is the touchstone of truth; likewise, practice in the Chinese society shall test the knowledge and value of this book on China's reality and decision-making. We shall continue with follow-up studies as this topic is highly complicated with many unpredictable factors in future development. Even after China crosses the threshold of high-income countries, the challenge of the "high income trap" would also ensue, which calls for forward-looking and professional research and abiding

[6] Xi Jinping, *Speech at the Dialogue between Asia-Pacific Economic Cooperation (APEC) Leaders and APEC Business Advisory Council (ABAC) Representatives* (November 10, 2014), People's Daily, November 11, 2014.

commitment to the notion of "knowledge for the people, and for the service of the country".

In a nutshell, practice knows no boundary, and so do knowledge, research and innovation.

At Tsinghua University Hu Angang
July 7, 2017

The manufacturer's authorised representative in the EU is Springer Nature Customer Service Centre GmbH, Europaplatz 3, 69115 Heidelberg, Germany. If you have any concerns regarding our products, please contact ProductSafety@springernature.com

Printed and bound by CPI Group (UK) Ltd, Croydon, CR0 4YY
30/09/2026
02225494-0003